FEMALE ACTIVISTS

Irish Women and Change 1900-1960

GW00644967

Female Activists

Irish Women and Change 1900-1960

Mary Cullen and Maria Luddy

Editors

Best wishes Evelyn.
Mary Cullen

The Woodfield Press

This book was typeset in Ireland by
Gough Typesetting Services for
THE WOODFIELD PRESS
17 Jamestown Square, Inchicore, Dublin 8, Ireland.
Web: http://myhome.iolfree.ie/~woodfield
E-mail: terri.mcdonnell@ireland.com

Publishing editor
Helen Harnett

The catalogue record for this title
is available from the British Library.

ISBN 0-9534293-0-X

Printed in Ireland
by Genprint Limited

Contents

Companion volume also edited by Mary Cullen and Maria Luddy

Women, Power and Consciousness in Nineteenth-Century Ireland: Eight Biographical Studies

(Attic Press, 1995)

Anna Doyle Wheeler (1785-c.1850)	*Dolores Dooley*
Margaret Louisa Aylward (1810-1889)	*Jacinta Prunty*
Frances Power Cobbe (1822-1904)	*Deirdre Raftery*
Anne Jellicoe (1823-1880)	*Anne O'Connor*
Anna Maria Haslam (1829-1922)	*Mary Cullen*
Isabella M.S. Tod (1836-1896)	*Maria Luddy*
Charlotte Grace O'Brien (1845-1909)	*Anne O'Connell*
Anna Parnell (1852-1911)	*Jane Côté and Dana Hearne*

Where *Female Activists: Irish Women and Change 1900-1960* studies twentieth-century women, this volume focuses on nineteenth-century activists. This original and scholarly work charts the lives of eight women whose activism in political, social and economic reform radically altered the public perception of women's role in Irish society. Their pioneering campaigns covered a wide range of contemporary questions and forced many issues that establishments preferred to ignore under the public spotlight.

Targets included specifically feminist issues such as votes for women, married women's control of their own property, improved educational and employment opportunities for women, violence against women and sexual double standards. Other campaigns involved the reform of the appalling conditions on emigrant ships, innovation in the public provision for the care of poor children, building a network of poor schools in Dublin, organising and running the Ladies' Land League and running the Land League itself for a period.

Individually and together these two volumes highlight the contribution that biographical studies can give to our understanding of the multi-faceted layers of experience, awareness and contribution that go to making the history of a society.

Notes on Contributors

MARY CULLEN is an Academic Associate at NUI, Maynooth, and a Research Associate at the Centre for Gender and Women's Studies, Trinity College, Dublin.

MARIA LUDDY is a Senior Lecturer in History at the University of Warwick.

CATHERINE CANDY is assistant professor of history at the University of Maine at Augusta and is completing a critical study of the transnational biography of Margaret Cousins.

ROSEMARY CULLEN OWENS lectures in women's history for the M.A. and Higher Diploma at the Women's Education Research & Resource Centre, University College, Dublin. Her publications include *Smashing Times: A History of the Irish Women's Suffrage Movement 1889-1922* (Dublin, 1984, 1996), and *Louie Bennett, A Biography* (Cork, 2001).

DAMIAN DOYLE completed his M.A. at University College Dublin and his Ph.D. in literature at the University of Colorado, Boulder, where he teaches part-time. His dissertation, 'A Bio-critical Study of Rosamond Jacob and Her Contemporaries,' relocates Jacob's work within the Irish literary canon.

THERESA MORIARTY is a researcher and project supervisor at the Irish Labour History Museum in Dublin. Her main area of research is in women's labour history.

NELL REGAN lives and works in Dublin. Her first collection of poetry will be published by Salmon Press in 2002.

MEDB RUANE is a journalist and commentator. She lives in Dublin and writes for the *Irish Times* and the *Sunday Times*.

MARGARET WARD is assistant director of Belfast-based think tank, Democratic Dialogue. She is the author of a number of books on the history of Irish women, including *Unmanageable Revolutionaries, Women and Irish Nationalism* and *Hanna Sheehy Skeffington, a Life*.

Illustrations

Introduction

Mary Cullen and Maria Luddy

It is often assumed that once Irish women won the right to vote in 1918 their political interests, for those who remained politically active, were channelled into supporting the cause of Irish freedom. This overlooks a number of realities. In the first place, the majority of Irish suffragists were neither republicans nor nationalists. Secondly, the vote did not deliver the full feminist programme. Women who were actively involved in the independence campaign found they had to continually demand political equality with their male colleagues. For them and other feminists the struggle to achieve full and active citizenship for women continued over the decades. Thirdly, the objectives of many nationalist and republican women went beyond the attainment of independence to the kind of state they wanted and they, including six of the women in this book, continued to work for this.

After 1922 women tended to find themselves marginalised and restricted in the Irish Free State. One can catalogue the economic and legal restraints: the 1926 Civil Service Act legalised a sex barrier in competitions for posts; from 1927 women were effectively barred from jury service under the Juries Act; from 1932 female civil servants and teachers lost their jobs on marriage; in 1934 the Criminal Law Amendment Act placed a complete ban on the importation of all contraceptives; in 1936 the Conditions of Employment Act empowered the minister to restrict the employment of women in industry; the 1937 Constitution clearly signified the place of women as being exclusively in the home; 1951 saw the 'Mother and Child' scheme controversy. The impact of Catholic social teaching was also an oppressive force. These are topics that have received some attention from historians.[1] Less often explored are the lives of

---

[1] For accounts and interpretations of these events see the following, Maryann Gialanella Valiulis, 'Defining their role in the new state: Irishwomen's protest against the juries act of 1927' in *The Canadian Journal of Irish Studies*, 17, 1 (July 1992), pp. 43–60; *idem.*, 'Power, gender and identity in the Irish Free State' in *Journal of Women's History*, 6/4/7/1 (Winter/Spring, 1995), pp. 117–136; *idem.*, '"Neither feminist nor flapper": the ecclesiastical construction of the ideal Irish woman' in M. O'Dowd and S. Wichert (eds.), *Chattel, Servant or Citizen: Women's Status in Church, State and Society* (Belfast, 1995), pp. 168–178; Mary E. Daly, 'Women in the Irish Free State, 1922–1939: the interaction between economics

those individuals who played an active role in Irish political life throughout the twentieth century. Some of these women provide the subjects for the biographies that follow.

The lives of Mary Galway, Margaret Cousins, Helena Molony, Hanna Sheehy Skeffington, Louie Bennett, Kathleen Lynn and Rosamond Jacob were often interlinked and a number of these women were close friends, political allies and sometimes political opponents. Some of these women are already known, perhaps Sheehy Skeffington being the most recognisable.[2] For the others some aspects of their work are readily identified but beyond that they remain shadowy figures. There are many who still remember the work of Lynn and the role she played in establishing St. Ultan's Hospital. Bennett, Galway and Molony are known primarily to labour historians. Cousins is particularly associated with the suffrage campaign in Ireland but few are aware of her life in India where she went to live in 1915. These biographical studies show that far from being limited or confined to one activity these women were significant players in a number of campaigns and on a wide range of issues. All of them can be associated with the suffrage cause. Galway openly supported it within the trade union movement. Cousins and Sheehy Skeffington established the militant Irish Women's Franchise League in 1908 in order to revitalise a suffrage campaign that they felt lacked necessary vigour. Molony was also a supporter of suffrage, though more strongly allied to the nationalist cause than many other suffragists at this time. Bennett was involved in organising both the Irish Women's Suffrage Federation to link together the smaller groups and the Irish Women's Reform League in 1911 to include as far as possible the demands of working women.

---

and ideology' in *Journal of Women's History*, 6/4/7/1 (Winter/Spring, 1995), pp. 99-116; *idem*., '"Oh, Kathleen Ni Houlihan, Your Way's a Thorny Way!": the condition of women in twentieth-century Ireland', in A. Bradley and M. Gialanella Valiulis (eds.), *Gender and Sexuality in Modern Ireland* (Amherst, 1997), pp. 102-126; Yvonne Scannell, 'The constitution and the role of women', in B. Farrell (ed.), *De Valera's Constitution and Ours* (Dublin, 1988), pp. 123-136; Mary Clancy, 'Aspects of women's contribution to the Oireachtas debate in the Irish Free State' in M. Luddy and C. Murphy (eds.), *Women Surviving: Studies in Irish Women's History in the 19th and 20th Centuries* (Dublin, 1990), pp. 206-232.; Caitriona Beaumont, 'Women, citizenship and Catholicism in the Irish Free State, 1922-1948', *Women's History Review*, 6 (4), (1997), pp. 563-585; *idem*., 'Women and the politics of equality: the irish women's movement, 1930-1943', in M. Gialanella Valiulis and M. O'Dowd (eds.), *Women and History in Ireland* (Dublin, 1997), pp. 173-188; Sandra McAvoy, 'The regulation of sexuality in the Irish Free State, 1929-1935', in G. Jones and E. Malcolm (eds.), *Medicine, Disease and the State in Ireland* (Cork, 1999), pp. 253-266.

[2] See Leah Levenson and Jerry Natterstad, *Hanna Sheehy Skeffington: Irish Feminist* (Syracuse, 1986); Maria Luddy, *Hanna Sheehy Skeffington* (Dublin, 1995); Margaret Ward, *Hanna Sheehy Skeffington: a Life* (Cork, 1999).

Jacob and Lynn were also active suffragists. By 1911 there were about eighteen suffrage societies throughout the country, catering for a variety of political and religious backgrounds, though, surprisingly, there was no distinct nationalist women's suffrage society. There were also many individuals within the campaign who were sympathetic to the labour movement. It was, perhaps, these women's various involvement in this campaign that shaped their political outlook. The political equality of women with men was the central cause within suffrage. Gaining the parliamentary franchise in 1918 saw the dissipation of the political energies of many, but some feminists recognised that real equality in social, economic and political terms had not yet been achieved. Their campaigning continued, for the majority of the women in this book, right up until the times of their deaths.

Five of these women lived in Dublin for most or all of their working lives though Lynn grew up in Counties Mayo and Longford, and Jacob in Waterford. Cousins, from Boyle in County Roscommon, was also Dublin-based during her short but active Irish political career. Galway was the exception, born in Moira, County Down, and growing up and living in Belfast in a family of linen workers. Three, Galway, Sheehy Skeffington and Molony, came from Catholic families, though Sheehy Skeffington firmly abandoned formal religion in adult life. Bennet, Cousins and Lynn all came from Church of Ireland backgrounds while Jacob was of Quaker descent though both she and her parents were agnostics by conviction. Most were middle class, and Bennett, Cousins, Sheehy Skeffington, Lynn and Jacob were most often comfortably off, even if at times money was scarce. Their sensibility was middle class. Both Molony and Galway came from less affluent backgrounds and both understood poverty and the needs of women who worked from their own life experience.

The political activism of these women straddled the partition of Ireland. The Dublin-based women were all actively involved in separatist nationalist politics during the first two decades of the twentieth century. Lynn and Molony were active in the 1916 Rising while Sheehy Skeffington helped bring supplies to the combatants. Bennett was sympathetic to the cause but her pacifism rejected the use of force for any objective. Jacob and Cousins were both sympathetic but Jacob was living in Waterford at the time, and Cousins had emigrated to India. The working lives of these six continued throughout the 1920s, 1930s and 1940s, and in some cases longer, for five of them in the Irish Free State and later the Republic of Ireland, and for Cousins in India. Again Galway is the exception. Much less is known of her political views because the sources are so scarce. She spent the last eight years of her life from 1920 in the new Northern Ireland State.

The personal circumstances of these women allowed them to remain active in public life. Most were unencumbered with a husband and children. Only Cousins and Sheehy Skeffington married. The Cousins appear to have decided not to have children. Sheehy Skeffington was of course widowed under

horrendous circumstances and did have a son. But she also had a family circle
and friends whom she could call on to help look after him. Jacob, Molony,
Galway, Lynn and Bennett remained unmarried and financially independent.
However, it was an independence that they worked for. Friendship and
companionship also gave these women tremendous support. Sheehy Skeffington
had a talent for friendship and numbered Cousins, Lynn, Jacob, Molony and
Bennett amongst her close friends. Bennett lived for many years nearby her
friend and companion Helen Chenevix; Lynn lived with Madeleine ffrench-
Mullen, while Molony lived for thirty years with Evelyn O'Brien. Galway,
again, is an exception in that little is known of her personal life and friendships.
We must be careful not to read too much into these friendships but they clearly
offered vital emotional support to these women.

Sources for some of these women's lives are relatively generous. The papers
of Francis and Hanna Sheehy Skeffington, housed in the National Library of
Ireland, consist of letters, diaries, speeches, newscuttings, photographs and
ephemera. The collection reflects the history of Ireland from about 1900 to
1946 and is arguably one of the most underused sources available to Irish
historians. Surprisingly, given her current obscurity, there is also a superb
collection of papers relating to Rosamond Jacob, again available in the National
Library of Ireland. Jacob kept a daily diary from 1897 to the time of her death in
1960 that records her feelings, her friendships, and her political and social
involvement. There is also a substantial collection of manuscripts regarding her
plays, poems and novels. Her friendship with Sheehy Skeffington is evident
from the correspondence available in the Sheehy Skeffington Papers. Jacob's
papers offer a veritable history of feminist activism in Ireland to the 1960s. The
diaries and papers of Kathleen Lynn, housed in the Royal College of Physicians
of Ireland, are also a wonderful source and provide the historian not only with
personal information but particular information about health care and health
provision in twentieth-century Ireland. Cousins wrote a joint autobiography
with her husband James and this can be augmented by the collection of her
papers that exist in India. In contrast Molony, Galway and Bennett are rather
elusive figures and the search for their lives required substantial historical
detection. There are no collections of personal papers and much about their
lives can be gleaned only from working through official papers such as trade
union minutes, government reports and their correspondence that is preserved
in other personal collections. The absence of personal papers clearly has an
impact on how a public individual is remembered or written about. Sometimes
they are the ones most quickly forgotten. However, copious papers do not
always result in recognition and Jacob's life is proof of this.

The purpose of this book is to bring to light the range and extent of these
women's contributions to Irish life, to link that in with their personal experiences
and to raise questions about the connections between feminism and political
action. There are clear examples within these biographies of the correlations

that existed between personal circumstances and political activism, between issues of gender and the nature of the state which was in many ways profoundly patriarchal. It is impossible to generalise about the experiences of Irish women in these decades and while there are similarities in the lives of these women and even in their political activism, there are also many divergences and paradoxes. How could Sheehy Skeffington, for instance belong to a pacifist organisation and yet support militant republicanism? Further, she and Bennett held sharply divergent views on the relation between pacifism and nationalism but worked closely together for many years. How could Bennett and Molony head the Irish Women Workers Union, campaign vigorously for women's right to equality with men in the workplace, and yet both accept that women might be better off in the home? Hanna Sheehy Skeffington, noted for her egalitarianism, had servants yet seemed to have no conflict over her right to a public life while someone else did the housework. The search for solutions to such apparent paradoxes deepens our understanding of the political, social and economic realities of a specific period and of how important the historical context is in the formation of political thinking. These women must be viewed in the setting of their time and place. Understanding how they came to hold the views they did can also highlight possible anomalies and over-simplifications in some of our own present-day attitudes. What is most evident in the lives and work of all of these women is the level of tolerance they had for the views of others and the importance they gave to debate and argument as a means of resolving conflict.

Only in the case of Sheehy Skeffington did a fairly rounded portrait already exist, and in her contribution here Margaret Ward focuses on the interaction in Sheehy Skeffington's political thinking and activism between her feminism and her opposition to imperialism. The other chapters each present an outline of a life that was up to now little known in any detail. They open up the range of interests and activisms of six women whose lives, objectives and achievements were remarkable by any standards. In doing so they have incidentally exposed the equally remarkable neglect by historians of these women's contribution to Irish history and the development of Irish society. Damian Doyle's study reveals the intellectual and historical interest of Rosamond Jacob's novels. She located her characters at the centre of current and sensitive political events and explored a complex range of experiences and perspectives. Impressive also is her early critique of the tendency of nationalist movements to repeat the repressive conformity imposed by the imperialism they opposed. Nell Regan documents Helena Molony's achievement as an acclaimed leading actress with the Abbey Theatre and her commitment to socialist republicanism. Yet her commitment to the women of the Irish Women Workers Union (IWWU) was so great that she abandoned her acting career and curtailed her socialist activity for their sake. Medb Ruane explains the pioneering contribution of Kathleen Lynn to medical research on tuberculosis and her holistic approach to the healthcare of children, an approach which combined scientific medicine with the need for love. Noteworthy also is her interest in the educational ideas of Maria Montessori at a time when these were seen by many as dangerously radical. Catherine Candy's research opens up the long and remarkable career of Margaret Cousins in India, where she became a major figure in the Indian women's movement while retaining her attachment to Ireland. Throughout her life she believed both that the women's movement transended all national boundaries, and that at the same time the reality of cultural difference had to be accepted and respected. Rosemary Cuilen Owens shows Louie Bennett throughout her long life steadfastly combining an uncompromising pacifism and commitment to negotiation with an equally uncompromising opposition to imperialism and injustice. Allied to her strong leadership qualities these made her a formidable player in Irish society. Using the scanty available evidence Theresa Moriarty follows the achievement of Mary Galway, who rose through the ranks to become Ireland's first full-time female trade-union official. Galway as a person remains the most elusive of these women, which is particularly frustrating since, unlike the other women in this book, she was one of those women who as a group remain shadowy, the rank and file trade-unionists and workers. The authors of some of the studies in this book have already prepared or are in the process of preparing full-length biographies or studies and these should add substantially to our knowledge of Irish history in the twentieth century.

A number of areas emerge that invite further research. While it cannot be claimed that these women form a representative sample, it is striking how far to the left most of them were in their political beliefs and activism. Four of them, Sheehy Skeffington, Jacob, Molony and Lynn were separatists who rejected the Treaty. Yet theirs was no simple or narrow nationalism. From the beginning their nationalism was linked to their feminist commitment, and so from the start they were aware of the dangers of exclusion and polarisation. All developed towards more complex positions which incoporated awareness of inequality between classes as well as between the sexes. During the 1920s, 1930s and 1940s, while church and state became increasingly anti-communist and the red scare took hold, they remained committed to socialist principles. All four gravitated to the left wing which tried to push the republican movement towards a commitment to a socialist workers' republic. The studies in this book point to the potential of further research into the political thinking, in the broadest sense, of these women and their like-minded colleagues, particularly in the context of the current interest in the interaction of nationalism and republicanism in Ireland.

The studies of Galway, Molony and Bennett point to another area of interest, the differences between the experience of women in the older craft-based unions and the new unionism. In Belfast Mary Galway rose through the ranks of union members to become a paid organising secretary of the Textile Operatives' Society of Ireland. By contrast the impetus for the foundation of the Irish Women Workers Union in Dublin came from the new unionism which aimed at organising unskilled workers. The IWWU set out to bring hitherto unorganised women into a trade union. After Delia Larkin's initial brief tenure, Molony, Bennett and Helen Chenevix, middle-class women invited in from outside, dominated its leadership.

The political views of the women studied here evolved over their lifetimes, affected and influenced by their individual experiences, and by their contact with national and international politics. If Ireland was, as has often been claimed, insular these women proved to be remarkably internationalist in their outlook. Many travelled to America, Russia and through Europe attending conferences and seeking funding for their projects. They corresponded with colleagues of similar interests throughout Europe and in America. There was little that was parochial about their views or thoughts.

As research into the history of Irish women continues it will become even more obvious that there were many Irish women who remained politically active throughout the twentieth century whose lives deserve to be investigated.[3] One can think immediately of women such as Professor Mary Hayden, Máire Comerford, Helena Concannon, Lily O'Brennan, Agnes O'Farrelly, Lilian Spender, Helen Chenevix, and there are many others, whose activism has gone unrecorded. This volume places the lives of seven 'forgotten' women in their political and social contexts and opens the way for further study of their lives.

---

[3] For recent studies in nineteenth-century biography see Mary Cullen and Maria Luddy (eds.), *Women, Power and Consciousness in 19th-Century Ireland: Eight Biographical Studies* (Dublin, 1995).

Mary Galway (1864-1928)

Theresa Moriarty

For years the historical memory of Mary Galway has been kept alive as the antagonist of James Connolly on the Belfast Trades Council in 1911. Mary Galway was the general secretary of the Textile Operatives' Society of Ireland, the only women's trades union in the linen industry. James Connolly had launched a separate women's mill-workers' branch of the Irish Transport and General Workers' Union (ITGWU)in Belfast. In the bitterness of the argument about who had the right to organise the women workers, Galway accused Connolly of being 'an adventurer',[1] dividing the workers along sectarian lines.[2] Her historical reputation has suffered as a result despite the fact that she was Ireland's first woman full-time trade union official.

The decades that straddle the cusp of the twentieth century were among the most intensive years of trade union organisation in Ireland. Mary Galway was a pioneer in the Irish trade union movement in those years. She was appointed as a linen worker to organise the first women's union in that industry, she was the first woman to sit on the Irish Trade Union Congress national executive, and the first woman vice-president of the Irish trade union movement. In the years of her most public activity she was described variously as 'intrepid',[3] 'able and energetic',[4] and her pseudonymous obituarist, 'Hotspur', described her as 'an earnest and strenuous worker.'[5]

Mary Galway's early life story has disappeared almost without trace. What

---

[1] Belfast Trades and Labour Council, Minutes, 2 November 1911. (Hereafter, BTC).

[2] Irish Trades Union Congress, *Annual Report and Proceedings*, 1912. (Hereafter, ITUC, *Annual Report*), p. 42.

[3] Hilda Martindale, *From One Generation to Another* (London, 1944), p. 141.

[4] *Woman Worker*, 19 June 1908.

[5] *The Irishman*, 6 October 1928.

information we have comes from references to her working life in contemporary publications, more concerned with the plight of linen workers than in supplying biographical information about one of their principal champions, except in so far as it established her credentials as their spokeswoman. James Haslam, a journalist, told the readers of the socialist *Clarion*, 'She has been a weaver herself and a sweated stitcher; she lives among the lowly-paid factory workers and the sweated home-workers, and she knows them. She laughs with them and sorrows with them.'[6] The 1912 inquiry into the condition of women workers in the linen making-up trades, stated that Galway had been a 'warehouse worker', a woman employed in the finishing skills of embroidery, hemming and thread drawing on the linen goods.[7] Before her appointment as a full-time organiser with the union, Galway told a government inquiry in 1909 that she had worked eleven years as a machinist.[8]

Official documentation permits a more detailed glimpse into her family background. She was born on 6 September 1864 in Taglanneg, Moira, Co. Down,[9] one of at least five daughters.[10] At the start of her long years as a trade union organiser the family had already moved to Belfast, where she lived with her parents, Elizabeth (née Magennis) and Henry Galway and two sisters, Margaret and Martha. Everyone in her household was a linen worker. Her mother and father were retired linen weavers, and their three daughters all registered their occupations as handkerchief stitchers. They lived in the west of the city, at 85 Leeson Street, near St Peter's church in Divis. She still lived there when she was appointed secretary to her union in 1897.[11] Some time later, and after her father's death, the Galway family moved home to nearby Crocus Street, a short road of terraced houses off Springfield Road, near the junction with the Falls Road. The economically active women in this all-female household are listed as hemstitch machinists. The Galways were Roman Catholics.

Without knowing when the Galway family moved to Belfast it is only possible to speculate about the schooling the daughters might have received. Most working-class families, urban and rural, would have received elementary education at a national school. The linen industry was unique in Ireland in maintaining a half-time system of education, which divided the working week

---

[6] James Haslam, 'Barefoot half-timers', *Clarion*, 4 November 1910.

[7] *Committee of Inquiry into the Conditions of Employment in the Linen and Other Making-Up Trades in the North of Ireland*, Report of Evidence, H.C. 1912-13, [Cd. 6509] xxxiv.

[8] Mary Galway, 18 May 1909, *Report of the Departmental Committee on Accidents under the Factory and Workshop Acts: Evidence and Appendix*, 1911 [Cd. 5540] xxiii, Q.6714.

[9] Information from Galway's birth certificate.

[10] Census report, 1901.

[11] *Ninth Report of the Chief Labour Correspondent of the Board of Trade Unions*, 1897 [Cd. 8644] xcix, p. 77.

between work and school for children from the age of eight. Galway may have been schooled in either or both. The census forms of 1911 tell us that the Galway daughters could all read and write, in both English and Irish. Mary Galway's background was statistically unremarkable. Not only were her immediate family all linen workers, but so were most of the neighbouring families. She shared this linen background and employment with tens of thousands of other women in the city. In the 1901 census form, from which her domestic details are drawn, Belfast had 75,000 linen workers, 50-60,000 of them were women employed in the workplace and at home. Her shared background with the women she was to organise in the Textile Operatives' Society of Ireland (TOSI) is in contrast to her singularity in becoming, by her own account, Ireland's first full-time woman trade union organiser in July 1897.[12] As the pattern of Galway's life was woven by the world of women's work in the linen industry of Belfast, her biography can be best outlined against this background.

Linen dominated Belfast. By the end of the nineteenth century it was the largest industry in the city. It gave rise to, and supported, a vital part of the engineering industry that built its machinery and equipment. It was heavily capitalised, the result of almost a century of technical innovation with a division of the labour process by location, skill, workplace and gender. This made linen a highly stratified industry where each section of the workforce was accorded a subtly different status, shaped by their gender, type of employment or skill, custom and even dress. As a contemporary report noted:

> All round the hall were the neater girls in smart hats and jackets, probably the girls from the wareroom of the city, but all down the centre tables . . . were the mill girls themselves. Ragged and tattered, with pinched wan faces, aged before their time, holding round them the shawls that barely hid the slovenly vest beneath . . .[13]

The 'smart hats and jackets', 'shawls' and 'vests' of 1893 marked a clear distinction between the women linen workers attending that meeting at the Ulster Hall. The boundary of rank is further emphasised by the *Women's Trade Union Review* report that the 'neater girls' of the warerooms sat apart from the 'ragged and tattered' millworkers.

Women linen workers had joined the industrial workforce as machinery had been introduced. They were widely recognised, though not remunerated, as skilled labour. Women's textile work had emerged from pre-industrial technologies, when both spinning and weaving had been essentially domestic

---

[12] *Minutes of Evidence Taken Before the Truck Committee*, vol. li, Minutes of Evidence H.C. 1908 [Cd. 4443], lix, p. 256. [Hereafter, *Truck Committee, Inquiry*].
[13] *Women's Trade Union Review*, October 1893. (Hereafter, *WTUR*).

tasks, rather than female trades. Women spinners (spinsters) were acknowledged
to possess skills as 'natural' to women as cookery or child rearing. Women were
employed exclusively in certain of the linen processes. In the early stages of
production single young women worked as spinners, a traditional occupation
of women in domestic households, transformed by the industrial mills. They
worked in the final or finishing processes as stitchers, in the sewing factories or
warehouses. They were also employed as weavers of the linen cloth, though
this had traditionally been a male process.

   Industrial processing had been accompanied by appalling working conditions
and hazards. Wet steam spinning threw off airborne lint and showers of spray,
which clung to the mill workers and drenched their clothes. Unventilated
workplaces incubated infectious diseases. Poorly guarded machinery caused
injuries, with little right to compensation. Women were particularly victimised
by this industry. A Belfast health inquiry of 1908 into the city's death rates
found the highest death rates for consumption were among women of
childbearing age. In *The Making of Irish Linen*, Peter Collins notes that Irish
linen handkerchiefs dominated the luxury end of the world market.[14] It was
fine and detailed work, and badly paid by piece rate. In 1895, when Galway was
starting out in the textile union, handkerchief hemmers, sewing sixteen stitches
to the inch, were paid one shilling and ninepence for twelve dozen. The scale
increased with the number of stitches to the inch.[15] Galway once itemised to a
public meeting the thirty separate steps involved in handkerchief manufacture.

   In 1897, when Galway was appointed to a full time position in the Textile
Operatives' Society of Ireland, there were ten unions organising in the linen
industry. The other nine were organised around specific, and male, tasks in the
production process, such as flax dressing, damask weaving, linen lappers and
yarn bundlers.[16] None of these nine unions admitted women as members.
Although the linen industry was one of the most modern industries in Ireland,
its industrial relations were characterised by an earlier era. Chief among the
practices and customs retained from the earlier days, and another consequence
of its slow pace of mechanisation, was the weakness of linen trade unions
themselves, which reflected the stratification within the industry. Each union
represented a group of workers in a particular stage of the processing of linen
from the raw crop to the fibre, hacklers, roughers and dressers, and others.
Until the 1890s these were exclusively men-only unions. They had never built
a federation of the trades societies or unions such as the textile societies among
the cotton operatives of Manchester. In Belfast they operated independently,

---

[14] Peter Collins, *The Making of Irish Linen: Historic Photographs of an Ulster Industry*,
(Belfast, 1994).

[15] *WTUR*, October 1895.

[16] *Report of the Chief Registrar of Friendly Societies on Friendly Societes with Branches:
Abstract of Annual Returns for 1894*, HC [97-iii] lxxxii, 553, 1897.

fiercely jealous of their autonomy. Settlements of strikes invariably resulted in different terms of settlements between the tasks of production.

The trade union movement itself in the city was made up of small scattered local societies, based on old craft associations, with restricted access to membership, staunchly apolitical, and unsuited to the needs of workers in large-scale industrial production. They came together on the city trades council, formed in 1881, as a local forum to discuss industrial strategies in Belfast, respond to employers' initiatives, advocate municipal reform, and co-operate between the different unions and branches represented on the council. The only effective action at the disposal of the workforce was a strike, which all too often might defeat its aim, as it could be turned against workers into a lock-out by employers. There was intense hardship in taking strike action in those days. Linen strikes were almost entirely spontaneous, sparked off by a particular or general grievance, without any trade union to turn to for support, or a strike fund to support workers or their dependants.

The Textile Operatives' Society of Ireland was formed in 1893.[17] It was the first women's trade union in Ireland to survive as an established organisation in the Irish trade union movement. It was one of the new wave of women's trade unions in the 1890s and was affiliated to the Women's Trade Union League (WTUL), a trade-union recognised organisation of women industrial campaigners, with headquarters in London. Years of argument and effort by the WTUL, formerly the Women's Protective and Provident League, to end the exploitation of women's low pay and poor conditions had helped to erode men's opposition to women in the workforce. By the 1890s the trade union movement was reconciled to the view that the female workforce should be organised. Trade unions viewed women as difficult to organise. Many, like the Flax Roughers and Dressers union, excluded women from these entirely male processes. Women-only trade unions were recognised as a means to surmount the difficulties that women faced in becoming union members. Poor wages meant women were all too often unable to pay the weekly membership dues to a union. It was gradually becoming acknowledged that women should organise women into unions with a lower rate of subscription that reflected their low earnings.

When the annual 'parliament of labour' of the Trade Union Congress was held in Belfast in September 1893 it brought together British and Irish conference

---

[17] TOSI underwent a number of name changes in its early years. It was first called the Association of Textile Operatives of Ireland. It is then reported as the Textile Operatives of Ireland. Months later it appeared as the National Union of Textile Operatives. Then it was known as the Irish Textile Workers' Association. It is in 1899 that the Belfast Trades Council minutes record the union by the name it became known throughout its independent life, the Textile Operatives' Society of Ireland. These name changes suggest its uncertain fortunes in its early years.

delegates and organisers of the Women's Trade Union League as guests of the Belfast Trades Council who united to launch a new women's union for linen workers.[18] A previous attempt in 1890 by the Belfast Trades Council and WTUL had set up women's unions, replicating the structure of men's linen unions, by organising three separate organisations to represent the different processes of linen production done by women.[19] These Belfast societies of Weavers, Warpers and Winders, of Warehouse Workers, and the Spinners, Preparers and Reelers of 1890 had not survived the enthusiasm of their early recruits.

Both the WTUL and the Belfast Trades Council nurtured the fledgling organisation. A textile trade union leader from the north of England, Mr Lord, was based in Belfast to encourage the new union. William Walker, a leading figure on the trades council, was appointed its first general secretary. As in 1890, the original enthusiasm for the union evaporated. Membership fell steadily in its first twelve months from 750 to 250 women. Discontent surfaced between the women and their part-time secretary, Walker. By October 1894 the Belfast Trades Council agreed that the 'interests of the Irish Textile Association would be best served by obtaining the services of a lady organiser and secretary.'[20] Twenty pounds was raised by the trades council and Susan Cockbill was appointed the first woman secretary. Her appointment did not stem the tide. When a WTUL organiser, Mrs Marland Brodie, a former north of England textile trade unionist, came to Belfast for a recruitment drive in 1895 the Textile Operatives' Union had only 400 members. Meetings were held in eleven localities, 'choosing the most suitable for the workers', which doubled the membership.

Whilst no records appear to have survived of Mary Galway's involvement in the initial years of the union, her subsequent career suggests she may have been a member from its earliest days, either sitting decorously among the women in the Ulster Hall in 1893, or signing up in the recruitment drive in 1895. She must have been an early and committed member. The fact that she was already president of the Textile Operatives' Society during the linen strike in January 1897, holding a voluntary and elected position at the head of the union, would indicate that she had an established record of activism within it.

On 19 January strikes stopped the linen mills and factories in Belfast. The thousands of strikers were, 'mostly women and girls.'[21] The employers' association had posted up new rules that governed both the industrial discipline

---

[18] A brief account of the launch of the union and its early years can be found in Theresa Moriarty, *Work in Progress: Episodes from the History of Irish Women's Trade Unionism* (Belfast and Dublin, 1994), pp. 7-9.

[19] Norbert C. Soldon, *Women in British Trade Unions, 1874-1976* (Dublin, 1978), p. 43.

[20] BTC Minutes, 18 October, 1894.

[21] Board of Trade, *Reports on Strikes and Lock Outs*, 1898, C.9437, p. xli.

of the workforce and the quality of their product. These rules spelled out prohibitions, and set fines and deductions for various misdemeanours and infringements, whether by standards of work or conduct. Terms of engagement, notice, punctuality and absences were all regulated by such rules. The most resented were those rules that spelt out fines for spoiling the cloth and singing or talking. The system of deducting such fines from its meagre wages was long established in the industry. A new Truck Act in 1896 ruled that the table of deductions should be displayed in the workplace. Whilst many of these had previously been in force, the new law acted as a catalyst to ignite a long-standing grievance among the women.

Negotiations between the workers and the employers were led by the Belfast Trades Council, including Mary Galway, TOSI's president, as the workers' representative. The strikes were successful, 'and considerable modifications of the rules were posted.'[22] The circumstances in which Galway moved from an elective to an appointed position in the union are unrecorded. Perhaps she displaced Susan Cockbill, or stepped in to fill the empty post. Either way, her conduct of the strike and negotiations as TOSI President, led to her appointment in July 1897 when Cockbill left the job that summer. Galway was now the appointed organising secretary of TOSI. In 1900 it became a full-time position. Her new post and her long years of service marked the end of the patronage of the women's textile union by the Belfast Trades Council and the WTUL. TOSI remained affiliated to the WTUL, and a member of the trades council, but was regarded by both as a fully autonomous organisation, no longer operating under their guidance. Writing in the 1920s, Galway recalled that when she took over the work of the Textile Operatives' Society of Ireland she

> found the conditions of female employment deplorable. The workers were not organised, and employers took advantage of this to treat their employees in a manner which seems incredible. I found women of long experience and skill being paid 10s weekly for a 54 hour week, and men, equally skilled, 14s weekly.[23]

In 1908 Mary Galway described the pattern of her working life to a government inquiry, 'I do the book work, enter members' names, visit members, canvass for members, hold meetings, start new branches, superintend the collectors, look after fines.'[24] The work of the organising secretary demanded a range of talents. In addition to such routine tasks, a union secretary was also required to be a skilled recruiter and mobiliser. Galway's years as a machinist would have

---

[22] Board of Trade, *Reports on Strikes and Lock Outs*, 1897, C.9012.

[23] Mary Galway, 'The linen industry in the North' in William G. Fitzgerald (ed.), *The Voice of Ireland* (Dublin, 1924), pp. 296–7.

[24] Mary Galway evidence, 13 February 1908, *Truck Committee, Inquiry*, p. 256, Q. 16667.

provided little experience of book work. At the end of the nineteenth century, and beyond, there was a great social gulf between both the routine and status of the office and the industrial worker. She entered an unfamiliar environment for a young hemstitcher. But her years as a machinist would have worked to her advantage, as James Haslam pointed out, since her personal experience in the linen industry kept Galway close to her membership.[25] Evidence she was to provide at government inquiries over the years suggests there was a close association with her members.

Before the First World War membership of the Textile Operatives' Society of Ireland remained small. Although it had been formed as a union embracing all categories of women workers in the linen industry it never recruited anything like a majority of the workforce. The fluctuating total of one to three thousand was always a tiny fraction of the linen workers, estimated in tens of thousands. The small size of the women's union ensured a personal, almost household relationship between its only full-time official and the members. The geography of Belfast's linen districts reinforced the domestic pattern of this relationship. The linen industry had dug its foundations into the well-irrigated districts west of the city precincts, where the streams from the hills gathered into the rivers that powered the early mills and factories. Industrial districts were shaped by the proximity of home and work. Employment was sought out in the domestic neighbourhoods. Women's household responsibilities encouraged this close association between workplace and home. Many of Belfast's linen workers lived in homes owned by and adjacent to the companies for which they worked.[26] The Belfast Trades Council complained that one firm 'compelled' some of their workers to live in the company houses, 'which were dearer and less comfortable.'[27] Intimacy within the union was strengthened by the family ties that bound generations of linen workers, as older women recommended younger family members to their employers. Male unemployment or irregular work reinforced this pattern.

In the 1920s Galway described the generational model of women linen workers in a family profile that was close to her own circumstances.

> Three females are employed for one male. You will find whole families of girls in the mills or factories – sometimes the mother and several daughters. The spinners and weavers of today are the daughters of spinners and weavers, so that skill runs in the blood; there are to-day in no part of the world more competent textile workers than the women of Ulster.[28]

---

[25] Haslam, 'Barefoot half-timers'.
[26] Galway, 'Linen industry', p. 296.
[27] BTC Minutes, 21 May 1898.
[28] Galway, 'Linen industry', p. 296.

Membership of the union itself shared a similar kinship of close family links. At times this model may have even shaped Galway's view of trade unionism itself. When she took on the Belfast Trades Council in 1901 for their lack of support for her union she proposed that, 'If the Trades Council of Belfast was really in earnest, they should begin at home, and organise their own sisters and daughters.'[29] She was addressing the trade union movement's own self-image as a male organisation, in which she was accorded an uncomfortable place as a woman trade union official, and which categorised women as a subordinate workforce, asserting women's dependency as family members. When James Connolly organised Belfast linen workers in 1911-12, he took such family ties for granted. He recognised the women of York Street mill whom he organised, as family members of the dockers in the Irish Transport and General Workers Union (ITGWU). He was to use this association to justify his organisation of these women.

From the start the membership fee of TOSI was a few pence. The 2d weekly fees went into a common or single, fund. Galway's wages and all the running costs of the union were paid from this. Galway's responsibility for her union finances led to other binds between union and members. The collecting of membership subscriptions was one of her responsibilities as a trade union official. Members paid their union dues weekly to district collectors, who, customarily, were appointed by the membership. This system of collecting union dues was, by the Women's Trade Union League account, based 'on the Lancashire system', where members were visited at home by the collector.[30] By December 1897 there were twelve TOSI collectors.[31] The system employed by TOSI was probably unique in Ireland. These collections guaranteed a weekly personal contact between all the members and the trade union. It reinforced the domestic contact between them, and provided a conduit for information to the union office itself. Galway told a government inquiry that whilst, 'the workers do come and report', she often heard of their complaints from the district collector, 'and I go and visit the worker at her home.'[32]

Not all her union contacts with members were contained in the privacy of their homes, though this was always included in Galway's strategy of reaching women workers. Mary McGee, a linen worker interviewed by Peter Collins, recalled a picture of Mary Galway that describes not only the correspondence of the public and domestic place in her union work, but also how Galway's professional duties engaged with her personal commitments.

Miss Galway went to seven o'clock mass in St Paul's, Beechmount, every

---

[29] ITUC, *Annual Report*, 1901.
[30] *WTUR*, October 1893.
[31] *WTUR*, January 1898.
[32] Mary Galway, evidence, 13 February 1908, *Truck Committee, Inquiry*, Q. 16675

morning. After this she stood outside making herself available to the girls. She
also talked to small crowds of workers. Then she would send little girls round
the doors to post handbills.[33]

She could be an innovative organiser. She reported in her first year that TOSI
held an annual ball at the end of the year. In 1905, she recorded, 'We still
continue to hold monthly free concerts during the winter months, and they do
a great deal of good in keeping our members together.' At these events she
invited a trade council member to speak 'on the benefits of organisation, etc.'
Galway later recalled the 'uphill work' of her early years as organising secretary:

> I had not been long in office before complaints began to pour in from my
> members of starvation wages and unjust fines for alleged defects in work,
> instant dismissals instead of the usual two weeks' notice, for refusal to pay
> wages earned, overheating and improper ventilation of mills and factories,
> unsatisfactory sanitary arrangements, dangerous machinery improperly fenced,
> women and children compelled to carry from place to place parcels of goods
> of excessive weight; and the old trick of time-cribbing, i.e., manipulating the
> works' clock so that the workers began again after breakfast or dinner a few
> minutes before the proper time.[34]

Linen workers' representatives operated in an industry of hostile employers.
Visiting members in their homes was a necessity forced by the employers'
repeated refusal to accept workers' representatives on their premises. At times
employers took extreme measures. When, for example, twenty-three
hemstitchers approached their employers, McBride & Co, to protest at an
unnotified wage reduction they 'had the hose turned on them.'[35] Galway
described her own approach to recalcitrant employers.

> In some cases, when I brought these grievances before the employers, they
> were remedied; in other instances I was ordered out, and told they would
> deal with the workers direct. Frequently we had to take legal action to recover
> unjust fines and wages. But in most cases the employers settled before it came
> to court.[36]

The fines system remained a long running source of discontent. It built into the
relationship between employer and workers a constant cause of complaint over
the rights and remuneration of their labour.

---

[33] Peter Collins, 'Mary Galway', *Labour History News*, 7, (1991), p. 40. (This is the
first biographical account of Mary Galway).
[34] Galway 'Linen industry', p. 297.
[35] BTC Minutes, 16 December, 1898.
[36] Galway, 'Linen industry', p. 297.

Belfast linen companies had few rivals in pettiness. In 1910, when King Edward VII died, linen workplaces were closed by the employers in a demonstration of national mourning. A number of firms stopped the women's wages for the day of the royal funeral. Some firms, Galway reported, were 'mean enough to deprive the girls of their bonus payments as well as their wages.' The Flaxdressers' Union secretary, Dawson Gordon, said his spinners had lost 2/8d.[37] On Coronation Day, the following year, when a similar works holiday was declared by the linen employers, the workers' wages were 'stopped in all but one factory and ware house.'[38] Galway described the Belfast linen companies in 1908 as 'the most unscrupulous lot of employers in the world.'[39]

At a protest meeting in September 1910 on sweated work Galway told the audience, to cries of 'shame', 'If it was known that the workers had given any information they would be dismissed by some of their Christian employers.' When she borrowed handkerchiefs made by an unnamed woman to demonstrate her work at this meeting, the woman was sacked by her employer, despite her record of thirty years work for the company. In evidence gathered by Galway to the linen inquiry of 1912 all the direct testimony from the workers was presented anonymously. Workers 'would consent to appear at inquiry – on understanding it would be private.'[40] Ireland's first woman factory inspector, Hilda Martindale, said most complaints she received from workers came through the unions or anonymously. After twenty years of organising women, Galway still cited the linen employers' intimidation as making it difficult to build linen trade unions.

Six months after her appointment as organising secretary of her union, Galway was elected onto the executive of the Belfast Trades Council at the annual meeting in 1898. After serving for four years she headed the annual poll, drawing support from the range of the city unions and branches. She was an intermittent attender in her early years. At times her union meetings clashed with the Trades Council. The trades report section of the minutes is punctuated by a series of strikes and disputes, when she turned to the Trades Council to air her members' grievances, report on successful or unsatisfactory settlements, or to win support or representation from the council in disputes. Her occasional interventions at the Trades Council seem confined to issues affecting her members rather than on the routine or broader matters of Trades Council business. But it was on the Belfast Trades Council that she established her reputation as an advocate and representative of women linen workers. The same year as her first election to the Trades Council executive she brought her members' cause to a wider stage.

---

[37] BTC Minutes, 2 June 1910.
[38] BTC Minutes, 3 August 1911.
[39] ITUC, *Annual Report*, 1908, p. 49.
[40] BTC Minutes, 19 August 1911.

In 1898 Mary Galway, the new organising secretary of TOSI, and Lizzie Bruce represented the textile operatives as delegates to the fifth annual congress of the Irish Trade Union Congress (ITUC).[41] At this time the union had one thousand members. From 1898 and for the next fourteen years, the textile operatives were the only female representation in that body. Galway's attendance at the annual congress was not unbroken. The presence of the TOSI delegation at the annual ITUC charts her union's progress. After the 1898 conference she did not attend again until 1901. This suggests TOSI did not affiliate to the ITUC in those years. In 1901, the Belfast Trades Council discussed a motion to reduce the affiliation fees for the female societies to five shillings, indicating that the struggling Textile Operatives' union was finding it hard to meet its financial obligations. Galway broke her attendance at the annual ITUC again in 1906, detained by meetings and negotiations during the Belfast linen strike in May and June. A small union, with only one full-time official, could not send a delegation while there were such demands on their resources.

Mary Galway was a consistent contributor to the Congress debates where she addressed the issues of her own industry and her women members. She spoke at her first national trade union congress to propose that a woman factory inspector should be appointed to Ireland. The founding Congress of the ITUC in 1894 proposed that of the three additional inspectors needed, two of them should be women. The first woman factory inspector in Britain had only been appointed that year, and in Ireland all factory inspectors were men. When the new women factory inspectors reported on women's workplaces in Ireland, they only came on a visiting inspection. Galway's call for a woman inspector based in Ireland was described by the ITUC president in 1905 as, 'the repeatedly adopted resolution of the Textile Operatives' Society.' She moved this resolution annually until Hilda Martindale was appointed in 1909 as Ireland's first female factory inspector, with responsibility for all women's workplaces in the country. Galway spoke later, in 1915, of twelve years of 'strenuous exertion' to win from the government Ireland's first Resident Lady Inspector of Factories.

At times Galway spoke out about broader issues. At the Sligo Congress in 1901 she challenged the mentors of her own union, the Belfast Trades Council, for their lack of commitment to women's trade unionism. The ITUC annual report notes that

> Mary Galway complained that the Trades Council of Belfast made no serious effort to organise women in that city. After eight years work, she regretted to say that out of sixty thousand female workers in Belfast, only twelve hundred were members of the Textile Operatives' Society of Ireland. If the Trades Council of Belfast was really in earnest, they should begin at home.[42]

---

[41] A second delegate, the basic representation for any affiliated union of one thousand members to the ITUC annual conference, accompanied Mary Galway each year.

[42] ITUC, *Annual Report*, 1901, p. 38.

Whilst she rarely made such a forthright public attack on her colleagues, Galway maintained an undercurrent of dissatisfaction at any neglect of her members' concerns. In 1901 she argued for a woman factory inspector because, 'the men inspectors seem to have too much to do to pay any attention to the women workers.'[43] At the 1904 Congress she criticised the government for not appointing a woman inspector saying, 'It was time that women workers received some attention.'[44]

She spoke most consistently on industrial issues. In 1903 she raised for the first time a second annual motion, to demand legislation for shuttleguards. The unguarded shuttles of the looms were a constant threat and cause of injury to the weavers. In 1905 she called for the abolition of overtime for women workers. She criticised the fines system in her own industry and called for greater inspection of ventilation and sanitation. On the death in 1906 of Lady Dilke, who had launched the Women's Textile Union in 1893, Galway appealed to Irish trades councils to help set up a fund in her memory.

Away from the union halls she worked to build up her membership and publicise their conditions. In April 1906 she addressed a recruitment meeting of women linen workers organised by the Belfast Trades Council. The same week the Council's monthly journal, the *Belfast Labour Chronicle,* published the first article in a series on women linen workers, 'Our Sweated Girls', by 'Junia'. Galway may have been the author. The first article which appeared on 7 April dealt with handkerchief stitching, her own trade. In a campaign for homeworkers in 1910 she remarked how she had tried to arouse sympathy on sweating four years earlier. Action by linen workers followed quickly on these initiatives. In early May 1906, within weeks of the first 'Junia' article, spinners in the York Street mill demanded an extra shilling a week.[45] The spinners' strike began on 14 May. It spread quickly through the city, as groups of young women took their case around the mills. Soon 15,000 women had left work, as support for wage increases spread through all grades of the linen workforce. The flaxworkers and spinners won an advance. The weavers who joined the strike on 21 May were refused.

The 1906 linen strike lasted through May and into June. Thousands of workers in all departments were laid off by the striking weavers and winders. The Board of Trade estimated that 24,000 flax spinners and weavers were affected.[46] By the end of May thirty factories in the city were closed by the employers. Galway met with the powerloom employers to argue for a uniform rate in the industry. A great meeting of workers in the Ulster Hall, due to start

---

[43] *WTUR*, October 1901.
[44] ITUC, *Annual Report*, 1904, p. 43.
[45] For an account of this dispute see Mats Greiff, 'Marching through the streets singing and shouting', *Saothar,* 22, 1997, pp. 40-41.
[46] Board of Trade, *Labour Gazette*, vol. 14, no 6, June 1906, p. 188.

at 8pm, had to lock the doors half an hour early because of the huge attendance. The meeting was addressed by Trades Council members, William Walker and John Murphy. Mary Galway proposed the motion calling for sympathy and support for the women strikers.

Mary Macarthur, secretary of the newly formed, 'cross-channel'[47] National Federation of Women Workers, which united the majority of British women's unions into a single organisation, came to Ireland at the invitation of the textile operatives and the Trades Council to support the strike and negotiations. She joined Galway on strike platforms throughout the district. The public meetings signed up new recruits.[48] By June the dispute had spread throughout the linen factories surrounding, as well as within, the city. Disturbances, violence and mêlées were reported from different places. The dispute led to hardship. The Trades Council secretary applied to the city Poor Law Guardians for outdoor relief for the locked out women. A group of the women put their case to the International Federation of Miners' meeting in London, for support. This may have been at the initiative of Macarthur, who had proposed a financial appeal for the Belfast women.

Galway met with the Viceroy, Lord Aberdeen, to plead the women's case, and publicly criticised him when he later advised the workers to return to work.

> Whatever happens in this dispute the Belfast employers have not heard the last word on the subject. We intend to continue organising until the Irish operatives are as strong as they are in Lancashire, and we don't intend to stop until we have secured for the Belfast mill and factory female workers who now exists on the most miserable wages, a standard of pay similar to that which prevails in that great industrial centre of England.[49]

In mid June the weavers returned to work on the old terms, unsuccessful in their claim, despite the groundswell of support. Although the strike had spread through linen centres in Antrim, Armagh, Down and Tyrone, the only group to win the wage increase were the Belfast spinners. The general return to work marked the end of the dispute, save for one hundred machine boys in Ballymena who held out for the one shilling instead of the threepence they were awarded.

In the aftermath of the 1906 strike membership of TOSI grew significantly for the first time. A report from the WTUL noted that 'membership of the union [TOSI] has more than doubled and a strong branch has been formed in Lisburn. Concessions were obtained by negotiation in the outlying districts.'[50]

---

47 *Irish News*, 6 June 1906.
48 *Irish News*, 4 June 1906.
49 *Irish News*, 8 June 1906.
50 Women's Trade Union League, annual report, 1907.

There were five thousand applications to join the union, but only 900 joined. A short-lived Londonderry Textile Operatives' Society was formed, probably for shirt workers, since the secretary was named as Miss McCarron, sister of the Irish secretary of the Amalgamated Society of Tailors. Galway's public role in the 1906 linen strike brought her further prominence. Her increased standing at the Trades Council was demonstrated by her nomination to a local labour election committee in the Victoria ward in October.[51] This was a formal recognition of her reputation as well as her abilities, since women were disqualified from voting, and consequently rarely, if ever, appointed to election committees.

At the 1907 ITUC she was voted onto its executive body, the parliamentary committee, in third place. This was another distinction in her pioneering career. She was not only the first woman in Ireland to be elected to the national congress executive, but a pioneer of trade union women elsewhere. The first woman member of the British Trades Union Congress (TUC) parliamentary committee was not elected until 1917. Galway was re-elected to the Irish trade union executive every subsequent year until 1913. On the parliamentary committee Mary Galway was included on its delegations to meet the chief secretary of Ireland, Augustine Birrell. The men of the ITUC were delighted to boast that her inclusion on such a prestigious body meant they were ahead of their trade union brothers in Britain.[52]

During the 1907 Belfast strike, led by James Larkin, the newly arrived organiser of the British National Union of Dock Labourers, Galway gave consistent support. At the ITUC and at the Belfast Trades Council in May, she supported his motion backing the Belfast workers. She was among the Belfast trade unionists who spoke with him at his nightly meetings.[53] Her own experience of widespread industrial struggle during the linen strike the previous year may have inclined her to support his militancy during the dockers' and carters' strike in the city.

One outcome of the 1906 linen strike undermined Galway's position. Although the spinners had been successful in the final settlement, signs of discontent at TOSI's handling of the dispute surfaced in the application of two hundred spinners to join the Flax Roughers' Trade Union, which up to then had not admitted any women as members. Before the dispute was over Galway criticised the union's recruitment of spinners at the Belfast Trades Council. 'Poaching' members is always a source of contention between unions. This inter-union row almost led to the flax roughers' withdrawal from the council. The women spinners stayed with their new union. By 1907 the flax roughers'

---

[51] BTC Minutes, 4 October 1906.
[52] ITUC, *Annual Report*, 1908.
[53] Collins, 'Mary Galway'; Austen Morgan, *Labour and Partition: The Belfast Working Class 1905-23* (London, 1991), p. 99.

claimed a third of their members, 600, were women, with 1,197 men,[54] and changed their name accordingly to the Flax Roughers' and Yarn Spinners' Trade Union. This newly 'mixed' union of men and women continued to deny women entry to the 'male' trades it organised.

TOSI, formed as a women's union, began to take in male members. Galway explained in 1908,

> We take in the men weavers because there is no union for them except the Textile Operatives' Society. We take in the men who are in a department for which there is no union, but we do not take in any men if there is a union for them.[55]

The inclusion of men as members was undoubtedly linked to the decision of the Flax Roughers' and Dressers' to organise women spinners. TOSI included other male workers beside weavers. Galway told a government inquiry in 1909 that '. . . our league includes all unorganised men and women, and men doing odd jobs in the spinning room, such as the doffers or boys carrying the roves.'[56]

Galway's feminism only comes together as a pattern of interlocking parts. She may have eschewed the term feminist, and never appears to have described herself as such. But on the immediate contemporary issue of feminism, votes for women, Galway voiced public support. At the ITUC she called for women to have the same political rights as men. The first national discussion of the extension of the franchise in the trade union movement had been for manhood suffrage – all men of twenty-one years and over, without any property qualification. At the 1908 Belfast ITUC, speaking about the progress of the sweated industries bill, Galway added that women should have the same political rights as men, and they should be admitted to parliament. 'Men', she argued, 'had sufficient to do in looking after matters which directly concerned them, and women's interests were neglected because they were not properly understood.'[57] A year later she amended an ITUC motion on electoral reform to include, 'the extension of the franchise to all adults, male and female.'[58]

In 1912, when an ITGWU motion for adult suffrage to the Home Rule parliament was proposed, the bookbinders' delegate implied women were not interested in the vote. He argued that votes for women would 'take way from the peace of the home', and destroy 'that nobility of character for which their women were prized.' Galway answered that women had the right to the vote

---

[54] United States Bureau of Labour, *The Women's Trade Union Movement in Great Britain* (Washington, 1909).

[55] Mary Galway evidence, 13 February 1908, *Truck Committee*, p. 259, Q.16763..

[56] Mary Galway evidence, 13 February 1909, *Accidents Inquiry*, p. 246, Q.6674.

[57] ITUC, *Annual Report*, 1908, p. 50.

[58] ITUC, *Annual Report*, 1909, p. 28.

regardless of whether it was a minority demand. 'Those who obeyed the laws of the land', she noted, 'should have some part in framing them.' She denied that it would destroy home life, but invested the vote with regenerative powers for women. The vote, she believed, 'would have the effect of making more intelligent and better mothers, and would cause them to take a greater interest in the welfare of their country.'[59]

Nor did she limit her advocacy of votes for women to suffrage debates. She raised the vote with other issues. In 1910, at a homeworkers' rally organised by trades council in the Ulster Hall, Galway urged the women in her audience to 'agitate until they got the franchise and representation in Parliament.'[60] A few days later she joined a women's suffrage platform to speak at the Central Hall about sweated labour in the linen industry. Her support for votes for women was framed within the trade union and socialist formula for full adult suffrage. Her persistent call for a vote that did not discriminate between men or women suggests a stronger commitment to women's enfranchisement than many of her trade union brothers, especially those socialists who were suspicious of the feminist campaign for votes as strengthening the propertied vote against the working-class interest.[61]

At the 1909 ITUC Galway became the executive vice president of the national congress for the coming year. She would be expected to assume the position of ITUC president, by custom, the following year. She was the only vice-president not to assume the presidency. We can only speculate on why this was so. William O'Brien, who was then a delegate from the Amalgamated Society of Tailors, and later the general secretary of the Irish Transport and General Workers' Union, wrote almost half a century later, that she had refused the position.[62]

In 1910 there were four branches of TOSI, with 2,476 members, 65 of whom were men. That year Galway added to her public standing in the storm of controversy which broke out in the newspapers, in the council chamber, and in the meeting halls of Belfast over the sweated conditions of the city outworkers in the making-up trades.[63] Thousands of women and their children worked in the home at hemming, stitching embroidering and thread drawing. Galway was in the forefront of the homeworkers' campaign. The previous year at the ITUC she had called for the inclusion of all sweated labour in factory and home to be brought under the new trades board, suggesting it was time to follow Australia's example and establish a minimum wage.

---

[59] ITUC, *Annual Report*, 1912, p. 53.
[60] *Belfast Newsletter*, 2 September 1910.
[61] Rosemary Cullen Owens, '"Votes for Ladies, Votes for Women": organised labour and the suffrage movement, 1876-1922', *Saothar*, 9, (1983), pp. 32-47.
[62] *Irish Times*, 2 February 1955.
[63] An account of this campaign can be found in Moriarty, *Work in Progress*.

This vast network of 'out' or 'home' workers was employed at home by the linen factories in the highly skilled 'finishing' or 'making up' trades. Embroidery, handkerchief and shirt finishing were the main tasks of these women. In addition, the factory workforce of women often took unfinished work home, a practice that grew in the early years of the twentieth century. The thousands of homeworkers made up a highly exploited and almost invisible, inaccessible workforce, beyond the view of workplace inspection. Domestic obligations and absence of childcare services forced women into this multitude of homeworkers. Sarah Patterson, for example, was a home worker. Her daughter, Sadie, became a linen trade unionist in the 1930s, and described the association of the mother and child's work in the home.

> It was my job to go to the warehouse to collect the bundles of work and then the following day to return the finished goods. Mother was paid a pittance. I have her last pay packet: 'Wages 16s 3d for 50 dozen sheets and overalls, less 1 sh[illing] for thread'. On her last day on earth she worked to 6 p.m. and died four hours later.[64]

Sadie Patterson's mother died in childbirth in 1918. Her 12 year old daughter had last seen her mother a few hours earlier as they had worked together on the last batch of materials for the making-up factory. At her dying mother's bedside she felt the strength of her religious belief and 'became a socialist that night', as she took over the responsibility for a family of eight.

At the end of 1909 Margaret Irwin, secretary of the Scottish Women's Industrial Council, published her investigation into 'Homeworking in Ireland', described by the *Belfast Newsletter*, as a 'lurid account.'[65] An even greater impact was made the following year by the publication of the 1909 annual report of the Belfast city medical officer, H.W. Bailie, who incorporated the findings of the survey of women's homework in the city by Jean Agnew, his sub-sanitary inspector. Among the litany of examples, he reported that,

> Quite recently our inspector was shown handkerchiefs which were to be ornamented by a design in dots; these dots were counted and it was found that the workers had to sew 384 dots for one penny. Comment is needless; other classes of work are as badly paid.[66]

Bailie made clear that such rates of pay were not exceptional. But this brief anecdote captured the public imagination and the 384 dots embroidered for a penny were quoted repeatedly in articles and arguments in favour of the homeworkers' cause. Galway's voice was raised throughout the protests. She

---

[64] David Bleakley, *Sadie Patterson: Irish Peacemaker* (Belfast, 1980), p. 4.
[65] *Belfast Newsletter*, 4 May 1910.
[66] H. W. Bailie, *Report on Health in the County Borough of Belfast* (Belfast, 1910).

joined suffrage meeting platforms to argue the women's case and headed a great protest meeting before an audience of mainly working women and girls. Joe Devlin, the nationalist MP, lent his name to the cause. Galway wrote a series of letters to the newspapers. The public campaign and outcry, which continued into 1911, led to an inquiry into the linen industry and a trade board was set up eventually to regulate the workers' rates of pay. Galway recalled that she 'took up the matter with the Belfast Trades Council. But public bodies move slowly, and it was not until 1915 that the Trade Board was set up.'[67]

When she chaired the proceedings of the 1910 ITUC annual conference, Galway was the first woman to hold such a position within the Irish trade union movement. The next woman elected to this position was Louie Bennett of the Irish Women Workers' Union, in 1931, who was to become the first ITUC woman president the following year. Only three other women held this position in over one hundred years, including Inez McCormack, Irish Congress of Trade Unions (ICTU) president 1999-2001.[68] Galway's chairmanship of the ITUC was not without controversy. In her opening remarks she called for a vote of sympathy to be passed to the Queen on the death of the King. She spoke, she said as a woman. But there was opposition among the delegates. A new, more socialist and nationalist, section of the delegates was now attending. William O'Brien spoke for them in his opposing call for a vote of sympathy with the victims of the Whitehaven colliery disaster. Galway halted the discussion by taking a standing vote in the hall and declared it carried. A motion and collection for the Whitehaven miners raised £4.1s.3d.[69] Nevertheless Galway topped the poll to the prestigious parliamentary committee. She joined the parliamentary committee as the acknowledged champion of women linen workers whose cause she had upheld from public platforms and before official committees. Between 1908 and 1912 Galway was called to give evidence to House of Commons' committees on truck, accidents, shuttles and linen homeworkers. In 1911 she attended a new Advisory Trade Committee for Ireland as a workers' representative.[70] It was at the height of this fame that a row developed on the Belfast Trades Council which has shaped her historical reputation.

1911 was punctuated by a succession of disputes in the linen industries, with mixed results. A claim at the Albion Cloth Works was unsuccessful; McBride & Williams reduced wages; the dispute at the New Northern Spinning Company was settled by negotiations, but in the Ropeworks the dispute led to no advance in wages. Few of these women were in TOSI, or members of any trade union at all. In the autumn of 1911 the dispute developed between Mary Galway and

---

[67] Galway, 'Linen industry', p. 297.
[68] The other two were Helena Molony and Helen Chenevix, both of the Irish Women Workers' Union.
[69] *The Harp*, June 1910.
[70] *Irish Worker*, 19 August 1911.

James Connolly for which she is best remembered. The argument arose from a strike at the York Street mill. The women who had walked out went to Connolly to ask him for support. He insisted he told them to go to Mary Galway, and when the women rejected this idea, he then stepped in to help them. The consequence of this was the opening of a women's section of his union, which he named the Irish Textile Workers' Union, employing the same initials as his union used colloquially, as Irish Transport Workers' Union.

Mary Galway viewed this new textile workers' union as a rival. Only a couple of months earlier the Irish Women Workers' Union had been formed in Dublin as an adjunct of the Irish Transport and General Workers' Union, with Delia Larkin, the sister of its general secretary, at its head. Galway may have had more than local fears about Connolly's Belfast efforts. Her resentment is clear. Connolly's report in the *Irish Worker*, under the pen name 'Seamus', said Galway had told the women to return to work. She denied this vigorously. This was not the first time she had to warn off poachers. In 1906 she had resisted the move by the Flax Roughers and Dressers to recruit women spinners. Now she was a woman in her middle age, with fourteen years of organising experience behind her. She was at the height of her public career. Her name, person and identity were indistinguishable from the cause of linen workers. She had been their spokesperson for almost fifteen years, and had addressed the plight of all women linen workers, not only those who were members of her union. She argued at the Trades Council there had not been a strike of women workers which had not been assisted by her union. Connolly himself was an influential member of the Council. He had arrived in Belfast in March as a local organiser for the Irish Transport and General Workers' Union, formed by James Larkin. That union had earned itself a considerable reputation. Connolly himself had returned from America the previous year with an established record as a socialist agitator.

The dispute between Galway and Connolly about who should organise women linen workers extended a 1910 argument on the Trades Council about the ITGWU organisation in Belfast docks. Galway won many supporters in her argument but not everyone agreed with her. Damaging allegations were made at the Trades Council to back up Connolly's assertion that the York Street millworkers had little faith in Galway's readiness to back them.

> Mr Graham said he failed to see how Mr Connolly had done any harm. He had heard Miss Galway state that the spinners and women workers in themselves were absolutely hopeless, and she admitted she could not do anything with them. If she had gone to Mr Connolly and said 'Good luck to you; I will give you all the assistance I can' she would have been acting in the true spirit of trades unionism.[71]

---

[71] BTC Minutes, 21 October 1911.

Her frequent exasperation at the women who did not join her union had not stopped her from speaking up for them. But this less public opinion, repeated in the chamber of the Trades Council, was damning.

Whilst the harsh words of Galway are often cited in the accounts of this row, no attention is paid to the language used by Connolly of her. 'He [Mr Connolly] advised the members of the council not to be led astray by Miss Galway's petulance and tantrums, and concluded by saying that she had been raising a storm in a teacup.'[72] Galway's angry words about Connolly, describing him as 'an adventurer', are more deeply etched on the historical record, than his accusation of her 'petulance and tantrums.' This was a very political row. Divisions on the Trades Council in this dispute fell on either side of the fault line of trade unionism, separating the older, more craft and labourist members from the newer, more confrontational socialists, whom Connolly represented.

The following spring this row spilled over into the 1912 ITUC, when members of the Belfast Trades Council objected to the admission of the Irish Women Workers' Union. The IWWU had registered late and some Belfast delegates opposed its status as an independent union. Mary Galway accused James Connolly of building trade unionism along sectarian lines. The angry exchange of the Belfast delegates was lost on the rest of the hall, and the IWWU representation was accepted. Galway's antagonism towards the IWWU did not end there. She objected when Delia Larkin was called to second the TOSI motion on factory inspection. What may have been a gesture of reconciliation became a further acrimonious exchange. Galway insisted that TOSI's second delegate, Elizabeth McCaughey, was sent to the Congress 'specially to second the resolution.' She accused the chair of prompting Delia Larkin to second the motion. Delia Larkin withdrew. Later when the standing orders committee rejected TOSI's objection to the IWWU affiliation the newspapers reported that, 'Miss Galway shouted with some heat –"There is a clique in the Belfast Trades Council who back these people up".'[73] Whilst she made no alliance within the trade union movement with her contemporary, Delia Larkin, Galway seems to have co-operated at Congress with the only other woman trade unionist attender, Minnie Rogers, of the small local Lurgan Hemmers' and Veiners' Trade Union.

Galway was not entirely isolated from other women industrial campaigners. She maintained some networks to other women operating in her field. She kept her union's affiliation and contact with the Women's Trade Union League in Britain. Her criterion of engagement appears to be the commitment other women gave to her own causes and her union. She had worked with Mary Macarthur in 1906. Hilda Martindale, Ireland's first female factory inspector, recalled a welcoming invitation,

---

[72] *Ibid.*
[73] *Irish News*, 30 May 1912.

from Miss Galway, the intrepid General Secretary of the Textile Operatives' Society of Ireland, to give some weekly talks to the women workers of Belfast on those requirements of the Factory and Truck Acts which affected them, as workers in their every day life.[74]

Jean Agnew, Belfast City Council sub-sanitary inspector, who researched women homeworkers for Bailie's 1909 report was another woman who worked with Mary Galway. Galway's association with other women officials demonstrates her practical employment of these women's skills and status, in her members' cause rather than as a personal network of support.

In 1912 most of Galway's effort went into the comprehensive inquiry into linen workers' pay and conditions in the making-up trades. Hundreds of workers gave evidence. This led to establishment of the first trades board for the linen industry. She attended her last national trade union Congress in 1913, when the Belfast Trades Council withdrew from the ITUC. She was voted off the parliamentary committee that year. In 1913 Galway had other issues to deal with than her place at the ITUC. Her union was sued by Mary Rooney of Leeson Street, the mother of a TOSI member who had been refused insurance payment on her daughter's death. Galway had argued that the woman had been insured for such a short time that the union would lose out by paying the five pounds death benefit. The union's case was that the daughter was not in benefit when she died, since her insurance payments were in arrears. There was a legal dispute about the standing of the union rules. The judge, Walker Craig, ruled the union should pay up. He 'severely criticised' the union, saying the 'defence was not creditable to the society.' He singled out the rule that allowed the union executive the final authority to vote on the spending of its funds.

The following night's meeting of the Trades Council regarded his judgement as a comment on the 'honesty of the society.' Galway gave a detailed account of the member's subscription record, arguing that the committee had no power to pay the claim, since the union members had 'strongly objected' to payments made in a similar case shortly before. The concern at Judge Craig's ruling was not confined to Belfast trade unionists. The British Labour Party had expressed its interest at the outcome. Galway wanted the judge censured. He had already come to the notice of the city trade unions in a series of compensation cases where his partiality had been denounced, most especially by James Connolly. In 1912 he called for Craig's removal. In 1913 Galway echoed Connolly's move in a call to have Craig censured.

Finances may have been an issue in the union at this time. Its members still paid a low rate of subscription. Betty Messenger's researches into the linen workforce recorded that it was said that 'every time Mary Galway got an increase

---

[74] Hilda Martindale, *From One Generation to Another* (London, 1944), p. 141.

in pay for her women, the amount of their contribution was increased.'[75] By 1913 TOSI was struggling to meet its financial obligations under the insurance act which charged unions to collect the workers' contributions. In July Galway told the Trade Council that the national insurance sickness benefit for women members was inadequate. It was 'absolutely impossible' for the union, 'to meet the demands upon them owing to the extremely low health of the persons insured.'[76]

Galway continued to serve on the Trades Council and on many of its committees. She retained support on the council, illustrated by her topping the poll in the executive committee elections, in which James Connolly came last. In October 1913, she was provisionally elected by the Trades Council to sit on the proposed trade board for the linen industry. She maintained TOSI as an independent trade union, negotiating independently from other unions in the linen industry. During the war linen manufacturing came under the munitions legislation, as so much of the fabric was used in the war industries, notably the new weave of aircraft linen. The munitions regulation introduced national bargaining, and for the first time linen workers' pay and conditions were settled by national arbitration, not by walkouts and negotiations.

TOSI benefited from this new industrial climate. In 1915, in a talk on trade unions and women's employment to a Dublin meeting of the Women's Industrial Conference, Galway reported TOSI was active in many parts of Ulster as well as in Drogheda and Kilkenny in Leinster.[77] At the end of 1918 there were over 10,000 members.[78] It remained aloof from the other linen unions' plan to join a linen trades federation. Galway remained TOSI general secretary until her death. She continued her work on the trades boards under Stormont in the 1920s. Mary Galway died aged sixty-four years, at home in 31 Crocus Street on 26 September 1928 of heart failure. Her union organised her funeral from Belfast to the family burial plot in Kilwarlin, Co Down.

The character of Mary Galway's politics appear quite opaque. The late Paddy Devlin described her politics as 'Hibernian',[79] placing her in the predominant political culture of the period among Belfast's catholic working class. During her formative organising years the Irish trade union movement had a close working relationship with the Irish Parliamentary Party, especially through the lobbying of the ITUC parliamentary committee. Whilst Galway rarely contributed to the political debates on Irish self government within the

---

[75] Betty Messenger, *Picking up the Linen Threads: Life in Ulster's Mills* (Belfast, 1988), p. 209.

[76] BTC Minutes, 3 July 1913.

[77] *Irish Citizen*, 11 December 1915.

[78] Barbara Drake, *Women in Trade Unions* (London, 1984), p. 238.

[79] Interview with the author.

trade union movement, her contribution to the Irish Free State publication, *The Voice of Ireland*, suggests she favoured, rather than repudiated, the new state.

As a trade union organiser, she employed the yardstick of British workers' pay and conditions repeatedly as a contrast to her members and the women of her industry. This does not imply Unionist sympathies. This rhetoric was consistently applied by Irish trade unionists and industrial campaigners, even the most nationalist, to demonstrate Ireland's unequal standing in the kingdom, or emphasise the scale of their grievance. It addressed the disparities within the economic union in which they organised.

The abiding influence on Galway's politics before the First World War, when they were most clearly demonstrated, came from the Belfast Trades Council and the labourism of its mentor, William Walker, the Carpenters' Union official, in particular. Before this the Trades Council had abstained from politics with capital letters in an effort to maintain a unified platform in the face of the loyalties of Belfast's divided political culture. The Belfast labourism of the 1900s viewed the allegiances of the city's working class as the product of powerful manipulation by outside interests, which obstructed progress, and deferred economic justice. It predicated the weakness of the city's labour movement on these divisions.

Labour on the Belfast Trades Council sought to transcend division with an independent programme focused on the wages and conditions of working-class life in the city. Yet the practice of trade unionism by the men and women of the city's trade union movement was not isolated from the politically sectarian geography of Belfast. In a report of Galway's assumption of a full-time position in 1900, the British women's trade union journal had noted that bigotry had presented difficulties in organising TOSI. Such bigotry, it was noted,

> damages even the football of Belfast [and] is not without its effect on the Union. It has been impossible to get a room lent for a meeting in the Protestant quarter of the town whereas every facility of the kind has been offered in the Roman Catholic quarter.[80]

Fear of division left the city's labour movement unable to form any strategy towards the sectarianism they encountered. Sectarian practices were repeatedly regretted, but seldom identified or negotiated. Sensitivities towards sectarianism contributed to the Trades Council dispute between James Connolly and Mary Galway.

Within Belfast's labour politics Mary Galway found herself a women's sphere of activity. A Belfast branch of Women's Labour League was launched in 1908[81]

---

[80] *WTUR*, January 1900.
[81] *Woman Worker*, 26 June 1908.

and Galway became its vice president, providing talks on women and unions.[82] Her distinctive public position as Ireland's pioneering and premier woman trade unionist assigned her a marginal place in the all male Irish trade union movement that she countered by the intensity of her loyalties and commitment. The admission of a women's union in 1893-4, and the 1895 concession of a woman organiser, did not transform the terms on which the Irish trade union movement came together. Men's organisational forms remained the model of trade unionism. Trade unionism remained a difficult territory for women to navigate, as men demonstrated they had to be won over. Seeking male approval set limits on the opportunities to challenge it.

In her early years Galway relied on the sisterly support of the WTUL, and their attention and admiration, as her frequent reports and contact show. She continued her affiliation with the League as a resource where she could record her achievements and appeal for support in times of difficulty, at least until 1916, a few years before the League ceased operating as a forum for women trade unionists. Whilst a hard working official committed 'to better the lot of Irish women and girls', Mary Galway retained an ambivalence towards women workers. This was not uncommon among trade unionists who regretted, as she did, that women's early enthusiasm for trade unionism quickly evaporated. Her own sense of years of 'strenuous exertion' for the most modest advance, would have contributed to her exasperation with women workers revealed in the 1911 row on the Belfast Trades Council. Formed by her years in the discipline of the linen factory, and experienced in the constraints of formal trade unionism, Galway may have been incapable of imagining, as Connolly did in 1911, women challenging their working culture. When she reflected on 'Trade Unions and Women's Employment' for the Women's Industrial Conference in 1915, she did not cite apathy or servility as explanations for women's reluctance to embrace trade unionism wholeheartedly. She felt women were disadvantaged from their early years, as they were not brought up in a trade union atmosphere, 'as boys in well organised trades are.' The industrial workforce of young women had the example of their working mothers, who were not in unions and did without. The 'tender age' of girls who went out to work and the domestic duties that fell to them militated against their involvement.

The treatment of Mary Galway by labour historians has been cursory and dismissive. Many studies do not even mention her or her union. Neither John Boyle's *The Irish Labour Movement in the Nineteenth Century*, nor Andrew Boyd's *The Rise of the Irish Trade Unions*, established labour history texts, mention her. The single mention in Emmet O'Connor's *A Labour History of Ireland*, describes Mary Galway as 'a tenacious but none too radical lady who concentrated on signing up the better paid weavers', while Austen Morgan's study of the Belfast

---

[82] *Woman Worker*, 11 September 1908.

working class introduces her inaccurately, as

> A Belfast protestant, she had worked in the better end of the industry, and
> this is where she recruited her members. She shared the view of her male
> trade union colleagues, underestimating the domestic and social difficulties
> faced by many linen workers.[83]

Mary Galway consistently enters the labour history narrative as the instigator of
argument justifying Connolly's characterisation of her tantrums and petulance.[84]
Betty Messenger's study of the linen workforce is one of the earliest works to
treat Galway and her union as an integral part of the linen workforce.[85]
Historians' dismissal of TOSI arises most frequently because it was, as it is
repeatedly stressed, a small union. It most consistently organised around 1,500
members. After the 1906 membership rose to around 3,000, still a small section
of the workforce. This was not unique to TOSI. Overall membership of the
linen trade unions was low. In 1900 ten unions only counted 5,000 members in
all,[86] although this figure represents a higher rate of trade unionism among
men. In a 1908 list of the numerical strength of almost sixty unions with women
members, the overwhelming majority in the north of England local textile
unions, the Textile Operatives' Society of Ireland was in the top half of the
group with 2,900 women members. No other Irish union came close to this
number of women members. The Irish Drapers' Assistants, about the same size
as TOSI, had only 700 women in it. The Flax Roughers and Yarn Spinners
organised 600 women.[87]

    Mary Galway's evidence of her membership profile confirms the labour
history view that TOSI was better organised in the factories, not the mills. She
told a government inquiry in 1909 that of a total of less than two thousand

---

[83] Morgan, *Labour and Partition*, pp. 151-4. Similarly, John Gray's history, *City in
Revolt: James Larkin & the Belfast Dock Strike of 1907* (Belfast, 1985) has a handful of
references to linen workers, but none to Galway or her union except in a footnote
to William Walker's early career. It overlooks the 1906 linen strike as a prelude to
the 1907 strike. Henry Patterson's *Class Conflict and Sectarianism: The Protestant
Working Class and the Belfast Labour Movement, 1868-1920* (Belfast, 1980), does not
include her.

[84] W. P. Ryan, writing in *Labour in Irish History* in 1919, and reliant on the accounts
of Connolly's allies, William O'Brien and Cathal O'Shannon, devotes pages to
the Connolly row. Dermot Keogh's only reference to her recounts the row at the
ITUC about the vote of sympathy with the queen. See his *The Rise of the Irish
Working Class: The Dublin Trade Union Movement and Labour Leadership 1890-1914*
(Belfast, 1982), p. 148.

[85] Messenger, *Picking Up the Linen Threads* and Peter Collins, 'Mary Galway'.

[86] Andrew Boyd, *The Rise of the Irish Trade Unions* (Dublin, 1985), p. 70.

[87] Bureau of Labour, *Women's Trade Union Movement*.

members, 1,133 worked in the factory department, 971 of them weavers. A quarter of the members worked preparing and carding; 338 spinners and piecers, layers and doffers and reelers. Less than a hundred members worked in warehouses, in her own trade of 'making up' – 27 of them were men. Her own sector had the smallest membership. When her union is viewed in the context of women's and Irish linen unions, the textile operatives were the third largest of the ten textile linen unions in Ireland, it looks a healthier organisation than its numbers suggest. It was, in fact, a relatively substantial union.

Labour history's treatment of Galway and her union arises from a failure to engage with issues of gender and class within the main narrative. Labour history with women may need to shift perspectives, rather than add a set of extra paragraphs that extend the outline, but not the substance of women's labour history. The male model remains untouched. Women remain marginal in the big picture where traditional labour history replicates the conventions of the institutions under examination.

Mary Galway's life is reconstructed almost entirely from public records. The absence of personal documents may reflect the nature of her life. A working life as a machinist and trade union organiser, of daytime tasks and night-time meetings left her little opportunity for reflective writing. There was always a speech, a report or a letter to the editor to be drafted in pursuit of her members' interests. Equally the absence of personal records may imply personal reticence and restraint. In an account of writing historical biography, Carolyn Steedman wrote of her subject, Margaret McMillan, a minister in the first British Labour government, that one of the difficulties is that 'this public woman left no collection of letters, no journal with which to peel away the layers of public form, in order to reveal the true woman.' She concludes,

> She prevents delineation of an interiority: she demands a public life I think, that might perform the trick – not of dissolving the opposition between the inside and the outside, for that is not possible – but of letting us see, briefly, momentarily, how we might find new ways of interpreting lives that have been lived. It has to take as its central image that arresting rhetorical moment of the woman on the public platform[88]

Biography is an imprecise and artificial discipline of authorship. Historians may shape a life and shade in episodes to add further definition to a stark outline. But we are left with an enigma. Bereft of diaries, and collections of personal letters, we have only speculation. Or silence. In the process of mobilising information or evidence, we delude ourselves that we control the subject's destiny. Lives are not lived like that. They are shaped by accident, impetuous decision, and

---

[88] Carolyn Steedman, *Past Tenses: Essays on Writing, Autobiography and History* (London, 1992), p. 166.

emotion, as well as calculation and foresight. There is no guiding hand, as the historian biographer feigns. This account can only suggest ways that Mary Galway's life can be explored.

Louie Bennett (1870-1956)

Rosemary Cullen Owens

Louie Bennett lived through eighty-six years of global upheaval and transformation. Born into a world of nineteenth-century Victorian values, her life encompassed major developments in world history including the emergence of the democratic state, the rise and fall of fascism, and the development of nuclear power. The social and political upheavals effected by these events profoundly influenced her public and private life. Women, workers, and war emerge as the key issues that dominated her career.

Bennett was born in Dublin in 1870 into a Church of Ireland family. Her father, Charles Bennett, ran the family business of fine art auctioneer and valuer on Ormond Quay. Her mother, Susan Boulger, came from a family of some social standing in Dublin. Reflecting the strong class divide of nineteenth-century Dublin society, Susan's marriage to someone 'in trade' was greeted less than enthusiastically by her family. Bennett noted the significance of class, and even more particularly religion, in the new Dublin upper middle-class suburbs in her reminiscences to R.M. Fox.[1] Little detail is known of her life up to 1911. She appears to have had a happy childhood, growing up amidst the comforts associated with a privileged background. Educated initially at home with her brothers and sisters (there were ten children in all), Bennett later went to boarding school in England, and for a time to Alexandra College in Dublin. A fine contralto, she studied music for a short period in Bonn. She was keenly interested in literature, and from an early age was an avid reader. For a time she had ambitions as a writer and published two novels, *The Proving of Priscilla* in 1902 and *A Prisoner of his Word* in 1908. The growing women's movement however, came to dominate her life and determine its course. Fox presents her as a serious minded and practical young woman, a

---

[1] R.M. Fox, *Louie Bennett, Her Life and Times* (Dublin, 1957), pp. 11-14.

strong presence at times of financial crisis within the family – of which there were apparently many. Her father's death at an early age, and the marriage of most of her siblings would appear to have left Bennett with primary responsibility for her widowed mother, and later her invalided brother, Lionel.

Fox refers to an early essay by Bennett in which she indicated a parallel between the emergence of an increasingly articulate women's movement and the changing portrayal of women in fiction during the nineteenth century. The work of Charlotte Brontë, George Eliot, Olive Schreiner and Henrik Ibsen profoundly influenced the young Bennett, who observed that 'the new woman, conscious of untried energies and cramped intellectual powers, shrieked for freedom in her literature.' She described Olive Schreiner's *Story of an African Farm* as 'a cry of rebellion against many things in heaven and earth, but most of all, against the injustice of woman's position in the world.' Literature, indeed, would appear to have been the incubator of Bennett's latent feminism.

Bennett's work on behalf of women began with her involvement in the suffrage movement in 1911. Many new suffrage societies emerged in Ireland from 1903, reflecting the changing political and social environment. The use of militant tactics was viewed favourably by some of the new groups notably the Irish Women's Franchise League (IWFL) formed in 1908 by Hanna Sheehy Skeffington and Margaret Cousins. To co-ordinate the work of the many smaller societies that had developed by 1911, it was proposed that a federation be formed. At the inaugural meeting of this body – The Irish Women's Suffrage Federation (IWSF) – Bennett entered public life and was appointed joint honorary secretary with Helen Chenevix. Based in Dublin, the IWSF grew steadily, from fifteen affiliated societies in 1913 to twenty-four in 1916. There was now a suffrage society to suit all opinions, from the long established conservative Irish Women's Suffrage and Local Government Association (IWSLGA) and the militant IWFL, to the middle ground of the IWSF. It appeared, indeed, that the 'era of dumb, self-effacing women was over.'[2]

Through involvement with the suffrage movement many middle-class women were introduced to the problems facing working-class women. The organisation by Bennett of the Irish Women's Reform League (IWRL) as a Dublin branch of the IWSF indicated a broader agenda than equal voting rights. The IWRL investigated the social and economic position of women workers and their families, and its findings were published in the suffrage paper the *Irish Citizen*. Through the activities of the IWRL we can trace the development of Bennett from a suffragist to a trade unionist. In addition, her work with the

---

[2] J.H. and M.E. Cousins, *We Two Together* (Madras, 1950), p. 185. For detail on the suffrage movement see Rosemary Cullen Owens, *Smashing Times: A History of the Irish Women's Suffrage Movement 1889-1922* (Dublin, 1984 and 1996); Cliona Murphy, *The Women's Suffrage Movement and Irish Society in the Early Twentieth Century* (Brighton, 1989).

IWSF and the *Irish Citizen* reveal her pacifist/feminist convictions. Her views were also imbued with an international perspective.

The women's suffrage movement had become increasingly international in outlook from 1904 with the formation of the International Woman Suffrage Alliance (IWSA) by women from the United States, Australia and Europe. A series of international congresses were held, and in 1913 three Irish women attended the seventh such congress in Budapest – Bennett of the IWSF, Hanna Sheehy Skeffington of the IWFL, and Lady Margaret Dockrell of the IWSLGA. With the outbreak of war in 1914, the pacifist stance adopted by a significant section of the suffrage movement caused division within most national women's organisations. Throughout Europe feminist groups espousing pacifism quickly lost members. The overwhelming majority in all countries supported the war effort.[3] Carrie Chapman Catt and Jane Addams formed a Women's Peace Party in the United States in January 1915. These developments were followed with close interest in Ireland, where suffragists too were divided on the correct stance for women towards the war. Those with strong English/Unionist connections abandoned or postponed all suffrage work. Jingoistic references to 'our brave soldiers and sailors' peppered reports of the IWSLGA, offending both nationalist women and feminists. In despair Bennett wrote to Hanna Sheehy Skeffington that women's groups were 'like sheep astray and I suppose that when the necessity of knitting socks is over the order will be – Bear sons, and those of us who can't will feel we had better get out of the way as quickly as we can.'[4]

Bennett's international outlook becomes quite clear from this time, as does her commitment to pacifism. Early in 1915 the IWSF reversed its suspension of suffrage activities during the war, pointing out that votes for women was its primary objective. In the *Irish Citizen* Bennett stated unequivocally that 'Women should never have abandoned their struggle for justice, war or no war.'[5] Apart from differences among Irish women on the general war issue, those with pacifist beliefs faced a more direct challenge at home. In an environment where both nationalists and loyalists prepared for military confrontation, pacifism became an increasingly unpopular ideal. Louie Bennett and Frank Sheehy Skeffington were among the leading pacifist voices during this period. The latter continuously published anti-war articles in the *Irish Citizen* arguing that 'War is necessarily bound up with the destruction of feminism, feminism is necessarily bound up

---

[3] R.J. Evans, *Comrades and Sisters: Feminism, Socialism and Pacifism in Europe 1870-1945* (Sussex, 1987). For a detailed study of the pacifist movement in Ireland see Rosemary Cullen Owens, 'Women and pacifism in Ireland, 1915-1932' in Maryann Gialanella Valiulis and Mary O'Dowd (eds.), *Women & Irish History* (Dublin, 1997), pp. 220-238.

[4] Sheehy Skeffington papers, National Library of Ireland (Hereafter, NLI), Ms 22,667(ii).

[5] *Irish Citizen,* 11 December 1915.

with the abolition of war.'[6] A meeting of Dutch, Belgian, British and German women held in Amsterdam in February 1915 planned an international women's peace conference to be held in the Hague in April 1915. The IWRL held a meeting to discuss Irish participation. Fears were expressed by some that such activity might imply disloyalty to those fighting at the front.[7] Similar sentiments were being expressed throughout Europe. In the British press intending participants were derided as 'pro-Hun peacettes' going to 'pow-wow with the fraus', their desire for a negotiated peace being opposed as treachery.[8] Almost all governments tried to prevent their women attending The Hague. A joint committee of Irish women's groups chose seven delegates, but only Bennett was granted a travel permit – a concession invalidated by an Admiralty ban on travel that prevented her attendance. In Dublin in 1915 international feminist pacifist ideals came into direct contact with burgeoning domestic militarism. A public protest meeting was held in Dublin against this government action with James Connolly and Thomas MacDonagh among the speakers. In a letter of support to the meeting Padraig Pearse declared that much good would be done if the incident ranged more of the women definitely with the national forces. Bennett was much troubled at the militarist undertones of this protest meeting. Earlier that year she had argued in the *Irish Citizen* that 'Suffragists of every country must face the fact that militarism is now the most dangerous foe of women's suffrage, and of all that woman's suffrage stands for.' Now she voiced her concern in a domestic setting:

> Militarism in the most subtly dangerous form has its hold upon Ireland. Those women who take up the crusade against militarism must not tolerate the 'fight for freedom' and 'defence of rights' excuses for militarism.[9]

Writing privately to Hanna Sheehy Skeffington, Bennett noted that the tone of the meeting had been far more anti-English than anti-militarist, and that while the present war was reckoned barbarous and immoral, it would appear that a war for Ireland would be considered justified. She objected to this superficial form of pacifism. The issue of justifiable militarist action for nationalist objectives would be a source of contention within the Irish peace movement over the next fifteen years.

---

[6] *Irish Citizen*, 12 September 1914.
[7] Diaries of Lucy Kingston, March 1915, private collection. Kingston's involvement in the suffrage and pacifist movement are documented in Daisy Lawrenson Swanton, *Emerging from the Shadows: the Lives of Sarah Anne Lawrenson and Lucy Olive Kingston* (Dublin, 1994).
[8] Anne Wiltsher, *Most Dangerous Women: Feminist Peace Campaigners of the Great War* (London and Boston, 1985), pp. 89-90; see also Margaret Mulvihill, *Charlotte Despard: a Biography* (London, 1989), p. 115.
[9] *Irish Citizen*, 22 May 1915.

One of the factors that gave rise to the number of new suffrage associations formed since 1908 was a desire to be recognised as independent Irish societies. The long established IWSLGA had been criticised regularly in the press as 'an English society.' Thus the IWSF and the IWFL consistently emphasised their independence. In 1913 Bennett promised that the IWSF would remain truly and purely an Irish organisation, but nonetheless made clear her internationalist stance stating that 'we suffragists recognise the bond of sisterhood uniting women of every nationality.'[10] While fully committed to the internationalist ideal, Bennett lost no opportunity to obtain independent representation for Irish women. One such instance arose with the formation of the International Committee of Women for Permanent Peace (ICWPP) following The Hague Congress of 1915. Initially Ireland was included as part of the British branch. From the beginning the Irish branch sought separate representation. A formal resolution to the ICWPP by Bennett in October 1915 expressed the discontent of Irish members and demanded that the principle of nationality be clearly established in the constitution of the Party. She pointed out that 'the peace process in Ireland must be indigenous and independent to be in any sense successful.'[11] In January 1916 the Irish women took matters into their own hands and renamed their branch the Irishwomen's International League (IIL). The status of small and subject nations was discussed in depth by the ICWPP during 1916, and raised by Bennett at every international executive meeting. In December 1916 the IIL was formally accepted as an independent national organisation. An even longer campaign finally achieved national recognition for Ireland within the IWSA in 1922.

R. M. Fox claimed that Bennett maintained 'anti-national' views until after the Easter Rising.[12] However, Bennett and Frank Sheehy Skeffington were of one mind in their attitude to war and militarism, and writings by both of them during 1915 indicate clearly that they sympathised with the desire for independence but disagreed with the use of force to attain it. Bennett's persistent campaign for independent Irish representation at the ICWPP and the IWSA indicate that what Fox describes as her 'dormant national feeling' was roused long before the killings of 1916. Her vision of 'nationality' however, was a broad one, implying freedom for all peoples and nations, large and small. The outbreak of war in 1914, the implications for the fate of small nations during and after that war, and attempts by women world-wide to stop the killing and find a peaceful resolution, were the issues that drove Bennett to take the stand she did. The murder of Frank Sheehy Skeffington in 1916 was a particularly

---

[10] *Ibid.*, 17 May 1913.
[11] Louie Bennett to Chrystal MacMillan, 29 January 1916, Women's International League for Peace and Freedom Papers, University of Colorado, Boulder. (Hereafter, WILPF Colorado).
[12] Fox, *Louie Bennett*, p. 12.

severe loss for her. She hoped that the story of his death would do more to weaken the prestige of the militarist system than years of propaganda. Her role in continuing that propaganda can be witnessed through the work of the IIL. She informed ICWPP headquarters that their priority as an organisation would be the encouragement of a more conciliatory spirit among different sections of the nation.[13] The abandonment of an active suffrage campaign in Britain in favour of various war-works prompted Bennett to describe English women as a 'servile sex.' Noting that Irishwomen were more independent, she urged caution 'for our political women hang on blindly to their particular political half-good fetishes, whether Sinn Féin or Redmondites.' Documenting various committees with little female involvement, where men made decisions on women's issues, Bennett wrote in despair to Hanna Sheehy Skeffington that 'women in general are a poor crowd, willing to be under the thumb of men.'[14] The IIL lobbied Irish and British leaders for the inclusion of women's voice in any Irish settlement. The formation of a League of Nations was strongly supported by Bennett and the IIL, which welcomed the reorganisation of Europe on the principle of nationality. Irish and English branches of the ICWPP worked closely during this period, notably on the treatment of Irish political prisoners and opposition to conscription to Ireland.

In May 1919 the second congress of the ICWPP was held in Zurich. Of the sixteen participating countries, Ireland was one of the smaller countries represented for the first time, Louie and Hanna Sheehy Skeffington its delegates. The ICWPP was renamed the Women's International League for Peace and Freedom (WILPF) and its headquarters moved to Geneva.[15] An 'Appeal on Behalf of Ireland' presented by the Irish branch sought support for Ireland's 'legitimate struggle for the rights of self-determination.' These were tempestuous times for a pacifist organisation. Writing to WILPF's International Secretary at Geneva in October 1920 Bennett noted 'things are very difficult here and we are hard put to it to keep our little group together. We are really living in a "war-zone" in Ireland, and our minds and hearts are racked daily.'[16] Despite often radically differing political loyalties, Irish women's groups came together on a number of controversial issues, notably the 1918 campaigns against conscription and the implementation of venereal disease regulations. A further example of such co-operation produced in 1919 'An appeal on behalf of the Principal Women's Associations of Ireland' demanding the establishment of an international committee of inquiry into the conditions of Irish political prisoners.

---

[13] Louie Bennett to Dr. Aletta Jacobs, 5 June 1916 (WILPF Colorado).
[14] Sheehy Skeffington papers, NLI, Ms 22,279(vi) in folder of undated letters to Hanna Sheehy Skeffington between May and September 1916.
[15] This is still the current name and headquarters of the organisation. Proximity to the League of Nations was among the reasons for this location.
[16] Louie Bennett to Emily Greene Balch, 2 October 1920 (WILPF Colorado).

Signatories included Constance de Markievicz, Hanna Sheehy Skeffington, Maud Gonne MacBride and Louie Bennett. WILPF lobbied strongly on this issue. When a Commission of Inquiry into Irish affairs was established, Bennett travelled to Washington as an IIL delegate. From a somewhat different perspective Mary and Muriel MacSwiney also gave evidence to the Washington Commission. Cogniscent of women's influence, Cumann na mBan instructed MacSwiney in her subsequent tour of the United States to assure Americans that 'the women of Ireland are standing with the soldiers and that "no surrender" is the watchword.' MacSwiney's biographer noted that 'the organisation did not want women represented as a pacifist group urging the men to lay down their arms.'[17]

Bennett and the IIL sought to make the Irish question a moral rather than a political issue, concentrating on the constructive activities of Dáil Éireann rather than a chronicle of atrocities. Acceptance of the Treaty by Dáil Éireann and the ensuing civil war had profound effects both on the IIL organisation and on individual members attempting to ally pacifist convictions with political commitment. Somewhat naively, WILPF headquarters believed that acceptance of the Treaty meant that Ireland could put the nightmare of violence and outrage behind it. Explaining that in fact the Treaty was not popular, was accepted with bent head and a significant degree of grief and shame, Bennett asked 'Can you be surprised? We are asked to accept Common Citizenship with an Empire whose deeds we loathe.' She hoped that de Valera would be strong enough to lead his followers away from political division and concentrate on education and economic reconstruction, thus providing a 'healthy opposition to the Free State', but she was unsure, noting that the 'women here are a dangerous element, fierce, vindictive, without any constructive ability but with immense ability for obstruction and destructive tactics.'[18] This highly critical opinion of republican women was later repeated by Bennett when she addressed the issue of working-class women's involvement in the labour movement.[19] When simmering post-Treaty tensions finally escalated into civil war in June 1922 Bennett, with Mary O'Connor of the Irish Women Workers' Union (IWWU), organised the evacuation of families living near the Four Courts. A group of concerned women met in the Mansion House to co-ordinate peace efforts, sending delegations with peace proposals to both leaders. Political division over the Treaty eventually caused its collapse. During these months, the IIL experienced its own civil war. Bennett informed Geneva of the branch's impending dissolution explaining 'the civil strife in the last few months has driven the larger majority of people into one or other political camp: both sides have raised objections to the attitude

---

[17] Charlotte H. Fallon, *Soul of Fire: A Biography of Mary MacSwiney* (Cork and Dublin 1986), p. 68.

[18] Louie Bennett to Emily Greene Balch, 30 January 1922 (WILPF Colorado).

[19] Louie Bennett, 'What the workers can do in the new day' in *Voice of Labour* (Dublin, 1924), p. 301.

of the IIL.'[20] She disagreed strongly with Geneva's suggestion that a separate
northern section of WILPF be formed, arguing that whatever type of WILPF
organisation emerged in Ireland should have as its primary aim the establishment
of links between north and south. Her correspondence with Geneva reflects
the turmoil and crisis of conscience experienced by pacifists throughout Europe.
It was decided to keep the IIL going for the moment, Rosamond Jacob taking
over as secretary for the time being. At its annual general meeting Bennett
formally resigned as secretary, warning the group against allowing onto its
committee women who took a prominent place in contemporary politics.
However, the committee elected for 1922/23 did include many high-profile
political women. Charlotte Despard was its chair, with Rosamond Jacob, Hanna
Sheehy Skeffington and Maud Gonne MacBride also involved. Not surprisingly
such a volatile committee led to numerous disagreements. A special meeting
was called on 23 January 1923 to consider a resolution by Bennett which stated
'[t]hat membership of the Irish Section is open to all who hold that in resisting
tyranny or striving for freedom only such methods may be used as will not
involve the taking of life.'[21] In a country in the midst of civil war this resolution
stripped the *raison d'etre* of a group such as the IIL to its core. After heated
discussion the resolution was lost by one vote. The issue of legitimate use of
force remained a thorny one that would continue to dog the IIL. The group
managed however to stay in existence for the moment.

Bennett cited the 1913 strike and lock-out in Dublin as a major influence
in determining her future direction. Writing of her clandestine visits to Liberty
Hall she recalled:

> At that time I belonged to the respectable middle class and I did not dare
> admit to my home circle that I had run with the crowd to hear Jim Larkin,
> and crept like a culprit into Liberty Hall to see Madame Markievicz in a big
> overall, with sleeves rolled up, presiding over a cauldron of stew, surrounded
> by a crowd of gaunt women and children carrying bowls and cans.[22]

Appalled at the condition of the women and barefoot children she observed,
Bennett undertook relief work to help strikers' families, but held back from
direct involvement in Liberty Hall. While accepting many common aims
between the labour and women's movements, she and the IWFL leaders advised
women to remain independent of any political alliance. Her account of James
Connolly, sent to an American friend during Easter week 1916, makes clear
that it was pacifist conviction that held her back from joining in his trade union

---

[20] Louie Bennett to Emily Greene Balch, 12 October 1922 (WILPF Colorado).
[21] Annual Report of Irish Section, Women's International League 1922–23 (WILPF
Colorado).
[22] Fox, *Louie Bennett*, p. 42.

work. While she and Connolly had disagreed publicly a number of times, she admired him intellectually, noting 'he was a thorough feminist in every respect.' Shortly before the Rising Helena Molony sought her help in re-organising the Irish Women Workers' Union. Bennett, although anxious to do so, made clear that she could not support any organisation threatening force. Challenged by Connolly that she did not really want to help women workers, she told him plainly that she was a pacifist first and before everything and would not give up that principle for trade unionism. Imprisoned after the Rising, Molony made a further appeal to Bennett for help. This time she responded. In August 1916 Bennett and Helen Chenevix attended the Trade Union Congress in Sligo, and from this point onwards Bennett became publicly identified with the IWWU. Bennett, Chenevix and Molony would form a formidable triumvirate on behalf of women workers. In 1917 Bennett was invited by Liberty Hall to organise 'the aristocrats of industry' – the women printers. She later recalled, 'I had absolutely no idea how to go about it. But I was burning with enthusiasm. I had no money. No office. No furniture. Nothing. But I went out and I got one member to start me off. I put her name down in a twopenny jotter and hoped fervently for more.'[23]

Thus began what she described as a 'timid campaign' of waiting outside printers' workshops thrusting handbills upon disinterested women workers. Meetings were organised and an office rented. Perseverance paid off. By the beginning of 1917 membership was over 2,000 and growing. From the outset Bennett insisted that the women's union operate independently from Liberty Hall and remain solely a women's union, a point of much debate over the years. Not surprisingly this intense involvement was reflected in the pages of the *Irish Citizen* then edited by Bennett. Increasingly articles and editorials focused on the pay and conditions of women workers. The union's first industrial action soon occurred. When the Dublin Master Printers' Association refused to recognise the IWWU and its pay claim on behalf of women printers, a six-week strike and lock-out ensued. Financial support from the Dublin Trades Council during the strike, and the subsequent successful outcome to the dispute, gave a further boost to the unionisation of women workers. Bennett observed that the spirit of self-sacrifice among the strikers in refusing suggested increases without union recognition was crucial. She noted what would be a recurring theme of hers over the years, that the religious spirit of women was a significant factor in the organisation of Irish women workers, 'helping to redeem it from the sordid and the mercenary atmosphere which haunts trade unionism in general.'[24] From the beginning IWWU's policy would concentrate as much on

---

[23] *The Irish Press,* 2 May 1955 (profile of Bennett by Ann Daly); see also Louie Bennett 'With Irish Women Workers' in *The Irish Economist,* vols. 7-8, (August 1922), pp. 294-301.
[24] *Ibid.,* p. 297.

improving working conditions as on wage increases. Describing current industrial practices as soul destroying, Bennett sought a standard by which human values would gain precedence over industrial values. In November 1919 she initiated a debate in the *Irish Citizen* on the issue of separate trade unions for women. A lively exchange took place between Bennett and Cissie Cahalan of the Linen Drapers' Assistants' Association, on this option versus the 'one big union' concept. Arguing for such separation, Bennett noted 'there is a disposition amongst men workers not only to keep women in inferior and subordinate positions, but to drive them out of industry altogether.' Pointing out that within mixed trade unions men were almost always dominant, she queried the likelihood of women's issues being pursued with any vigour. Cahalan disagreed, blaming women themselves for lack of involvement. While disagreement with Bennett's views concentrated mainly on the issue of single-sex unions, little criticism was voiced on her views regarding women's right to work. In the 'equal pay for equal work' scenario, Bennett did not believe the time was right for women to invade men's industrial preserves, claiming that 'the class war must be fought out before women could fight for equality of opportunity.' In the meantime she believed a women's organisation could do much to raise the general status of women in industry. Bennett maintained her views on women's unions over the years. In 1922, commenting on continued male superiority in trade unions, she noted that the feminist movement had never touched Irish industrial workers, again arguing the need for women's control of their own unions.[25] Similarly, in 1930, she noted that the woman's voice was rarely heard at Trades Union Congresses or Trades Council. Pointing to large areas of female employment – teachers, clerical workers, shop assistants – which were almost always represented by men, she commented wryly 'what a touching and flattering confidence in the male sex.'[26]

In March 1920 Bennett took over editorial and financial responsibility for the *Irish Citizen*. That there was some disquiet at this development can be gauged from her comment to Emily Balch of her intention to run the paper primarily as a journal for women workers, noting that 'Mrs. Skeffington is unwilling to give me full control and we don't see eye to eye on labour questions.'[27] Bennett was personally optimistic however, advising Hanna that she could 'pull me up whenever you like, [but] I do not fear serious disagreements with you.'[28] But disagreements there were. The first of these arose with Bennett's publication of a 'Home Hints' column aimed at women in the home. Kathleen

---

[25] *Ibid.*, pp. 297-8.
[26] Louie Bennett, 'Women and the labour movement' in *Dublin Labour Year Book, 1930* (Dublin, 1930).
[27] Louie Bennett to Emily Balch, 11 March 1920 (WILPF Colorado).
[28] Louie Bennett to Hanna Sheehy Skeffington, 7 March 1920, Sheehy Skeffington papers, NLI, Ms 24,110.

Connery, of the IWFL, scathingly attacked what she termed 'this kind of literary dish wash.' To her, and many suffragists, such a column indicated a regressive attitude to women's progress. Bennett in response asked 'is not housekeeping woman's primary duty, and should not the art of doing so be a prominent feature in any woman's journal?'[29] She argued that while housekeeping was in need of better organisation and methods, it compared most favourably with the life of man in shop or factory, which she deemed 'dull and full of drudgery.' Correspondence to the paper showed strong feelings on both sides. Interestingly many of those who agreed with Bennett were single, while most who disagreed were married, indicating perhaps an idealised image of life in the home by those who were not confined there. Ironically, Louie's key position as secretary of the IWWU placed her in a strong position to demand equality of opportunity for women in all areas of work. Reflecting current conservative attitudes towards women and home however, Bennett argued that as the majority of working men were sole supporters of wives and children 'it would be madness for women workers to attempt to disturb fundamentally the present distribution of industrial work.'[30]

The other main area of disagreement was the changing ethos of the *Irish Citizen* from being a feminist suffrage paper to a feminist trade union paper. From 1918 more and more space was given to women workers, union activities and pay disputes. An editorial late in 1919 by Hanna Sheehy Skeffington emphasised the continued need for a distinctly non-party feminist paper, as 'no party, unhappily, is yet quite free from sin where women are concerned.' Despite this clear non-party stance, the first issue published under Bennett's management in the spring of 1920 announced the decision of the IWWU and the Irish Nurses' Organisation to use the paper as their official journal. Tensions increased between the two women, Bennett pointing out to Sheehy Skeffington in July 1920 that changes would have to be made if sales were to increase. Accepting that many former readers might object to 'our particular line of stuff' Bennett hoped to make the paper popular with workers. Shortly afterwards she told Sheehy Skeffington she would like to take over the paper completely and develop it as a feminist labour paper. This proved to be the last straw for Sheehy Skeffington, who cancelled their agreement. Unease with IWWU involvement in the *Irish Citizen* did not always rest on feminist principles. When news broke of the cancelled agreement one suffragist wrote to Sheehy Skeffington hoping that the paper would continue under her direction, commenting 'we want moral and temperance points raised, not anti-[Liberty] hall squabbles. . . . I fear women workers are likely to be no use re morality and temperance.'[31]

---

[29] *Irish Citizen,* May – August 1920.
[30] *Irish Citizen*, November 1919.
[31] Marion Duggan to Hanna Sheehy Skeffington, 10 September 1920, Sheehy Skeffington papers, NLI, Ms 22,693(v).

Following an invitation from the IIL, it was decided by Jane Addams and her executive committee to hold WILPF's fifth international congress in Dublin in 1926. Key women among the Irish organisers were Bennett, Rosamond Jacob, Lucy Kingston and Helen Chenevix. Correspondence between Geneva and Dublin in the lead-up to the congress shows the Irish group advising on sensitive political issues and protocol. The problem of location was solved when the National University building in Dublin was made available, though Kingston cautioned Geneva 'we are careful not to put our Branch too greatly under the Government "wing", this would incriminate our League with a certain section of the public.'[32] The congress in July 1926 was attended by 150 delegates from twenty countries, and was the first international gathering to be held in the Free State. Both Éamon de Valera and W.T. Cosgrave attended its opening ceremony, the first public function attended by both leaders since the civil war. At a public meeting in the Mansion House during the congress Jane Addams paid tribute to Frank Sheehy Skeffington, 'the Irish pacifist known the world over.' Thanking Addams, Hanna (representing the Republican group) concluded that WILPF should continue to stress peace and freedom, quoting Pearse's 'Ireland unfree can never be at peace.' Her speech aroused great enthusiasm. Fox later recounted that 'one could sense the emotional pull between the pacifist and the militant Republicans, who were still unreconciled to peaceful methods.'[33] One of the British speakers related how dissident members of Irish WILPF, the 'black women', remained outside the congress because they had taken part in the civil war and were still involved with revolutionary republicans.[34] While some reports criticised the use of an international and pacifist congress as a platform for intense nationalist propaganda, official WILPF records made no comment on the issue, but praised Irish WILPF for its organisation of a very successful congress.

Bennett was elected to the executive of WILPF during the Dublin congress, but increasingly trade union activities left her less time for WILPF involvement at home and abroad. WILPF's sixth congress was scheduled for Prague in August 1929, and unwittingly would cause the next major crisis within its Irish branch. Records show apprehension by some at WILPF headquarters regarding possible delegates from Ireland. Mary Sheepshanks wrote frankly to Louie, 'The prospect of having those Republicans at Prague fills me with dismay. They did their best to spoil the Dublin Congress and did succeed in doing a certain amount of mischief. I do hope you can do something to keep them off Prague.'[35] It was decided that the Irish delegates would be Bennett, Sheehy Skeffington and Rosamond Jacob. In fact, Bennett did not travel to Prague, her mother's

---

[32] Lucy Kingston to Madeleine Duty, 1 January 1926 (WILPF Colorado).

[33] Fox, *Louie Bennett*, p. 89.

[34] Helena Swanwick, *I Have Been Young* (London, 1935), pp. 450-452.

[35] Mary Sheepshanks (International Secretary of WILPF 1927-30), to Louie Bennett, 20 November 1928 (WILPF Colorado).

deteriorating health the apparent reason. She had, however, forwarded a copy of the paper she had been invited to present on 'The Machinery of Internal Peace.' A copy of this came to the attention of Sinn Féin, whose publication of extracts and hostile comments plunged the IIL again into fierce controversy. Sinn Féin complained to Geneva regarding Bennett's 'misleading and prejudicial comments', quoting Bennett's description of certain types of cranks, vagabonds and villains attracted to Sinn Féin, and her comment that 'An irregular minority of this sort inspires fear in Government and constitutional circles. Such activities have led to a vicious circle of arrests, victimisation, terrorism and reprisals.' Sinn Féin further refuted Bennett's claim that it was not in sympathy with the ideals of labour, but would not hesitate to use labour to secure complete independence for Ireland.[36] Immediately the Irish section was thrown into turmoil, Lucy Kingston noting at the next committee meeting:

> L[ouie] B[ennett] is attacked for her paper on Irish conditions [Prague] by (1) S[inn] Féin (2) Fianna Fáil (3) Repub[lican] members of our committee. Find myself on her side for once, and certainly Mrs. S[heehy] S[keffington] and the rest show no mercy. An implacable crew where 'The Rock of the Republic' is concerned.[37]

Informing Geneva that 'Mrs. Skeffington, who has always been a friend of mine, is especially outraged', Bennett explained:

> All through the past year there has been considerable dissatisfaction amongst the really pacifist group, owing to the presence on the Committee of people who openly state that they consider the use of force essential to achieve a social revolution, or to achieve national freedom. They lay emphasis on the W.I.L. object of *freedom* rather than peace. Things have now reached a climax and I think a split is inevitable.[38]

The secretary of the IIL, Mrs M'Clintock Dix, wrote to Geneva explaining her unsuccessful attempts to obtain the resignation of Mme MacBride, commenting that 'a peace committee with Mme MacBride on it was a farce.'[39] A series of stormy committee meetings ensued, debate focusing on acceptance of the Washington Object which excluded from membership those who justified defensive warfare and armed revolution. A smaller gathering subsequently reversed a majority decision in favour of the Object. While this show of sharp practice was disliked by Dix, it provided a way for the group to remain in existence, albeit without Bennett and Chenevix who resigned from the

---

[36] Sinn Féin to WILPF, 25 October 1929 (WILPF Colorado).

[37] Kingston diaries, 1 November 1929.

[38] Louie Bennett to Mary Sheepshanks, 30 November 1929 (WILPF Colorado).

[39] Una M'Clintock Dix to Mary Sheepshanks, 1 February 1930 (WILPF Colorado).

committee. The IIL's 1930 annual general meeting, in fact, voted a return to the Washington Object, and many former members rejoined, including Bennett. But within a few months, a further controversy proved fatal. In the spring of 1931 the IIL invited Patrick McGilligan, Minister for External Affairs, to be guest speaker at a public meeting to discuss a disarmament declaration initiated by WILPF. Some within the IIL considered McGilligan unsuitable to stand on a platform for peace and freedom on political and personal grounds; other felt he should be heard. Threats of disruption forced the cancellation of the meeting, with both president and secretary resigning in protest. Rosamond Jacob wrote to Geneva desperately trying to retain some WILPF presence in Ireland, asking if there were precedents for two groups to operate within one section where controversial matters arose. Explaining that the cleavage that had always existed within the IIL now threatened to break the group, she noted 'some of us would put peace before freedom, and others would put freedom before peace.'[40] Despite her efforts, WILPF in Ireland did not continue this time. From this point on, involvement in the disarmament campaign provided many former members with the means to remain involved in the peace process without divisive political arguments. Bennett was among a group who remained involved with WILPF on a personal basis. In response to enquiries from Geneva in April 1932 regarding a revival of its Irish section, Lucy Kingston explained that such a revival was not possible at that time, but perhaps could be contemplated 'if things change greatly in this country.' It would be almost sixty years before WILPF was re-established in Ireland.[41]

With the voluntary separation of the political and industrial branches of Labour in 1930, Bennett urged women to become involved in the political arena. Towards the end of 1933 members finally agreed to the formation of a political wing of the IWWU, prompted no doubt by moves restricting women's employment that had been developing since the late 1920s. The trade union movement generally supported restrictions on women workers, viewing their lower wage rates as a threat to male workers at a time of high unemployment. From 1934 attention focused on Sean Lemass's forthcoming Conditions of Employment bill. The IWWU sought, and were refused, consultative status in the framing of this bill.[42] At their 1935 annual convention, IWWU delegates voted in favour of affiliation to the Irish Labour Party and indicated their intention to resist all attempts to restrict women's employment. Bennett took a high profile stance in demanding equal status for all workers and a wage scale based on value of work without sex discrimination. Her trenchant defence of women's

---

[40] Rosamond Jacob to Camille Drevet (International Secretary of WILPF 1930-34), 9 April 1931 (WILPF Colorado).
[41] WILPF Ireland was reformed in 1991 in the wake of the Gulf War.
[42] Mary Jones, *These Obstreperous Lassies: A History of the Irish Women Workers' Union* (Dublin, 1988), pp. 122-133.

right to work was modified somewhat by her concession that women were more suited to certain industries than men, and that many monotonous mechanical processes could be better endured by women than men. Over the summer of 1935 the battle over the Conditions of Employment bill was at its height. While assuring the IWWU that the status of women workers would not be affected, Lemass refused to delete Section 12, which gave the government power to restrict or prohibit the employment of women in industry. The IWWU looked to the Labour Party for support, but to no avail. Following a meeting with leader William Norton, it became clear that no support would be forthcoming. Debate at the Irish Trade Union Congress (ITUC) in August 1935 showed the extent of trade union hostility to any amendment to the bill, it being argued that 'it was a very wrong thing that young girls should be sent into factories and young men kept out.' Some women trade unionists supported this stance commenting that 'too many women inside the factory were a menace to the industrial classes.'[43] Norton was adamant in his opposition to the IWWU, citing Helena Molony's assertion of women's right to be carpenters and blacksmiths as proof of a wish to displace men.

The IWWU stance was supported by women's groups at home and abroad. The early 1930s saw intense debate in women's journals worldwide on the issues of women's right to work, to retain their nationality after marriage, and their relegation to the domestic sphere under fascist regimes. With the establishment by the League of Nations of an inquiry into the civil and political status of women, a meeting was held in Dublin's Mansion House at which many well known women voiced their opposition to the Conditions of Employment bill. Bennett restated her view that Lemass's concern was not for the welfare of women but for their control.[44] Shades of suffrage activity emerged with the formation of a Standing Committee representing various women's organisations. A co-ordinated publicity campaign was initiated to oppose the bill and inform the public of its implications. In the Senate the bill was strongly attacked by Kathleen Clarke and Jennie Wyse Power who argued that it contradicted the equality declared in the 1916 Proclamation.

Public reaction during this controversy reflected popular attitudes to women at work that accepted that after marriage women's place was in the home. Legislation during the 1930s consistently restricted the employment of married women in the public service. Parallel with this was the acceptance of three different pay rates for the same work, for married men, single men, and single women, the last being the lowest. It was also accepted that women should not be promoted beyond basic grades. In 1932, arguing against the civil service marriage ban, Mary Kettle commented that 'from their entry until they reach the age of 45 or 50 women are looked upon as if they were loitering with intent

---

[43] *Ibid.*, pp. 128-9.
[44] *Republican Congress,* 30 November 1935.

to commit a felony (the felony being marriage).'[45] Of particular significance was the fact that many women trade unionists accepted restrictions on the employment of married women, and the ambivalent attitude of Bennett and the IWWU executive reinforced such acceptance.

Throughout her life Bennett argued trenchantly for equal rights for women in political, social, educational and professional spheres. However, her 1919 argument that under the existing industrial system women workers could not fight for equality without regard for wives and mothers, alongside her assurance that women would not invade men's industrial preserves, display a personal attitude consistent with conservative popular opinion. While it has been argued by Mary Daly[46] that the practical effects of the 1936 act on women's employment was negligible the psychological effects cannot be underestimated – effects which were further embellished with the constitution of 1937. Bennett denounced Articles 40.1 and 41 2.2 as an invitation to anti-feminist prejudice and a danger to the employment of married women, while at the same time suggesting that 'government policy should be a wage standard sufficient to maintain wife and family in frugal comfort.'[47] An attitude not totally removed from that of de Valera who introduced that constitution to the Dáil by declaring that the breadwinner 'who is normally and naturally the father of the family should have sufficient income to maintain the whole household.'[48] Similarly, an IWWU executive statement on the draft constitution, referred to the 'vague and chivalrous sentiments of 41.2' and suggested that 'mothers would prefer concrete proposals which would release them from the pressure of economic necessity to work outside the home.'[49] The women's groups that joined together to campaign against the constitution recognised the potential in these clauses for discrimination against women in all spheres. Even the recently won franchise could be endangered under Article 16 with the removal by de Valera of the words 'without distinction of sex' present in the 1922 constitution. Following protests from groups including Bennett and the IWWU this clause was re-inserted. Bennett and the IWWU were also particularly concerned with implications for women workers in articles 40 and 45, and ultimately succeeded in having the phrase 'inadequate strength of women' removed from Article 45.

---

[45] Mary E. Daly, 'Women, work and trade unionism' in Margaret MacCurtain and Donncha Ó Corráin (eds.), *Women in Irish Society, The Historical Dimension* (Dublin, 1978), p. 76.

[46] Cited in Liam O'Dowd, 'Church, state and women: the aftermath of partition', in Chris Curtin, Pauline Jackson and Barbara O'Connor (eds.), *Gender in Irish Society* (Galway, 1987), p. 27.

[47] Louie Bennett to the editor, *The Irish Press*, 15 May 1937.

[48] Margaret Ward, *Unmanageable Revolutionaries: Women and Irish Nationalism* (Dingle, 1983), p. 240.

[49] Jones, *These Obstreperous Lassies*, p. 142.

With this however, the IWWU ceased its involvement in the women's campaign against the constitution. The other groups involved, The Women Graduates' Association and the Joint Committee of Women's Societies, were disappointed, recognising the weakening effect of such withdrawal. Why did the IWWU abandon the women's cause at this stage? Their annual report stated that they were not prepared to engage in a campaign of opposition on the grounds of sex discrimination, pointing out that there were other articles in the constitution which posed more serious threats to the interests of both male and female workers. Experience of male trade unionist and Labour Party attitudes during the 1935-6 controversy were still live in the memory of the IWWU executive. Alliance with what was disparagingly dismissed as an elite of intellectual middle-class women campaigning for sex equality would not have helped IWWU efforts to improve women's status within the labour movement. Crucial however, was the acceptance by Bennett and her executive of contemporary church and state attitudes regarding the role of women within society. Daly has pointed to the mental confusion which persisted in this regard within the IWWU into the 1950s when its 1953 Congress supported an equal pay proposal but sought to debar from its benefits the young married woman and the single girl. Jim Larkin reacted to this contradictory action by commenting that before any success could be achieved 'women would have to propagate the idea of the principle among their own sex and get acceptance for it.'[50] Undoubtedly the action of Bennett and the IWWU was short-sighted and in the long term damaging to the position of women in Irish society.

Approaching her seventieth birthday in 1940 it might have been expected that Bennett could reduce her involvement in public affairs. On the contrary, the 1940s were to be a particularly busy decade. In 1945 laundry worker members of the IWWU voted for strike action to obtain a fortnight's paid holiday. The Federated Union of Employers intimated that no increased holidays would be granted until the government declared a statutory fortnight's paid holiday. The Minister for Industry and Commerce informed the Dáil of his opposition to any such concession. On 21 July, 1,500 women commenced strike action that would last fourteen weeks. Despite the great inconvenience caused it soon became clear that the striking women had public opinion on their side. Eleanor Butler (later Lady Wicklow) recounted Bennett taking her on a tour of Dublin laundries:

> She made me wade into the steamy laundries, with floors flooded. The women wore overalls and nothing underneath because they couldn't stand the heat and the steam. Their conditions were appalling, so much that a very high proportion of these women got TB and suffered from rheumatism.[51]

---

[50] Daly, 'Women, work and trade unionism', p. 77.
[51] Rosemary Cullen Owens interview with Lady Eleanor Wicklow, May 1987.

Despite the fact that at this time the trade union movement was torn by dissent – and had in fact split into rival congresses – support for the strikers came from all sides. The strikers themselves kept morale going with regular meetings, parades, media coverage, and the sale of a strike song – sung to the air of the war-time song Lily Marlene – sold at 1d a sheet. Ultimately the women were successful in their claim and – as in the case of official tea-breaks – set an example quickly followed by male workers.

Speaking to a teacher's group in 1947 Bennett recounted the horrific conditions of women workers in 1917, underpaid and exploited, working a fifty-four hour week (sixty in laundries) with no paid holidays. She credited women for the considerable reforms achieved in working conditions over the previous thirty years, noting that '[w]omen's influence has in fact proved a humanising factor in industry.'[52] 1946 has been described as 'a watershed in labour history.' The Industrial Relations Act of that year established the Labour Court, through which pay claims would now be processed. Bennett accepted the need for conciliation procedures, but feared too close a bond with government, nothing 'my generation can never get free of the "'agin the government" instinct.'[53]

During these years Bennett was also busy on other issues involving women. Between 1939 and 1943 she served on the Commission on Vocational Organisation established by the Fianna Fáil Government. Michael Browne, Archbishop of Galway, chaired the Commission, which received both written and oral submissions. Browne was particularly aggressive in his questioning of women's groups. Questioning their commitment to women as 'home-makers', he asked if all such groups were not feminist/suffragist in origin, whose real aim was the achievement of equality with men. Probing the implications of women at work, he suggested that the rise in factory employment for women contributed to male unemployment, and in fact acted as a deterrent to marriage. The IWWU strongly refuted such suggestions, Helena Molony informing Browne that we 'all believe that woman's place is in the home provided she has a home.'[54]

During the war years Bennett was involved in a series of developments relating to workers' housing and their rights to organise. Her interest in housing had been articulated as early as 1925 when she had advocated slum-clearance for both medical and moral reasons. She was particularly concerned that any proposed housing scheme should not be of inferior quality – thereby creating slums for the future. A number of initiatives were undertaken by the IWWU in this regard during the 1920s and 1930s, but plans for direct union investment

---

[52] Fox, *Louie Bennett,* pp. 67-8.
[53] Louie Bennett to John de Courcy Ireland, 7 July 1946, University College Dublin Archives, 9A' 40(l).
[54] Minutes of Commission on Vocational Organisation, vol.4, pp.1309-1331, NLI, Ms 295; see also volume 9, pp. 3,065-3,080, NLI, Ms 930.

had to be abandoned due to spiralling costs. Bennett continued to place a high priority on this matter, recruiting young architects like Eleanor Butler, and forming the Citizens' Housing Council with Father Canavan and Dr. Bob Collis. Ultimately, due to her perseverance and support, a development of housing for the low paid was built close to her home in Ballybrack.[55]

When a number of women's groups came together to demand a fair rationing system to cope with wartime shortages of essential goods, Bennett and the IWWU supported their demands. A petition presented to government by this group before the 1941 budget was dubbed 'The Housewives Petition' by the press. Bennett advised the group's leaders, Hilda Tweedy and Andrée Sheehy Skeffington, to build on the momentum generated by the petition and start a new women's organisation, offering the use of the IWWU hall for its inaugural meeting. So was formed the Irish Housewives Association in May 1942.[56] Under the auspices of the Dublin Trades Council, a number of women's groups joined with the Labour Party to exert pressure on government for price control on rents and essential goods. In October 1947 Bennett chaired 'The Women's Parliament' in Dublin's Mansion House, from which was formed the Women's National Council of Action (WNCA). The opening in January 1949 by Dublin Corporation of a producer-consumer market in Francis Street and the establishment in 1951 of a Prices Advisory Body, were two significant achievements of the WNCA.[57]

There were other areas of public life that absorbed Bennett's time during the 1940s, among them the building of sanitoria to cope with the enormous public health problem of TB, the provision of worker education, and the establishment of closer links with people in Northern Ireland. Lady Eleanor Butler and others have acknowledged the support given to Dr. Noel Browne by Bennett, both on the issue of TB, and during the later 'Mother and Child' debacle. In 1951 she represented the IWWU on deputations to Browne in support of his proposed scheme, and privately was much in contact with him during this period.[58]

Regarding worker education, Bennett had consistently advocated improved educational facilities for women. While serving on an education committee of the ITUC national executive in 1925, she and Marie Mortished had moved that girls be included in proposed day training classes for apprentices. Following a recommendation that a Workers' Educational Institute be formed, evening classes were started, enthusiastically supported by Bennett. The IWWU provided

---

[55] Robert Collis, *To be a Pilgrim* (London, 1975), pp. 91-92. Also interview with Lady Wicklow, May 1987.

[56] Hilda Tweedy, *A Link in the Chain: The Story of the Irish Housewives Association 1942-1992* (Dublin, 1992), p. 15.

[57] *Ibid.*, pp. 99-105.

[58] Interview with Lady Wicklow, May 1987.

lecture rooms and their hall to the committee. While this initiative lasted only a couple of years, the IWWU executive continued its commitment to the idea, including educational projects in its budget, and provision of a library and classes for members. In 1948, following a proposal by Bennett to the ITUC national executive, the People's College was founded, with Bennett as one of the key members of its organising committee. Despite subsequent controversy regarding the ideological bias of the College's constitution, and the vexed issue of non-sectarian education resulting in a rival workers' college being established by the Jesuits in Ranelagh, the People's College grew in strength with a distinguished team of lecturers and administrators, and the continued support of the IWWU.[59]

From her suffrage days Bennett had always maintained close links with women in Ulster. Contact with the northern province was extended during her years with the IWWU and the ITUC. A further link was provided by her involvement in the Irish Association for Cultural, Economic and Social Relations. Branches of this Association were formed in Belfast and Dublin during 1938, aiming to promote co-operation and goodwill between Irish people north and south. The outbreak of war in 1939 placed huge strain on the new association, exacerbated by the very different policies to the war adopted by the Belfast and Dublin governments. The association was revived after the war, and continues today.[60]

Right up to the end of her life Bennett remained keenly involved and interested in all aspects of Irish life and current affairs generally. Letters from her last years show a lively enquiring mind, a person concerned with the individual, encouraging in difficult times, and supportive of independent thought and action. Constantly the themes of spirituality and religion recur throughout her correspondence. She wrote to her niece in 1950, 'I bore my colleagues by constantly asserting that the restlessness and discontent of the workers arises from a sub-conscious craving for their rights as human persons.'[61] Recounting Emily Balch's advice that the best years of one's life are the sixties, 'all passion spent, futile regrets abandoned, futile hopes forgotten, – one can devote oneself with serenity to one's special task', Bennett agreed with this, but commented that the 'serenity is a bit of a poser':

> Personally I think we don't in the course of our lives give enough thought to other people and their need for sympathy and understanding. The 'personal touch' counts for so much. . . . We might have a better world if less attention

---

[59] Ruaidhri Roberts, *The Story of the People's College* (Dublin, 1986), pp. 1-33.

[60] Mary A. McNeill, *The Beginnings of The Irish Association for Cultural, Economic and Social Relations* (Belfast, 1982).

[61] Louie Bennett to Henrietta Wilson, 22 February 1950 (in author's possession)

were given to sex relationships & more to personal relationships in other spheres.[62]

It is clear from her letters, and interviews with family and friends, that Bennett had a keen interest in young people and their views. Young people enjoyed her company, finding her not just a sympathetic listener, but a stimulating and supportive friend. As late as 1954 she told Mary O'Malley of her plan to organise around her some young people to debate the part Ireland might play in the struggle of the colonies versus imperialism, commenting, 'We won't get away from the Atom Bomb threat until the Colonial peoples get fair play.' Constantly she urges her correspondents to get involved in social issues and not sit idly by.[63]

She was quite despondent about the Labour Party during these years, considering the Trade Union movement much more progressive. Her disenchantment continued into the 1950s. In 1952 she described the party conference 'a wash-out, important matters were shelved and we were cornered by the opportunistic politician's cliques.'[64] By 1955, at the age of eighty-five, she had at last retired from the IWWU noting 'I live the life of a real lady now. I do nothing and don't want to do anything. To an onlooker without responsibility, life can be tremendously interesting and even exciting.'[65] Her international awareness was still a strong feature. Regarding Ireland she pondered:

> It seems to me very sad that we remain so isolated from the outside world and so apparently indifferent to the great events likely to revolutionise our system of civilisation. I think the North as well as the South are mentally island bound – they care only for their own interests. Or is it that those who have a wide vision become missionaries or emigrants?[66]

That year she was hospitalised for some time. Back home again she told her friend Seamus Scully she would not mind so much being an awful crock if only the sun would shine, advising him 'console yourself, you are living through the hardest stage of your life. Old age is not so bad.'[67] Still she kept herself informed, constantly urging others to be active. Much of her attention was absorbed by the development of nuclear power, strongly supporting opposition to the

---

[62] Louie Bennett to Henrietta Wilson, fragments from two letters, undated, c.1950, private collection.
[63] Louie Bennett to Mary O'Malley, 29 April 1954; Louie Bennett to Seamus Scully, 22 April 1955, private collection.
[64] Louie Bennett to Mary O'Malley, 21 May 1952, private collection.
[65] Louie Bennett to Mary O'Malley, 3 June 1955, private collection.
[66] *Ibid.*
[67] Louie Bennett to Seamus Scully, 21 June 1955, private collection.

hydrogen bomb, characteristically noting, 'I feel we all ought to be *up and doing* in the campaign against it.'[68]

Bennett's emphasis on spiritual values had been articulated many times over the years. In her presidential address to the ITUC in 1947 she had declared that the trade union, now an integral part of the social fabric, in its origin was inspired by spiritual values. Now, at a cross-roads in its history, she believed it had a vital part to play in the evolution of a civilisation based on such values. In an article published ten years earlier she had criticised the dominating motive of industry as evil from every point of view, declaring that 'the motive of all work, whether it be of the manager, the expert, the machine minder, the apprentice, needs the element of religion in the sense of service to life.'[69] Her idealistic view that the motive of the artist creating beauty should be the same as that of the street cleaner, mechanic, weaver or politician persevered over the years. Bennett wrote to her niece of Einstein's theory of a cosmic religion based on order and natural law – all life being inspired by a force which is God, with human religions all being expressions of this Godhead. Just months before her death she told her niece – 'As you know I am very unorthodox religiously, and it occurred to me that I ought to think out my position clearly and hand on my reflections to you.' She believed we lead a double life, on the one hand the material, physical life giving scope of action and energy, on the other an inner life, seeking the unseen – the difficulty being in balancing the two to create harmony. In the course of this letter Bennett writes what might have been her epitaph:

> Standing as I do at the end of my life, I have a strange conviction of the *value* of life. I think of it as a tremendous adventure, carrying a challenge to us. I am glad to have lived, to be a part of life, however insignificant. I have known the dark days of the soul. I look back on failures, and disappointments and contemptible sins of omission and commission, and still I am glad to have lived, and I look ahead to a great future for man. It seems absurd to write this, but I have a conviction about it which rises up against every doubt and is in a sense stronger than myself. I don't want to live in the new world that's coming for the younger generation, but I like to think of it and to hope for a further revelation of God, and that all the present restlessness and seeking for a 'spar' to hold on to will lead to a deeper understanding of the mystery and greatness of life

Her closing comment to her niece reads – 'I think love outlasts death.'[70]

Looked at from the perspective of Dublin in the twenty-first century, Louie Bennett would appear an unlikely candidate to become involved in public life

---

[68] Louie Bennett to Seamus Scully, 22 April 1955, private collection.
[69] Louie Bennett, 'Motive in industry' in *Ireland Today*, vol. 3, no.1 (January 1938).
[70] Louie Bennett to Henrietta Wilson, 6 June 1956, private collection.

on behalf of women. Like most women at that time she had no career training. There was no family tradition of politics or public service to absorb. While we know that she had ambitions as a writer, we know little else of her early development and desires. What caused her to break away from traditional class and gender expectations at the age of forty? Unfortunately none of her personal papers survive to cast light on these early years. Information on her life up to 1911 is based on reminiscences relayed by Bennett to R. M. Fox in the last year of her life, and on family recollections and anecdotal information. Her public career from 1911 can be assessed through her work in the suffrage, trade union and pacifist movements, primarily through archives such as the Sheehy Skeffington, WILPF and Trade Union papers. The lack of personal archives however, makes difficult the development of a fully rounded picture of Louie Bennett, and as a consequence she remains a somewhat enigmatic figure.[71] What does emerge quite clearly from available sources is a woman of great determination and strong character, with firm ideals regarding pacifism and women workers. The catalyst that determined her future career was her involvement in the suffrage movement. From the formation of the IWSF in 1911 her leadership qualities became immediately apparent. Debate within the suffrage movement internationally on pacifism focused Louie's attention from 1914. Allied to her suffrage campaign, increasingly she concentrated her attention on the issue of women workers.[72] Ultimately, she would spend the rest of her life attempting to implement her convictions on these issues in an Irish context.

An understanding of her commitment to pacifism is vital in assessing her life's work. While she could be confrontational in pursuit of goals, her preference for negotiation and peaceful resolution to conflict determined her attitude to all forms of conflict – political or industrial. All issues were filtered through her pacifist consciousness. Her conciliatory attitude and lack of working-class perspective has led to some criticism. Yet, she has been acclaimed by Ruaidhri Roberts as 'one of the most significant trade union leaders of the period.'[73] Despite her solid bourgeois background, there can be no doubting her commitment to promoting the status and conditions of women workers. However, her argument for full equality for women within all facets of society

---

[71] Family sources refer to one or two unsuccessful romantic episodes with the opposite sex. From 1911 she was particularly close to Helen Chenevix, both on a personal and professional basis. However, in the absence of papers from either woman, the nature of this relationship is difficult to assess.

[72] Her career with the Irish Women Workers' Union spanned almost forty years. She was its General Secretary from 1917 until her retirement in 1955. Bennett was the first woman President of the Irish Trades Union Congress in 1932, a position she held again in 1948.

[73] Ellen Hazelkorn, 'The social and political views of Louie Bennett, 1870-1956' in *Saothar*, 13 (1988), pp. 32-44.

was undoubtedly compromised by her ambiguous attitude towards married women working outside the home. Her personal preference for economic conditions in which the latter would not be necessary was not unusual for her time, and was allied to a pragmatic understanding of what the trade union movement and society in general would accept in this regard. She continued to fight on behalf of women throughout her lifetime. Arguing in favour of a separate women workers union in 1919 Bennett had asked 'Did we dream that when we won the right to the Parliamentary vote we had finished with the woman's struggle for her place in the world?'[74] Writing of women in the Labour movement in 1930 she declared 'we women have our part's to play in it, and if the men fail to open doors for our entry, then we must open them for ourselves.'[75] As late as June 1955 she organised a support meeting in her home for the sole female candidate from Dun Laoghaire in that year's local elections.[76] In one of the last public interviews she gave in the year before her death she again emphasised the need for international co-operation between women. 'Despite the progress we have made', she noted, 'women still must unfortunately fight to hold their corner. They must organise with women all over the world. That is their weapon. That is their strength.'[77]

---

[74] *Irish Citizen,* November 1919.

[75] Louie Bennett, 'Women and the labour movement', p. 39.

[76] Louie Bennett to Seamus Scully, 21 June 1955, private collection.

[77] *The Irish Press,* 2 May 1955.

Kathleen Lynn (1874-1955)

Medb Ruane

In 1874, the world was changing faster than ever before. Powerful nations pushed out frontiers into faraway continents. Scientists postulated evolutionary ways of describing the universe that shocked many, and made control of nature seem just a simple step away. Through armaments, commerce and the alchemy of money markets, wealth was accumulated at staggering rates, bringing pleasure to some but misery and im-poverishment to more.

Kathleen Lynn's long life tackled issues of inequality and exclusion that wealth and power created. She did so not as a philan-thropist, but as a committed political campaigner working to change inequities from franchise to healthcare to national self-government. Dr. Lynn is known for founding St. Ultan's Hospital in Dublin, which promoted a whole-child treatment of infants and pioneered Irish-based research into T.B. That represents only part of her story.

Born on 28 January 1874 at Mullafarry, near Killala, County Mayo,[1] Lynn was a smart, compassionate woman who broke every convention expected of women from her background in her time. She was a committed Protestant in an Ireland where Catholic values came to define Irishness itself, a radical republican within the Protestant community, and a highly-qualified professional woman within a predominantly male public world. Her sensitivity to all forms of exclusion and injustice grew from that position. Innovative and often visionary, her interventions in the public world of twentieth-century Ireland touch on the core issues of power that resonate today: the distribution of wealth, the rights of minorities and the 'national question.'[2]

---

[1] Mullafarry (Ballysakeery) baptismal records, courtesy Very Rev. Dean E.G. Ardis.
[2] Direct biographical information includes Dr. Kathleen E. Murphy, 'Obituary,' *Journal of the Irish Medical Association*, 37 (1955), p. 321; Hazel P. Smyth, 'Kathleen Lynn, M.D., FRCSI', in *Dublin Historical Record*, 30 (1977), pp. 51-7; Dr. J.B.

Lynn's family was devoutly unionist. Katharine Wynne, her mother, descended from planters granted land in Sligo/Leitrim along with the title Earl of Hazelwood, could trace a blood relationship with most of the estimated two hundred families who formed Her Majesty's power base on the island. Her foremothers included Mary, Queen of Scots. Robert Lynn was a doctor's son from Sligo, who graduated in divinity from Trinity College, Dublin.[3] Kathleen was the second of their four children. Annie Elizabeth, known as Nan, was the eldest (1873); then came Emily Muriel, known as Muriel (1876), and John (1877). Lynn always called Katharine 'Mother.' Robert became 'Fardie' for good when the children couldn't quite manage the formal 'Father.' They lived at Mullafarry until 1882, when Robert secured the living at Shrule in Longford. Within four years, his reputation won him the prestigious living in the gift of Arthur, Lord Ardilaun, scion of the Guinness family, at St. Mary's, Cong, a garrison town in south Mayo. The family moved into the well-appointed rectory there in 1886.

Mullafarry was a marginalised place, whose people were decimated by successive famines that reduced their numbers by two-thirds in thirty years. Her mother's work included almsgiving and visiting local people: Lynn accompanied her, usually on foot, and vividly recalled the poverty she saw as a young child.[4] Shrule framed Lynn's girlhood adventures: part of the territory described by Oliver Goldsmith and Maria Edgeworth, it was more prosperous and 'county' than north Mayo. Two incidents there made a special impact. The work of her friends' father Dr. Smartt is the likely source for the assertion attributed to Lynn that '. . . The local doctor was the fount of help and hope, and so I decided to become a doctor.'[5] The second invokes a scene she recalled when she was eavesdropping on adult conversation and overheard how a valued piece of Waterford crystal had survived the 1798 rebellion. It struck her as odd to take pleasure in its survival when so many people had died.[6]

Lyons, *Brief Lives of Irish Doctors 1600-1965* (Dublin, 1978), p. 159. Medb Ruane, 'Kathleen Lynn', *Ten Dublin Women* (Dublin, 1991), pp. 61-7; *idem.*, *Western People*, December 1995; *Irish Times*, 3 May, 21 June 1999.

[3] *Burke's Family Records* (London, 1976); 'Wynne Family Tree, 1888', courtesy the late Canon Billy Wynne. Also B. Leslie, 'Tuam Biographical Succession List', Representative Church Body Library, Dublin, Ms 61.2.15, p. 162.

[4] Interviews by the author with George Taylor 1994-8, subsequently a member of Mullafarry's select vestry. See also Census figures, 1841-1871, National Archives of Ireland (hereafter cited NAI): population declined from 6,034 to 2,163.

[5] Quoted in Hazel Smyth, 'Kathleen Lynn'. No contemporary medical figure in Cong or Mullafarry shows the same bonds she forged with the Smartt family; the Smartts were cousins, hence this conclusion. Shrule parish records and vestry minutes courtesy Rev. B.W. Kingston.

[6] Author interviews with Geoffrey Wynne, her executor, June, July 1994: Lynn's Statement to Military History Tribunal, for the Bureau of Military History, in private hands. (Hereafter, 'Statement').

Cong gave Lynn the chance to observe the rich at close quarters. Kathleen was twelve when the family moved there. She was sent away to school so Cong was a home she visited, rather than lived in continuously.[7] Although she maintained some links with Lady Ardilaun and her powerful friends, including later the formidable Lady Aberdeen, wife to the Lord Lieutenant, Lynn's subsequent actions suggest she did not like what she saw.[8]

The Guinness residence at Ashford Castle was a place where rich people partied: on at least two occasions, the parties were led by the Prince of Wales. It was a virtual theme park for the aristocracy. Forests were planted to encourage species of wildlife that could afford one a good day's shoot; lakes and rivers were redirected to ensure appropriate vistas and offer a pleasant afternoon's cruise. Throughout the grounds, follies and tea houses welcomed lovers' trysts and sheltered the delicate bloom of gentlewomen's skin from the spiky malicious rain sheeting inland from Lough Corrib.[9] The mud-clad hovels and tiny stone cottages of Mullafarry could not have been farther away.

The mindset in which Lynn was reared took its cue from Lord Ardilaun, who was a leading advocate for retaining the rights of the landlord class.[10] She knew no other perspective until years later,[11] and her actions are all the more remarkable because of the class and political transgressions they implied. After her 1916 activities, her father disinherited her[12] and refused to let her return home. 'Fardie' did not relent until 1920, when she had to promise not to receive

---

[7] She was lated educated in England and Düsseldorf, Germany.

[8] See Kathleen Lynn diaries, (1916-1955), four volumes, courtesy of the Wynne family. These diaries have been transcribed by Margaret Conway for the Royal College of Physicians in Ireland (RCPI), and are held by the RCPI. Hereafter cited as KLD. Transcriptions used here before 1930 were made by the author. The diaries' extraordinary style reflects Lynn's personality by simultaneously giving data while making it hard to decipher. Each day has three lines, but is written from the bottom up, with as many as twenty-one days over twenty-one years crammed together on a single spread. Slips of paper included suggest the shorter diary entries may not be first drafts.

[9] Cong and Clonbur Parish records and papers courtesy Very Rev. Dean Anthony Previte. See also Bridget Clesham, *St. Marys's Church Cong* (Cong, 1994). Cong's Medical Centre was named in Lynn's honour, as is the Medical Council's HQ at Lynn House, Dublin.

[10] See his statement quoted in Michael McCarthy, *Five Years in Ireland* (London and Dublin, 1901) p. 496.

[11] Lynn, 'Statement'.

[12] Robert Lynn's will dated 19 September 1916, leaves his estate valued at £393.13.10 to Nan and Muriel. He witnessed Nan's will, leaving everything to Muriel, on 15 June 1916 while Lynn was in detention, having assigned proceeds of a private trust to Nan and Muriel only, NAI.

any visitors or mix with unsuitable people in the town. When she did, he preached a sermon that embarrassed Lynn publicly, and hurt her deeply.[13]

Lynn began a new life when she entered Alexandra College Dublin in 1891, aged 17.[14] Alexandra was a pioneer of women's higher education. Spearheaded by Anne Jellicoe, Alice Oldham and Henrietta White, who was Kathleen's headmistress, Alexandra saw itself as '. . . watching over the interests of girls especially with regard to the Intermediate Education and Royal University.'[15] The College inspired students to achieve in what were considered exclusively male academic areas. Achievement was not only personal: academic success represented the honour of the College and demonstrated the intellectual potential of women in general. When Lynn started there, women could only receive degrees from the Royal University of Ireland (RUI), which was an examinations board and not a place of study; despite being allowed sit exams, women were excluded from attending many third-level lectures, including all courses at Trinity College.

The debate about the higher education of women was waging across the drawing rooms of the United Kingdom, Europe and the United States. Some scientists believed educating women was an unnatural act, because their brains were not big enough to cope with the extra blood flow required. Other people thought it a waste of money. But admitting women to higher education implied their subsequent admission to the professions and thereby to influential positions in the public world. Many found the prospect unacceptable. Lynn's father never supported her desire to be well-educated, to work or to become a doctor.[16] Her mother, however, was distantly related to Archbishop Trench, one of Alexandra's founding patrons. Lady Ardilaun, the Rev. Lynn's employer, took a strong interest in the school, following the fashion set by its patron and namesake, Alexandra, Princess of Wales.[17] That may have helped tip the scales

---

[13] KLD, '. . . Nan said they would like me at home only no-one must know I am there.' (25 Sept. 1919). Lynn did not return on those terms. Lady Ardilaun intervened (21 Dec. 1920) and Lynn was invited home for Christmas '. . . if I won't have demonstrations (do they picture bands?) or see people who are not their visitors...' (24 Dec. 1920). But her father preached a '. . . god and country . . . ' sermon which '. . . annoyed me much, hate my father to be unfair.' (26 Dec. 1920).

[14] Lynn first appears on the register in October 1891, Alexandra College Archive, Dublin, courtesy of Ms Jean Hazlett.

[15] Anne O'Connor and Susan Parkes, *Gladly Learn and Gladly Teach: A History of Alexandra College and School* (Dublin, 1983), p. 48.

[16] Author interview with May Cummins, who said 'If he'd had his way, he [Robert Lynn] would have kept her at home.' Lynn's sisters did not attend Alexandra, did not marry, and stayed at home.

[17] Lady Ardilaun provided an emergency fund to help urgent cases uncovered by the Alexandra guilds, following the College's special celebrations to mark her silver wedding anniversary in 1896, O'Connor and Parkes, *Gladly Learn*, pp. 70-4.

in Lynn's favour. Her own determination must have made an impact too, as her sisters were not educated to that level.

Alexandra's ethos freed Lynn's intellect to achieve its potential, and she excelled. Arithmetic, geography, Latin, history and music were her chosen subjects. Her extra-curricular activities included hockey and cycling, as well as her headmistress's passion for horticulture, which stayed with her all her life. As a Junior candidate in 1892, she came second in the Stern Scholarship to Katherine Hinkson.[18] She matriculated in the 1893 RUI exams, spending six months preparing in Cong, and sitting German too.[19]

Alexandra also offered Lynn a context within which her life could take shape. The school was closely associated with the Irish Women's Suffrage and Local Government Association (IWSLGA) led by Anna Haslam, who visited regularly.[20] As well as hearing about the suffrage movement, the girls were encouraged to think about the public world and were lectured on such thorny topics as local government reform, employment conditions for women, poverty, housing, Irish history and the Irish language. Lynn adopted ideas generated at Alexandra as templates in her later work. The Alexandra College Guild, founded in 1897, involved the girls with past-pupils and supporters in devising practical means of improving social conditions. While emerging in many ways from the nineteenth-century tradition of female philanthropy which was one of the few female routes into the public world, the Guild was also a network to counteract the tight professional community of the 'old boy's club.' Leading Protestant boys' schools had already introduced past-pupils' groups, with Catholic boys' schools such as Castleknock (1896) and Clongowes (1897) following suit.

When Dr. Katherine Maguire addressed its first annual conference on 'Social Conditions of the Dublin Poor,' the Guild acted on her suggestion that it invest in run-down tenement houses, repair them and let them out at a fair rent. A special company formed to manage the project was the only public company in Great Britain and Ireland directed entirely by women.[21] Lynn adapted the guild model for inner-city housing and community projects later generated by St. Ultan's. Maguire, a past-pupil who took her MD in 1895, become Lynn's friend and mentor, acting later as a consultant to St. Ultan's.

Lynn's ambition to become a doctor could not be realised at Trinity College, her father's alma mater, which in 1892 had rejected a petition in favour of women's education signed by 10,000 people. Although women had been

---

[18] Better known as the writer Katherine Tynan. Alexandra students night report, 9 December 1892 and elsewhere; Registers 1890-1896, Alexandra College Archive.

[19] National University of Ireland, Dublin, courtesy of John Foley. Lynn's records, Mercer Library, RCSI, Dublin, courtesy of Mary O'Doherty.

[20] See Rosemary Cullen Owens, *Smashing Times: A History of the Irish Women's Suffrage Movement 1889-1922* (Dublin, 1984).

[21] O'Connor and Parkes, *Gladly Learn*, p. 70.

distinguished traditionally as healers and physicians, ranks had closed against them by the early nineteenth century, coinciding with the emergence of the professional classes which identified themselves as exclusive. Legislation introduced in 1876 finally allowed medical bodies to grant qualifications 'to all persons without distinction of sex.' Gradually, women were admitted to lectures too. The Royal College of Surgeons in Ireland (RCSI) was the first Irish medical school to admit women and licence them to practise medicine. RCSI classes included women from 1885; the Catholic University School of Medicine in Dublin's Cecilia Street admitted women from October 1896. Lynn, along with a Miss Frances Dreaper, attended lectures at both centres to prepare for RUI medical degree exams. Her exclusion from Trinity had the accidental effect of educating her in part alongside a generation of mainly Catholic doctors, like all female medical students. Cecilia Street-trained doctor/politicians Lynn would later encounter included Richard Mulcahy, Ernie O'Malley and Ada English.[22] Trinity College finally agreed to admit women to arts degrees in 1902, and soon after to medical education.[23]

By June 1896, the Alexandra College magazine applauded Lynn's 'brilliant success' in the first year RUI medical exams where she came first in practical anatomy, winning £3 and a medal, '. . . a distinction not hitherto achieved by a woman.' In December 1898, the magazine reported her victory as winner of the Barker Anatomical Prize awarded by the Royal College of Surgeons, and congratulated her '. . . recent successes as one of the most gifted women student doctors.' Kathleen Florence Lynn was awarded the degrees of M.B., B.Ch., B.A.O. (bachelor of medicine, surgery and obstetrics) from the RUI in 1899. She had interned at Holles Street Hospital (1897/9), the Rotunda Hospital (1899), the Royal Victoria Eye and Ear Hospital (1899) and at the Richmond Lunatic Asylum,[24] all in Dublin.

Holles Street and the Rotunda gave Lynn hands-on experience of the appalling conditions into which so many Dublin children were born and confirmed her interest in what we now call the nature-nurture debate. Infant mortality rates from preventable diseases struck almost two out of every ten children under the age of five, while mortality under one year was even higher. She noticed that although no hospital wanted to admit sick infants, there was no special hospital for them.[25]

Lynn's earliest recorded experience of professional discrimination because

---

[22] F.O.C. Meenan, *Cecilia Street: The Catholic University School of Medicine 1855-1931* (Dublin, 1987), pp. 83-95.

[23] See J.B. Lyons, 'Women in medicine,' *Irish Medical Times*, special supplement, January 1992, pp. 38-40.

[24] National University of Ireland, Dublin, courtesy of John Foley.

[25] Uncatalogued document 'Memorial to Dr. Kathleen Lynn' in Minutes of Dr. K.L. Lynn Memorial Committee, uncatalogued papers, RCPI.

of her sex occurred in 1898. The Adelaide Hospital, whose first woman student was Katherine Maguire, found itself unable to offer Lynn employment as a resident doctor on the grounds that it had no female residence and therefore nowhere to put her.[26] She did obtain residency at the Royal Victoria Eye and Ear Hospital (RVEEH), and was the first woman to do so. She worked as an ophthalmologist and as a duty doctor at hospitals including Sir Patrick Dun's. The consultancies were part of a wider general practice she managed from her home at 9 Belgrave Road, Rathmines, where she moved in 1904. (She had lived previously at 61 Lombard Street West, South Circular Road). Lynn rented the terraced, two-storey over basement house from the Plunkett family until her death.

Discussions about Irish language and culture, about workers' rights, women's rights, health and education were gripping the new century. Dublin was a small place, where ideas flowed freely and quickly across social groupings, which themselves sometimes overlapped. Lynn's middle-class neighbourhood was a centre for various activists. The Plunketts belonged to the rising Catholic middle classes and were interested in the new cultural nationalist movements; their son Joseph Mary would later sign the 1916 Proclamation, and be executed as a traitor. The Haslams lived nearby, as did the theosophist and feminist Margaret (Gretta) Cousins, while from 1918 Lynn's next-door neighbours included Hanna Sheehy Skeffington into whose garden Lynn's dogs used to leap.

Lynn's professional education flourished.[27] She was awarded the rare distinction of Fellow of the Royal College of Physicians in Ireland (FRCPI) in 1909, aged 35. In 1910, the RVEEH promoted her to the post of clinical assistant. She remained in that position until what the RVEEH records call a 'mysterious absence' starting in Easter week, 1916.[28] 1916 was a defining rite of passage in her life, symbolising a threshold crossed in political and personal terms. Lynn's involvement in the rebellion represented a coming together of the political interests she had pursued through feminism, republicanism and labour. The three strands were intertwined and, happily, coincided with her religious beliefs. She asserted that nationalism led to internationalism, and that internationalism '. . . equals Christianity.'[29]

---

[26] David Mitchell, *'A Peculiar Place': the History of the Adelade Hospital, Dublin 1839-1989* (Dublin, nd.), p. 258. Dr. Mitchell disputes the claims in Smyth, 'Kathleen Lynn', and elsewhere that Lynn was refused because of sexism, then describes how the Adelaide's first woman doctor was finally employed in November 1914, when no men applied because of the war.

[27] Geoffrey Wynne understood Lynn's reported study in the United States during this period arose with Lady Ardilaun and Lady Aberdeen's help. See Women's National Health Association journal, *Slainte*, vol.1, (1909).

[28] Gearoid Crookes, *Dublin's Eye and Ear: The Making of a Monument* (Dublin, 1993), pp. 45-6, 68, 80, 88, 105-7.

[29] KLD, 2 May 1936.

Lynn's politics grew from her commitment to votes for women. Suffrage, as then applied, excluded not only all women, but also men who were not classified as householders: labourers, working men, and the unemployed. Her view of a universal suffrage broadened, and she became involved with the labour movement, which she identified as a core expression of her republican principles. 'I was converted', she observed, 'to Republicanism through suffrage. I saw that people got the wrong impression about suffrage and that led me to examine the Irish question.'[30] The 'wrong impression' ignored the tenet that all God's children should be treated equally, and instead saw female suffrage campaigners as discontents determined to embarrass their government and their families, never mind upsetting the 'natural' balance of society.

Lynn was already an active board member of the non-militant IWSLGA. But she also belonged to the more radical, militant, Women's Social and Political Union (WSPU), founded by the Pankhursts and working across the United Kingdom of Great Britain and Ireland. The WSPU's close links to the labour movement created a pattern of female activism that included the exploits of women such as Eva Gore-Booth, who organised mill workers in Manchester, and Emily Hobhouse, the first non-combatant to enter the British concentration camps for Boers in South Africa and tell the world about the excesses of the imperialist agenda there. Lynn initially subscribed to its London-based headquarters and then to an Irish branch, serving as its secretary for a while.[31] Lynn's membership of the British-based WSPU was a potentially controversial position within the local politics of Irish feminism, and she was criticised for it.[32] Yet it enabled her to maintain a broad span of alliances with women whose opinions were as likely to be unionist as nationalist. By June 1912, Lynn was campaigning at mass meetings in Dublin for the inclusion of votes for women in the Home Rule Bill. The following year, she replaced Dr. Elizabeth (Eliza) Tennant as medical examiner to imprisoned suffragettes, after Tennant's loyalties were found lacking and reported as such in Hanna and Frank Sheehy Skeffington's feminist journal, the *Irish Citizen*.[33]

Helena Molony, a member of Inghinidhe na hÉireann and editor of its journal, *Bean na hÉireann*, claimed she was responsible for Lynn's conversion to republicanism, when she contacted her because Constance Markievicz, Lynn's

---

[30] Included in contemporary obituary and funeral reports, copy courtesy of Bridget Clesham.

[31] WSPU records from the Suffragette Fellowship name Lynn from 1908, Fawcett Library, London. See also *Women's Who's Who* (London, 1913). Information courtesy of Gail Cameron, Museum of London, and of London Guildhall.

[32] Marguerite Palmer to Hanna Sheehy Skeffington, 11 Aug. 1914, Sheehy Skeffington papers, Ms 22,666, National Library of Ireland, Dublin. (Hereafter, NLI). My thanks to Margaret Ward for this reference.

[33] See Margaret Ward, *Unmanageable Revolutionaries: Women and Irish Nationalism* (London, 1983).

distant kinswoman, needed a doctor for a minor complaint.[34] Markievicz, a powerful role model for Lynn because of her ascendancy background and their shared family connections,[35] told her sister Eva that she had brought Lynn into the fold.[36] Years later, Lynn herself ascribed the immediate spur as her contact with Molony, while placing it in the wider context of the questions to which suffrage led her.[37] A personal route was provided by her growing friendship with Madeleine ffrench-Mullen, a Roman Catholic as devout in her religious practice as was Lynn. ffrench-Mullen, a founder member in 1908 of *Bean na hÉireann*, was Molony's colleague. Her regular column about children entitled 'An Grianán' was penned under the pseudonyms M. O'Callaghan, or Dectora.[38] One story of how they met pictures Madeleine as a robust young woman who fell off her chair and collapsed with laughter at a first-aid meeting. Lynn reportedly helped her up and the two became firm friends.[39] ffrench-Mullen would help Lynn build the infants' hospital she had already identified as an essential but missing part of the healthcare infrastructure. The two women shared a caring professional and personal partnership, living and working together until ffrench-Mullen died in May 1944.[40] They were a great team.

Lynn's work as a doctor moving across class boundaries brought her into direct contact with people whose lack of rights inspired labour leaders such as James Connolly, then Ulster organiser of the Irish Transport and General Workers' Union (ITGWU). Her general medical practice became increasingly devoted to working with Dublin's poor. Sympathetic doctors supported a developing system of baby clubs that fostered such initiatives as 'Little Mothers' schemes to promote better diet and combat T.B. The models were closely related to current practice in large cities like London, Manchester and Liverpool, and would also be adopted at St. Ultan's.

---

[34] 'Cathal O'Shannon and Helena Molony', Helena Molony's spoken recollection recorded 11 Nov. 1964, RTE Sound Archives, Dublin, no. 172/68.

[35] Katharine (Wynne) Lynn's first cousin Owen Wynne had married Fanny Gore-Booth. Fanny's brother Henry Gore-Booth married Georgina Hill, who produced five children including Constance (b. 1868) and Eva (b. 1870).

[36] Letters between Constance Markievicz and Eva Gore-Booth can be found in Ms 21, 815, and Ms 21, 816, NLI.

[37] Lynn, 'Statement'.

[38] See *Bean na hÉireann*, 1908-1911. Also Sydney Gifford Czira (aka John Brennan) *The Years Flew By* (London, 1974).

[39] See fn 16, above.

[40] See Carroll Smith-Rosenberg, 'Discourses of sexuality and subjectivity: the new woman 1870-1936', in Martin Duberman, Martha Vicinus, George Chauncey, Jnr., (eds.), *Hidden from History: Reclaiming the Gay and Lesbian Past* (New York, 1990), pp. 264-280; Rictor Norton, *The Myth of the Modern Homosexual* (London and Washington, 1997), pp. 180-214. Those interviewed by the author did not think that this was a sexual relationship.

A clear political division characterised the principal health-promoting voluntary agencies, including those sponsored by women. Women activists could work in health care without sanction, and were increasingly choosing to do so. There was wide consensus about how to achieve better healthcare – free school meals for children, locally-available dispensaries, open-air treatment for consumptives – but a very different analysis of the root causes by leading organisations like Inghinidhe na hÉireann or the Women's National Health Association of Ireland (WNHAI). The contest between the two opposing views marks how politicised health care and health intervention had become since the nineteenth century. The Inghinidhe [Daughters of Ireland], who were founded by the nationalist Maud Gonne, saw poor healthcare as the direct result of British imperialism and recognised it as a field for opposing government policies. The WNHAI, however, continued to see healthcare within the ascendancy traditions of almsgiving and philanthropy that had flourished from the nineteenth century, rather than believe poor health might result directly from political choices.

Wealthier by far than the Inghinidhe, the WNHAI was supported by many women from Lynn's birth community. A measure of how politically sensitive healthcare was regarded in practise is that Lady Aberdeen, the Lord Lieutenant's wife, was the WNHAI's President. Lady Aberdeen herself travelled to investigate new healthcare models in the United States. By 1909, when the Inghinidhe's profile was rising, the WNHAI found the funds to launch a travelling healthcare caravan on a country-wide basis. Perhaps in a nod to the times, it was called 'Eire'.[41] Dr. Ella Webb, Lynn's colleague and later a leading practitioner at St. Ultan's, ran a WNHAI-assisted dispensary that distributed pasteurised milk to mothers and children, while Ella Young, Lynn's writer friend, taught history to inner-city children as part of her contribution to the Inghinidhe.[42] The WNHAI remained the dominant organ after the Free State was founded, and absorbed some Inghinidhe women.

Lynn's labour activities developed as part of her emerging republicanism. She became a vice-president of the Irish Women Workers' Union, founded by Delia and James Larkin in 1911, and a patron of various activities it encouraged, such as a shirt-making co-operative. Lynn worked as a medical officer during the 1913 lock-out, a key confrontation between labouring and professional classes. In the Liberty Hall food kitchens, where she oversaw dietary rations, nationalists and feminists joined socialist activists in various tasks, such as doling out food supplies shipped over from sympathetic workers in Liverpool and

---

[41] *Slainte*, vol. 1. no.3, (March 1909). See also *Women's National Health Association of Ireland: Golden Jubilee 1907-1957* (Dublin, 1958) and *Bean na hÉireann*, no. 7, (May 1909), where a letter from 'Kathleen' challenges class-based assumptions about T.B.

[42] Ella Young, *Flowering Dusk* (London, 1945), pp. 71-72.

Manchester. But the food supplies dried up when British public opinion became persuaded that the lock-out was primarily a nationalist ploy rather than a symptom of class struggle. The lock-out brought enormous hardship to Dublin's working people, and provoked questions about how middle-class Irish nationalists, such as the newspaper proprietor William Martin Murphy, might be expected to treat the working classes in the event of Home Rule being granted. What little labour legislation there was favoured employers and the professional classes, with the police defending those interests when required to do so. Concerns grew in parallel that growing militarism elsewhere, including the formation of the Ulster Volunteers and the Irish Volunteers, would leave labour interests behind.

James Connolly, then Ulster organiser of the Irish Transport and General Workers' Union, invited Lynn to join the new Irish Citizen Army (ICA), which was ostensibly intended to protect workers and their families from the police. The ICA was committed to an equality agenda for men, women and children which Connolly was instrumental in promoting when the 1916 Proclamation was drafted. Lynn was appointed its medical director. Connolly believed she was exceptional, and told his family: 'The most amazing of them all is Dr. Lynn: that she with her early training and environment should find her niche in the Citizen Army, be so thoroughly at home and be so completely accepted by them is something to be constantly amazed at.'[43] Initially, Lynn's work took the form of first-aid classes to women and men, with the classes set up on a mixed basis, as was membership of the ICA itself. She had little time for militarism and did not attend ICA drills,[44] yet it is not accurate to call her a pacifist in the true sense.[45] She actively or tacitly supported armed opposition to successive governments until the mid-1930s.

Easter 1916 exposed the latent fractures in Lynn's personal and professional lives. While the ICA and the Volunteers were fighting in the city of Dublin, doctors she had worked alongside were manning medical units for army personnel. The RVEEH, her employer, was taking in wounded British soldiers.[46] On Monday, 24 April, she drove with Markievicz, ffrench-Mullen and Molony from Liberty Hall where they had packed her car with medical supplies, intending to stop briefly at City Hall before going on to her posting at the College of Surgeons. But at City Hall, situated immediately beside the centre of British administration at Dublin Castle, ICA Captain Seán Connolly had shot and killed a policeman, and was himself mortally wounded. Lynn saw the policeman's body lying dead on the ground and climbed out with Molony, who had acted

---

[43] Nora Connolly O'Brien to Eamon de Valera, 8 March 1957. De Valera papers, box 1421, Franciscan Archive, Dublin.
[44] Lynn, 'Statement'.
[45] Canon William (Billy) Wynne, *Irish Times* column 'WW', April 1994.
[46] O'Connor and Parkes, *Gladly Learn*; Crooks, *Dublin's Eye and Ear*, pp. 104-6.

with Connolly in the Abbey Theatre, leaving Markievicz to drive on to Surgeons.

Lynn attended Connolly and comforted his younger brother who was also stationed there. She could not leave to take up her post at the College of Surgeons. By nightfall, the tiny ICA unit was surrounded. Soldiers burst into the room where Lynn and others were sheltered. She gave the surrender, and reportedly caused a minor flurry of protocol as the soldiers were unsure whether regulations allowed them accept it from a woman.[47] Her diary entry for that day is typically understated:

> Easter Monday. Emer [Molony] & I in City Hall, Seghan Connolly shot quite early in day. Place taken in evening. All women taken to Ship St. about 8.30. Emer, Mrs. Barrett, 2 Norgroves, B. Davis & I, joined later on by B. Lynch, J. Shanaghan & B. Brady. We were locked up in a filthy store, given blankets thick with lice & fleas to cover us & some 'biscuits' to lie on, not enough to go round.[48]

The insurgents surrendered. On Monday, 1 May, Lynn, along with an estimated twelve women and fifty men, was marched from Ship Street barracks up Thomas Street to what she called a 'great ovation – only separation women hooted.'[49] The men were deposited at Richmond Barracks; the women moved on to Kilmainham Jail. Lynn was overjoyed to see ffrench-Mullen there the next day: they shared a cell with Molony until Lynn was taken with Countess Plunkett to Mountjoy on Tuesday 9 May.

Conflicting loyalties hit home when her father visited on Wednesday. 'It is hard to grieve one's Father, but I *could* [sic] not do otherwise.'[50] Two days later, she wrote a rare personal cry in her diary:

> A very black Friday, Fardie & Nan were here, oh, so reproachful, they wouldn't listen to me & looked as if they would cast me off for ever. How sorry I am for their sorrow! Erin needs big sacrifices . . . Why do they always misunderstand me?[51]

Lynn's diaries record rumour and counter-rumour as men were taken out and shot. A clergyman who berated her un-Protestant politics prompted the curt

---

[47] Lynn, 'Statement'; see also *Cumann na mBan*, vol. 2, no. 10, (Easter 1926). An anecdote that she always opposed women wearing trousers is unfounded: women leaders met before the Rising and decided that wearing trousers would make them seem even more offensive to the public.

[48] KLD, 24 April 1916.

[49] KLD, 1 May 1916. Separation women were the wives and dependents of soldiers serving overseas in the British forces.

[50] KLD, 10 May 1916.

[51] KLD, 12 May 1916.

retort that she would follow her conscience. Her entries cease on 17 May. Weighing under eight stone and still itchy from lice, she was deported to England in June. Her family and their powerful contacts made strong representations to spare her incarceration in an English jail. Their solution was to find a friend of a friend who would take Kathleen into care on the basis that she was '. . . a sort of lunatic,' as Lynn later recalled.[52] This was a traditional way of classifying women's transgressive behaviour.

Lynn refused to go on those terms. However, doctors were at a premium because a world war was being fought and so Jennie Wyse Power, her IWSLGA colleague, was allowed to arrange that Lynn work instead with an Irishman called Dr. Cusack, who was a locum at a medical practice in Coleford House, at Abingdon, some miles from Bath.[53] Lynn wrote to Kathleen Clarke:

> It is simply a black horror to look back to that time at Kilmainham when every morning we heard the fatal shots & knew some of our best and bravest had gone . . . Thank God for their brave and noble deaths, which will never be in vain, all down the ages their effect will be felt, proving that the spirit can never die.[54]

Muriel Lynn's illness offered an excuse to return Kathleen to Cong on 11 July. 1916. Following representations from Lawrence Ginnell MP, and her family, the authorities had already decided to release her by the time she returned to Coleford House on 14 August to fill in for Dr. Cusack.[55] She travelled to Dublin promptly.

Lynn was out of paid employment. The RVEEH refused her offer to return to work in autumn 1916[56] and no other hospital would employ her.[57] She had new challenges. Using nationally-based organisations such as the Irish Volunteer Dependents' Fund as a network, deputy leaders like Kathleen Clarke were working from June 1916 to keep the national movement intact. Public opinion, which had not supported the Rising in significant numbers, was outraged by the Government's policy of executions. The people were ripe for turning.

In January 1917, Clarke appointed Michael Collins as the Fund's secretary. Collins became a master tactician in military terms, and built up a unique cycle of resistance. But power struggles within the movement threatened its success.

---

[52] Lynn, 'Statement'.
[53] *Ibid.* The Cusacks were a nationalist family from Galway.
[54] Lynn to Kathleen Clarke, 19 June 1916, courtesy Helen Litton.
[55] Lynn, 'Statement'. Lynn's Home Office 1916 files have been destroyed (D.R. Taylor, Home Office, to author, 19 February 1996). See the correspondence between the Home Office, Dublin Castle and the Dublin Metropolitan Police, in Chief Secretary's Office Papers, 13503/16, NAI.
[56] Crooks, *Dublin's Eye and Ear.*
[57] Author's interviews with Dr. John Shanley.

Lynn's ICA was being overwhelmed by the significantly stronger interests represented by Sinn Féin, the Volunteers, the Liberty Clubs (led by Lynn's landlord, the papal Count Plunkett), and the secret Irish Republican Brotherhood. Neither feminist nor social agendas were a priority for those groups. Clarke was also de facto leader of Cumann na mBan, the female adjunct to the Volunteers. However, unlike the ICA, the Volunteers had never formally acknowledged women's equality; women were regarded as auxiliaries, rather than equals. With the executions of committed pro-equality leaders Connolly, Mallin, MacDonagh, and, to an extent, Patrick Pearse, attitudes to women's rights were likely to prove completely inadequate unless women's groups could present a unified front. Clarke's support was vital.

Lynn visited Clarke for a week in Limerick in March 1917,[58] and by May Cumann na mBan had joined women from the ICA, Inghinidhe and the IWWU to form a League of Women Delegates. In October, it was named Cumann na dTeachtaire (CnaT). CnaT wanted to secure women's role in the national movement and to promote their claims for equality, including suffrage. There is some evidence that Lynn believed CnaT did not fulfil its full potential to effect change, but its immediate impact was strong.[59] Cumann na mBan were changing; their 1917 Convention introduced a new policy that the organisation would work directly to ensure women should '. . . take up their proper position in the life of the nation.'[60] Previously they had relied on the good faith of the Volunteers.

Lynn's visit to Clarke was prescient. At Dublin's Mansion House in April, Count Plunkett made a bid for power on behalf of his Liberty Clubs, and began formal negotiations with Arthur Griffith's Sinn Féin for control of the nationalist movement. Countess Plunkett, his wife, was the only female member of the nine-person negotiating team. By June, CnaT had persuaded Countess Plunkett to appoint Lynn, the senior female official then at liberty, as her substitute on the team. Markievicz was released later that month and co-opted to the Cumann.

Griffith's and Plunkett's groups merged under the name Sinn Féin. They proposed to hold a convention where an enlarged executive would be appointed, including six men released from prison. CnaT argued that six women should also join the executive: Lynn, Clarke, Áine Ceannt, Wyse Power, Alice Ginnell and Molony. Their attention focused on the tenth Sinn Féin convention, scheduled for 25 October 1917. The Sinn Féin organisation had changed utterly

---

[58] KLD, 12-17 March 1917.
[59] Cumann na dTeachtaire minute book, Sheehy Skeffington papers, NLI, Ms 21,194; see also fn. 73 below; see correspondence with ffrench-Mullen, NLI, Ms 22,682. Also called the Conference of Women Delegates, it met until January 1919. See, KLD, 25 January 1919 on having tea with Count Plunkett: 'I like not his hush party tactics,' and by 26 January 1919, 'we must wake up Cumann na dTeachtaire.'
[60] Quoted in Ward, *Unmanageable Revolutionaries*, pp. 126-7.

since the founding of Griffith's original pro-monarchist group. It had become the unifying grouping of Irish nationalism, and its political complexion was rapidly taking shape. It was also gaining credibility with the electorate. The pro-Home Rule Irish Party had supported the British Government's role in the world war, only to find itself wrong-footed when official responses after the 1916 rebellion and subsequently proved too harsh to be popular.

The convention witnessed the amalgamation in theory between the Volunteers, identified with radical republicanism, and non-combatants who had belonged to the old Sinn Féin. Tensions between militants and politicians remained, however, despite consensus on a new constitution. Like many other women republicans, Lynn belonged to the radical wing, believing then in a republic for all the people governed by all the people, but later coming to view it in 'transcendent' terms.[61] Éamon de Valera, who was with Markievicz one of the two surviving 1916 commandants, was unanimously appointed president of Sinn Féin, with Griffith and Fr. Michael O'Flanagan elected vice-presidents. Lynn was elected to the Sinn Féin executive of twenty-four in total, as one of four women and three Protestants. The other women were Markievicz, Clarke and Grace Gifford Plunkett; the other Protestants were Ernest Blythe and Darell Figgis.

Lynn's key intervention argued that the equality of men and women be emphasised in all Sinn Féin speeches and pamphlets. Applause greeted her remarks, and not because the convention members were committed feminists. Lynn's profile in the republican movement was rising. She was now *de facto* Surgeon General to Sinn Féin, a position that was soon made official. One month previously, Thomas Ashe had died on hungerstrike while her fingers felt his pulse ebb away.[62] The massive response to his death – some 30,000 people attended his funeral – measured how far public opinion was changing in support of Sinn Féin's strategy to win the status of a republic instead of the Irish Party's preferred Home Rule.

Although her diaries show Lynn could be acerbic, her words to the convention were suitably modest. Using a metaphor from ophthalmology, she underlined how the Irish republic would see only as much as a one-eyed man did, unless women were accorded equal involvement and status. She continued:

> There would have been no Easter Week except for the women who urged the men to take action boldly. We have no doubt now that Easter Week saved Ireland . . . We (women) are inexperienced, different and timid, we ask

---

[61] See Michael Laffan, *The Resurrection of Ireland: The Sinn Féin Party 1916-1923* (Cambridge, 1999).

[62] KLD, 26 Sept. 1917. The diaries rarely record specific details of meetings, and are short on giving her own analysis. This may reflect Lynn's innate privacy, and the fact that her house was frequently raided, making confidentiality important.

the men with centuries of experience to give us a little help and encouragement at the start, so as to give us a fair share in the work before us.[63]

The motion, an amended resolution lodged initially by CnaT, was seconded by Jennie Wyse Power and supported by Seán T. O'Kelly, who told delegates that it would be unIrish to oppose it. It was carried with widespread support.

Lynn served on the Sinn Féin standing committee until it was disbanded in 1922. (She served later on the anti-Treaty standing committee). The organisation's fluid identity was reflected in an immediate way by the changing languages and spellings that named her – Caitlín ní Fhlynn, Caitlín ní Fhloinn, Kathleen Lynn. She adjudicated structural proposals on issues including the disbursement of funds, the setting up of departments, Sinn Féin courts (where women served as judges and on juries), publishing of public health pamphlets, as well as overseeing the selection of election candidates at local level.[64]

Lynn viewed Sinn Féin with both pragmatism and scepticism, noting later that '. . . it held us together only to let us down at the critical moment.'[65] In a practical sense, she functioned both as a gatekeeper and as a watchdog, feeding into Sinn Féin the aims and aspirations of women across the span of alliances she had made in the labour and feminist movements. Central to her politics was a commitment to including the position of Protestants in the new Ireland. In 1918, she worked with Figgis to promote a ruling that, 'Sinn Féin clubs throughout [the country] give every facility to our Protestant fellow countrymen and women to sign the anti-conscription pledge.'[66]

Lynn spent weeks on the run because of her standing committee membership: her house was raided frequently over these years. Arrested on 31 October 1918, her deportation order was cancelled the same day when the Lord Mayor intervened.[67] Despite her many commitments, including founding St.Ultan's Hospital in 1919, her medical practice did not suffer. She treated patients while on the run, including wounded republicans.[68]

---

[63] Sinn Féin Convention Report, NLI, Ms 21,523. See also various memoirs, including that of Sean T. O'Kelly, NLI, Ms 27, 707, pp. 180-194.

[64] Minutes of Sinn Féin Standing Committee, NLI, Pos. 3269 (hereafter SFM). See 17 Jan. 1918, 18 Feb. and 1 March 1919, for spellings of her name. For post-Treaty minutes, see Chief Solicitors' Office Papers, 2B/82/117 (23) ff. NAI. See 'Methods for avoiding epidemic of syphilis in Ireland', *Sinn Féin Public Health Circular no.1*, 1918.

[65] Lynn to de Valera, 30 Oct. 1922, Department of the Taoiseach Files, S121/10B, NAI.

[66] SFM, 22 April 1918.

[67] KLD, 31 Oct. 1918. It seems the Lord Mayor's intervention was personal, as it is not cited in the minutes of the Municipal Council of City of Dublin 1916-19. City Archive Dublin, courtesy Mary Clarke.

[68] Lynn, 'Statement'.

The country was close to anarchy, and the standing committee worked to impose a structure and direction on its supporters. A simple measure of how close is the story of Lynn's car, which survives in film footage, notably showing Markievicz returning to a rapturous public reception on release from prison. Lynn loaned it to Sinn Féin's Department of Transport during the 1918 Cavan election, but later it was taken from outside her house without her permission. Lynn was furious. She made a formal complaint to the standing committee noting how it was returned to her '. . . minus lamps . . . unworkable horn, the lining stripped off and the cushions in rags . . .' Plunkett was instructed to inquire into 'the use of motor transport and safeguarding private persons.'[69]

Even on the run, Lynn continued to attend early morning service every day, and to take services up to three times daily on Sundays.[70] Her profound spirituality governed every aspect of her life, and informed her inclusive politics as deeply as it shaped her life and work with the poor. Lynn had never doubted that God was on the side of the oppressed. Delighting in the positive progress of the Russian revolution, she thanked Him: 'Bolshevism is gaining on all sides, D.G. [*Deo Gratias*], how puny are the efforts of the Rich to resist the Spirit of Freedom.'[71]

Lynn's medico-political approach to healthcare matured. When British soldiers were decommissioned after the war, she worked with ffrench-Mullen and Dr. Alice Barry to create an alliance of women activists in a venereal disease (VD) committee that simultaneously highlighted the widespread social disease and underlined the moral turpitude of the British army. The VD committee had the political advantage of drawing in non-nationalist doctors, who could then be lobbied to suppport the cause. Its work ran parallel to CnaT,[72] and followed on the tradition of female protest about sexual health following the Contagious Diseases Acts, which had been the focus for late nineteenth-century activists.

Lynn's idea of a republic envisaged a multi-denominational society. The Church of Ireland's special status as the established church had been removed in 1869. Its historic call 'For God and Country,' however, raised increasingly awkward questions about political allegiance within the wider debate about national self-determination and self-government. With Ulster edging towards a political break from the rest of the country, southern Protestants as a community faced an uncertain future within an independent or self-governed Ireland, where

---

[69] SFM, 20 March 1919; KLD, March 1919.
[70] Lynn, 'Statement'.
[71] KLD, 4 Feb. 1919.
[72] Minute book, Conference of Women's Societies, including details of anti-VD campaign (Stokes/Ruane inventory: strong box, iv, a), RCPI. See also fn. 60 above. With thanks to Robert Mills, Dr. Barbara Stokes, Dr. Rose Barry, Dr. Dermot Kelleher.

the rising Catholic middle-class was expected to increase its public power. The recent *Ne Temere* decree had further isolated them, by making it mandatory for the children of mixed marriages to be raised in the Roman Catholic faith. Lynn worked with Cumann Gaelach na hEaglaise, a Church of Ireland group which wanted the church to change its ethos. Founded in 1904, the Cumann's first secretary was writer, Sean O'Casey, who soon fell out with them as he did later with the ICA. Longer term, Lynn wanted to develop the Irishness of the church based on its Celtic past, rather than on its Anglocentric associations. It would take time, but might be achieved gradually through short-term objectives from having Irish-language services to translating the Book of Nurney into Irish.[73]

Divinity students, including Lynn's father, learned Irish to communicate and evangelise in rural communities. Before the language revival, the Bible was one of the few printed texts available in Irish. By the turn of the twentieth century, however, the Irish language was increasingly seen as enmeshed with the ideals of nationalist groups. The Cumann met with considerable opposition within the church. Cumann Gaelach members like Dr. Douglas Hyde, founder of the Gaelic League, were Irish Irelanders who wanted to deanglicise the church. Other members were not nationalists, but were sympathetic to the practical argument that if signs of Irishness such as the language were permitted to be owned exclusively by nationalists, the church would be weakened by the political and social consequences of Home Rule.

Lynn's work with the Cumann was a characteristically progressive act. She arranged to have Éamon de Valera honoured with a special reception by the Cumann on 10 November 1921, while the Anglo-Irish Treaty negotiating team was in London. Guests included Susan Mitchell, Louie Bennett, Helen Chenevix, Dr. Hyde, Jack Butler Yeats and many senior clergy. The reception was a useful political opportunity for him, and their many meetings before it suggest that she briefed him on what to expect. De Valera was reported as saying:

> The fact that the lines of political division ran to a certain degree parallel to the lines of religious division – a circumstance which they knew was accidental – gave an unfortunate foothold to those who wished to misrepresent the position. To foreigners it appeared as if the political differences had their origin in religious antagonism. . . It was better when (leaders) met for National affairs that the religion of those that came together should not be adverted to... If they wanted to realise the emotions and the hopes of those charged with guiding the present national movement in Ireland they had only to read [Thomas] Davis, a Protestant.[74]

Equality became more visible. At the age of forty-four, Lynn voted for the first

---

[73] See Risteárd Giltrap, *An Ghaeilge in Eaglais na hÉireann* (Baile Átha Cliath, 1990). Author's interview with Dr. Donald Caird.

[74] Giltrap, *An Ghaeilge*, pp. 78-83. See also KLD, Sept.-Nov. 1921.

time in the December 1918 general election, which gave the vote to women over thirty in Britain and Ireland, and to working men. Markievicz's success in Dublin's inner-city ward, St. Patrick's, as the first ever woman MP lifted her heart. 'Let us use our women's vote for good,' she recorded that election day. Her optimism was boundless, as was her belief in the ethical muscle of her sex:

> Women and men are complements one of the other . . . I think that women . . . work straight for their end without being held back by personal considerations. We see all around us a system rotten with corruption and intrigue. If women have their place it will be much easier to keep it honest and open and straight.[75]

Tragedy gave Lynn the opportunity to create the infants' hospital she had always desired. The arrival in Ireland of the global influenza epidemic threw public health services into crisis. There were no antibiotics then, nor reliable methods of inoculation: people worldwide died in their millions.[76] Lynn worked to combat the epidemic with former medical colleagues who disapproved of her republican sympathies – Drs. Katherine Maguire, Ella Webb, Elizabeth Tennant, and others. On 21 October 1918, she checked out an old building at 37 Charlemont Street for use as a temporary flu hospital, and on 2 November, opened a depot there with Dr. Alice Barry, who was known for her baby clubs in the area. They intended to treat and inoculate people of all ages against flu. Within a week, Kathleen had admitted a motherless baby called 'Peadhar': there was still no infants' hospital in Dublin. Babies continued to arrive.[77]

St. Ultan's Hospital for infants was born. Lynn and ffrench-Mullen opened the doors on Ascension Thursday 1919, with resources of two cots and £70. Ultan represented the Irish churches' common Christian past, a unifying theme for two such religious women. The sixth-century saint had cared for children orphaned by the yellow plague; Lynn read about him in the work of Sir William Wilde, father of writer Oscar (and a leading ophthalmologist), whose books about Celtic and early Christian Ireland were popular with the landed classes in Lynn's childhood.[78] Every September thereafter, they visited St. Ultan's Well at Ardbraccan, near Navan, to pray for the hospital and its babies. De Valera valued their political support sufficiently highly to visit Ardbraccan on 4 September 1921 two months before his Cumann Gaelach reception, where he threw in the ball at a charity football match.

---

[75] Sinn Féin Convention Report, Ms 21,523, NLI.

[76] Author interviews with Dr. John Cowell, Dr. Barbara Stokes, Dr. Rose Barry, Dr. John Shanley, Dr. Tom Kavanagh.

[77] KLD, 1918-1919.

[78] Lynn valued her copy of William R. Wilde, *The Beauties of the Boyne* (Dublin, 1849), where St. Ultan is described. She later presented it to Dr. John Cowell, who headed the T.B. unit.

Lynn's political behaviour between 1921 and 1926 demonstrates her provocative attitude to the relationship between democracy and power. She was not alone. The precise form of government Ireland might adopt was variously imagined by different wings in Sinn Féin. A minority, including Griffith, could envisage a monarchy; republicans like Lynn wanted government by the people for the people. But first the people must do right, Lynn believed. In the weeks leading up to the Anglo-Irish Treaty, she recorded her readiness to reject anything less than a republic with full independence from Westminister. Over those latter months of 1921, Terence MacSwiney died on hungerstrike, Kevin Barry was executed and a little girl called Annie O'Neill was killed by Black and Tans in Charlemont Street beside St. Ultan's Hospital. Tensions were mounting within Sinn Féin. As acting President of the Standing Committee, Lynn steered through an amendment to the Sinn Féin Constitution requiring members to give their 'undivided allegiance' to Dáil Éireann. De Valera had drafted the amendment to include allegiance to the president and cabinet of the Dáil, as well, but was obliged to drop it.[79] His desire to vest allegiance in his own position signalled what came next. Lynn wrote in her diaries:

> Peace Terms, but what a peace ! Not what Connolly and Mallin and countless others died for. Please God the Country [*sic*] won't agree to what Griffith, Barton, Gavan Duffy, Duggan and Mick Collins had put their names to, more shame to them, better war than such a peace. It is terrible how many who should know better seem quite pleased with terms![80]

The oath of allegiance was anathema to her socialist and republican convictions. As well as betraying her dead comrades' beliefs, it would subject Ireland to the British government and its class-ridden political systems. Her commitment to the republic was also underpinned by a theological belief that it alone represented God's will. She prayed that '. . . our prayers be answered and the right triumph in the end.'[81] Contrary to the single received image of Catholic women praying during the Treaty negotiations and debate, Lynn's prayers were part of a non-Catholic prayer vigil centred at St. Anne's Church in Dawson Street, Dublin.

Lynn was opposed to compromise and alert for pro-Treaty manoeuvres within Sinn Féin. At the standing committee, she opposed Michael Collins's attempts to regularise voting rights at club level, and to manage the Treaty vote by ballot, rather than by open vote.[82] But the Treaty was carried in the Dáil (following an open vote, despite the decision to hold a ballot), and June's elections confirmed the electorate's support for it. Once again, Lynn occupied a minority position.

---

[79] SFM, 27 October 1921; KLD, 13 November 1921.
[80] KLD, 7 December 1921.
[81] KLD, 10 December 1921.
[82] SFM, 31 January 1922.

Blooded by a vicious civil war, the new Free State government executed many of its political opponents, and imprisoned more, including some 400 women for whose welfare Lynn fought through the Women's Prisoners' Defence League. On de Valera's invitation, Lynn stood in the August 1923 general election, and became one of 44 abstentionist TDs. She was one of only five women, the others being Markievicz, Mary MacSwiney, Caitlín Brugha and Margaret Collins O'Driscoll, the sole woman elected on the pro-Treaty side.

Anti-treaty TDs met regularly as a Republican Dáil, but it was a parliament without power. De Valera became eager to find a formula that would let him lead his T.D.s into the Free State Dáil. Lynn had already had several confrontations with de Valera, particularly over the ending of the old Sinn Féin standing committee under her presidency of it, which she had opposed but been unable to stop.[83] Her fragile alliance with him was now severed. In the company of persuasive like-minded friends such as Mary MacSwiney, Lynn's abstentionist position became entrenched.

In March 1926, Sinn Féin's Ard-Fheis at Dublin's Rotunda wrestled with motions and amendments designed to test such a formula.[84] Lynn thought that Sinn Féin should ignore immediate electoral ambitions and attack the government instead on economic and educational issues.[85] Her attitude made a limited sense; living conditions in the Free State had worsened dramatically as the new state's perilous financial situation was skewed further by growing recession in Britain. However, her previously sharp political instincts may have become blunted. Whatever the ideals of his earlier rhetoric, de Valera was intent on accessing parliamentary power.

De Valera could not bring Sinn Féin with him, so he left it behind, taking many leading republicans with him, including Markievicz. Lynn saw the split as a victory for principle. In fact, the victory was Pyrrhic, and sounded the death knell for Sinn Féin as she knew it. Her diary records '[Dev] left us, Die-Hards, in possession [of the Republic]. It is best so may there be no bitterness, D.G. [*Deo Gratias*], the uncompromised Republic stands.'[86] In April, he founded Fianna Fáil, the 'Soldiers of Destiny', and on 23 May his former Sinn Féin colleagues refused his proposals for a coalition arrangement. By the end of 1926, Lynn believed rumours that '. . . Rome was at the bottom of [Dev's] new policy.'[87] In 1927, Fianna Fáil entered the Dáil. Lynn's stance was moving her closer to men like Count Plunkett, whom she had previously scorned, rather

---

[83] Lynn/de Valera letters, 28 and 30 Oct., 1922, Department of the Taoiseach Files S121/10B, NAI.
[84] KLD, 12 March 1926. See Laffan, *Resurrection of Ireland*, p. 441.
[85] KLD, 15 March 1926.
[86] KLD, 28 March 1926
[87] KLD, 31 October 1926.

than women like Markievicz whose political judgement she had always valued. In July 1927, Markievicz died, and bequeathed Lynn her Wicklow cottage.

Had Lynn supported de Valera, she could have expected political rewards within the new Fianna Fáil, given her proven record as a strong candidate. Instead, in the absence of a viable political alternative to the Free State, she gradually withdrew from mainstream politics. She used opportunities such as the Women's International League for Peace and Freedom (WILPF) 1926 meeting in Dublin to lobby for the anti-Treaty cause by alerting delegates to the Free State's economic failure. She annoyed WILPF organiser Louie Bennett by inviting unemployed men along to mingle with the delegates.[88] Lynn supported the 'Ghosts,' a self-appointed group named after the 1916 system of identifying shadow leaders to act when leaders were dead or in prison. The Ghosts produced pamphlets and organised mass meetings to oppose the Free State, including its gradual erosion of women's rights, beginning with the 1927 Juries Act.[89] Lynn also maintained many of her republican contacts, but the movement was fragmenting, at best. By 1936, she was forced to agree that '. . . alas, the IRA is no longer upright.'[90] Lynn did hold her seat on Rathmines U.D.C., to which she had been elected in 1921, until it amalgamated with Dublin Corporation in 1930. As a councillor, her particular interests were public health, housing, working conditions, education and holiday schemes for workers.[91]

St. Ultan's occupied almost every waking moment of her life. The infants' hospital became a place where she could expect herself to deliver her feminist, Christian, and republican ideals. It was staffed entirely by women for many years. ffrench-Mullen was responsible for administration and nursing staff, while Lynn took charge of medical provision and planning. Nan Dougan was the first matron; former first-aid pupils from the ICA, IWWU and Inghinidhe worked as nurses in its early years. Cleaners in those days included Maud Gonne, Markievicz, and Geraldine Dillon.

You can still find old Dublin women and men who will light up at Dr. Kathleen Lynn's name.[92] From 1919, St. Ultan's belonged to the community it served. It was operated on strictly professional principles from the outset, with

---

[88] KLD, 12 July 1926. See also Rosemary Cullen Owens, 'Women and pacifism in Ireland, 1915-1932', in Maryann Gialanella Valiulis and Mary O'Dowds (eds.), *Women and Irish History* (Dublin, 1997), pp. 220-238.

[89] KLD, 22 May, 5 July, 1927. Sheila Humphreys and Sydney Gifford Czira were among the women involved.

[90] KLD, 17 June 1936.

[91] KLD, 1920-1930; see also U.D.C. Minutes in the custody of Dublin City Archive.

[92] Harry McCarthy, Molly Lambe, Mary Corbally, and other former patients and tenants interviewed by the author. In August 1999 Essie Keeling was still refusing to be evicted from St. Ultan's flats.

articles of association, medical, house and board committees, along with special committees for new initiatives.[93] Visiting doctors covered specialities outside those of the Ultan's staff. Infants under the age of one year were admitted at first, with the age limit then extended to two years. Children up to five years were treated in out-patients later to comply with the Maternity and Child Welfare Act. By 1930, it included thirty-five cots, a modern out-patients department and a laboratory.[94]

Medical policy adopted a progressive, experimental approach, initially in diet and education, and later in T.B. research. An early experiment involved grazing two goats (one named 'Carson') on the nearby canal bank to provide milk for the babies, although Dr. Webb expressed doubts about its quality. What distinguished it in its time was Lynn's insistence on what is now called child-centred medicine and healthcare. She understood medicine as being genuine care in the fullest sense, devoted to the child's imaginative and intellectual needs, as well to their physical health. She acted on her belief that a few hours of cuddling and comforting could help ease a child back to health – a common enough view now, but an example of radical childcare in her time. Watching Lynn walk around the hospital with a baby in her arms, younger doctors raised their eyebrows.

Lynn's love of radical ideas and innovation didn't stop with politics and medicine: as a hospital director, she commissioned pioneering young architect Michael Scott to design the outpatients' unit which became his first public building and Ireland's first modernist project.[95] St. Ultan's flats were built to house former slum tenants. Her commitment to treating the whole child led her to introduce one of the world's first hospital Montessori units, which Dr. Maria Montessori came to see in 1934.[96]

Financial insecurity dogged the early years. Fundraising ventures used traditional Inghinidhe and Cumann Gaelach methods of céilís, sweeps, concerts, sales of work, as well as persuading grocers and farmers to donate fresh food, with many women contributing newly-knitted and second-hand baby clothes. Jack B. Yeats was among leading artists who contributed to a special Book of St. Ultan's. Guiney's shops donated bed linen. Networks were used extensively.

---

[93] See Minutes of Board 1919, 1923-33; Minutes of Medical Committee 1919-1936, uncatalogued papers, RCPI.

[94] *Ibid.*

[95] Records of building work beginning with Scott's out-patient unit are detailed in minute books, RCPI. See, *Michael Scott Architect in (Casual) Conversation with Dorothy Walker* (Kinsale, 1995), pp. 39, 41, 58, 229.

[96] Lynn corresponded with Maria Montessori, whose educational theories were considered extremely radical in her time. Dr. John Cowell told me that Mario Montessori continued the special relationship with St. Ultan's after his mother's death in 1952.

Lynn's upper-class contacts such as Lady Ardilaun and her circle were invited to see the hospital and the babies, after which they usually opened their purses. Politicians, and politicians' wives, were regularly taken on guided tours. Irish-American contacts already working for the 'Republic' on a range of fronts, including the White Cross and the Celtic Cross committees, raised more cash, while a Jewish nurse raised funds from the Jewish community. Lynn and ffrench-Mullen made their first US fundraising tour in 1925, targeting medical and Irish-American communities in Chicago and New York.[97]

By 1934, the desperate grind of fund-raising had been relieved considerably by the new national 'Sweep,' a lottery that funded the Hospitals' Commission and, through it, enabled the healthcare sector to modernise and equip itself. The Commission replied to separate expansion plans from St. Ultan's and from the National Children's Hospital at Harcourt Street with the recommendation that the two should merge. Land was available: St. Ultan's had anticipated expanding by starting to buy up slum property nearby.[98]

Ireland, however, was indeed becoming a Catholic state where the 'good citizen' equated to the 'good Catholic.' Lynn was aware of the trend, but seems not to have realised how acutely it would affect her professional plans. The education system was already operating on sectarian lines, and strategies developed to extend that model to medical care. The Roman Catholic Guild of St. Luke and the Regnum Christi sought to promote the influence of Catholic doctors, and through them of a fixed, Catholic medical ethics.[99] They reckoned that 62.5% of hospital care was controlled by non-Catholics, including the exclusive Freemasons, while more than 90% of patients were Catholics.[100]

Activity quickened with the news that the British Medical Association's 1933 conference was to be held in Ireland, where the British-Irish body would visit St. Ultan's hospital, among others. The Guild's Dr. Stafford Johnson reported to Archbishop Edward Byrne that Church of Ireland Bishops were to be given precedence over the Catholic bishops at public meetings. The reason was because the Anglican Church was the established church in Britain and the Church of

---

[97] Memorial Committee, (B. xix, vault/store room, Stokes/Ruane Inventory), RCPI.

[98] Minutes of Board and Joint Committee, RCPI.

[99] The Irish Guild of Catholic Nurses was established in 1922, and given the Archbishop's imprimatur in 1928. See *Irish Nursing News* for regular articles on being a good (Catholic) nurse. See also Dr. Hugh Daly to Archbishop Edward Byrne 25 Dec. 1933: 'My primary obligation [by request of the President of Maynooth College] is the development of the guilds.' Byrne Papers, hospitals files, AB7/B/XV, Dublin Diocesan Archives [hereafter, DDA]. Thanks to Archbishop Desmond Connell and David Sheehy.

[100] Stafford Johnson to Byrne, nd, with pages dated 19 February, 1934, Byrne Papers, hospitals files, AB7/B/XV, DDA.

Ireland was seen as its regional branch, despite some thirty years work by the Cumann Gaelach to dispel that perception.[101] This was considered wholly insulting to the majority population.

Byrne's illness created an opening for the rise of the younger Fr. John Charles McQuaid of Blackrock College, which happened to be de Valera's alma mater. Dr. Monica Lea-Wilson, a Harcourt Street pediatrician, was a central source of information to him; her husband had been killed in 1920 on Michael Collins's order, following his reported behaviour towards Tom Clarke and other republican prisoners in the Rotunda grounds in 1916.[102] Lea-Wilson also kept a close eye on the workings of the new Irish Paediatric Association, which Lynn co-founded in April 1933.

Opposition to the Ultan's/Harcourt St. amalgamation was waged initially by Dr. James Stafford Johnson, and later under the personal direction of Fr. McQuaid. It was the first major battle of the Catholic medical ethics campaign, and was crucial in shaping what became known as the Catholic position, which would go on to affect public policy throughout the century in terms of hospital formation, social work, schemes such as Noel Browne's 'Mother and Child', and, more recently, contraception and abortion rights. That position also opposed certain kinds of research: some supporters believed that even apparently innocent experiments with serums could lead by degrees to sterilisation and vivisection practices.[103]

Ironically, six out of thirteen St. Ultan's board members were Catholics, as were half the medical staff,[104] but the Catholic position was about control, not balance. Dr. Alice Barry of St. Ultan's was targeted for special attention. Barry was approached by Lea-Wilson, who was a friend of Barry's cousin. By this point, Barry and Lynn had worked together for over fifteen years since the days of the VD Committee. Yet when pressed by the formidable Lea-Wilson, Barry confessed that '. . . the Protestant doctors' manners are so suave . . .' and that they had a 'superiority complex.'[105]

---

[101] Byrne to Stafford Johnson, 5 January 1933, asking to bring Dr. John Shanley, local secretary of BMA, to meet him, *ibid*.

[102] Tim Pat Coogan, *De Valera: Long Fellow, Long Shadow* (London, 1993), pp. 44-5. The national Gallery of Ireland's Caravaggio painting was formerly in the Lea-Wilson collection.

[103] For example, see Ethel G. Davidson, *Vivisection and the Hospital Sweepstake* (Dublin, 1935), McQuaid Papers, medical affairs files, AB8/A/IV. DDA.

[104] As fn. 100 above.

[105] Lea-Wilson to McQuaid 21 February 1936: 'She only spoke to me because her cousin Anita Daly was a life-long friend . . .' The same letter confirms Dr. Barry's contacts with Stafford Johnson. See also Lea-Wilson to McQuaid, 18 February 1935 on the Ultan's plan to create '. . . a fortress extending from Portobello to Charlemont Bridge.' McQuaid papers, medical affairs files, AB8/A/IV, DDA.

Barry blocked the amalgamation and was forced to resign from St. Ultan's Medical Committee on 20 November 1935, while retaining her membership of the overall board. But other general board members had been approached too, with varying levels of success. Although Harcourt Street carried the plan, St. Ultan's was set to reject the amalgamation overall.[106] On 20 December 1935, Lynn went to meet Archbishop Byrne, and answer his objections so that the amalgamation could go through.[107] We glean some of them through her subsequent personal letter to him:

> I would respectfully point out that only one of the Medical staff . . . is a graduate of Trinity College. . . . There is no idea of either religious or secular instruction being given [in the new hospital]. . . . None of the Medical Staff have ever heard of, much less practiced, the giving of instruction in sex matters or Birth Control at a Children's Hospital . . . I myself, and many others not belonging to your flock, consider such practices immoral. As to the sterilization of the unfit, such a thing could never arise with regard to children under 16. Our aim at St. Ultan's has always been to see that children were brought up healthy, and to prevent their ever joining the ranks of the unfit.[108]

St. Ultan's and Harcourt Street continued to plan for amalgamation, underestimating both their opponents' influence and the scale of objections to their plan. Dr. Dorothy Stopford-Price, one of Ireland's leading innovators in twentieth-century medicine, was using medical and clinical research methodologies at St. Ultan's.[109] That further antagonised McQuaid. Lynn had invited her to investigate a bacillus called B.C.G., developed recently by Swedish researchers. The bacillus offered a chance to combat T.B., which was devastating families and communities across Ireland. Both Lynn and Stopford-Price had first read about it in German-language journals; Stopford-Price had begun research at Baggot Street Hospital.

Before the end of December 1936, Dr. Stopford-Price had vaccinated thirty-five children there. Her St. Ultan's pilot became a model for the Dublin Corporation scheme and, after the War, for the National B.C.G. Committee, which opened at St. Ultan's in July 1949. By then, the link between St. Ultan's

---

[106] Minutes of Joint Committee, RCPI.

[107] Byrne was briefed by Stafford Johnson: see his handwritten 'Notes', nd, anticipating questions, particularly Lynn's 'carefully prepared case for the medical and scientific aspect' and detailed memo. See also Stafford Johnson to Byrne, 12 November 1935: 'I humbly suggest to Your Grace that you ask Dr. Barry what are the Catholics in St. Ultan's board going to do?', Byrne Papers, hospitals files, AB7/B/XV, DDA.

[108] Lynn to Byrne 27 January 1936, Byrne Papers, hospitals files, AB7/B/XV, DDA. Byrne also objected to infant girls and boys sharing the same ward.

[109] Dorothy Stopford-Price, *Tuberculosis in Childhood* (Bristol, 1942).

and T.B. treatment was so strong that Archbishop McQuaid's objections were overruled.[110] Meanwhile, McQuaid had forged ahead with his own aims. By 1939, with undertakings already won from de Valera and other leading politicians, he had secured funding and support for a Catholic Children's Hospital to be sited in Crumlin. It was.[111] McQuaid became a legendary Archbishop of Dublin.

Lynn and ffrench-Mullen publicised the horrors of rising TB, grossly inadequate housing and widespread poverty in Dublin. It was an unpopular position to take in de Valera's Ireland, whose political shortcomings were worsened by an economic war with Britain. The *Irish Press* asked its readers, 'Can you wonder that Dr. Kathleen Lynn, after years of patient, unselfish toil at times despairs of the work she and her associates are performing and asks herself "What's the use?"'[112] The state was reluctant to become involved directly in social and educational matters for fear of seeming communist. Under McQuaid, the Catholic Church preferred to see social and educational issues as its area of expertise.

Lynn's dislike of de Valera's Ireland grew.[113] Aged sixty-three, she opposed the 1937 Constitution, believing it fell far short of the inclusive equality agenda set out in 1916. She concentrated her energies on developing the TB scheme and new Paediatric Unit at St. Ultan's, while continuing to work with Cumann Gaelach na hEaglaise, as well as supporting locally-based childcare units like the Liberty Crèche in Meath Street.

Lynn recorded her opposition to Hitler in the lead-up to the Second World War.[114] After the war, the International Refugee Organisation was prohibited from helping starving people in Germany.[115] Lynn was persuaded by Dr. Kathleen Murphy of St. Ultan's to serve as a vice-president of the Save the Children committee, which campaigned to bring Christian German children to Ireland.[116] The Department of External Affairs reported Murphy's suspected IRA involvement to the British Foreign Office. Through de Valera's interventions,

---

[110] Lyons, *Brief Lives*, pp. 161-2. See H.E. Counihan, 'Dr. Dorothy Price: Obituary', *Journal of the Irish Medical Association*, 34, (1954), p. 84.

[111] McQuaid to Byrne 8 July 1938: 'the matter is receiving an unusually kind attention from Mr de Valera' and 11 July 1938: '[Dev] promised to see matters through.' De Valera accompanied McQuaid to meet the Hospitals Commission, McQuaid papers, medical affairs files, AB8/A/IV, DDA.

[112] *Irish Press*, 12 October 1936.

[113] KLD, 17 June, 24 June 1936.

[114] KLD, 24 July 1934.

[115] The IRO was forbidden in Annex 1, part II of its constitution from helping anyone, anywhere, of German ethnic origin.

[116] Its 'Bulletin' became increasingly dominated by a conservative Roman Catholic editorial line. Copies of those, and material on Operation Shamrock, courtesy Simon Wood.

the Irish government minimised its political exposure by arranging for the Irish Red Cross, led by Dr. John Shanley, to take overall charge of Operation Shamrock.[117] Murphy honoured Lynn's involvement: when the German government commissioned a sculpture for St. Stephen's Green to thank Ireland for its support, she arranged for the piece to be unveiled on Lynn's birthday in 1956, four months after her death.

Lynn died on 14 September 1955, aged 81. She attended St. Ultan's daily until that April, after which she entered St. Mary's Nursing Home, Ballsbridge. She was buried at Deansgrange with full military honours, beside her mother, sister Nan and brother John. St. Ultan's survived until the late 1970s, when it finally closed. The site is now a private clinic.

Some papers from St. Ultan's sentimentalise Lynn. 'Remember me in the nurseries of heaven,' one contemporary obituary is entitled.[118] Her kindness was legendary, yet the sentiments mask the unsentimental strategies she used to make infants and their care a bigger issue than ever before in Irish public discourse. Lynn's medical achievments as a facilitator of key research into T.B. are not acknowledged in either Noel Browne or James Deeny's autobiographies;[119] only with the naming of the Medical Council headquarters in her memory has the medical establishment begun to grasp the extent of her professional contribution.

Lynn's determination to follow her conscience ensured her status as an outsider in both her public and private life. The only ideology she allowed to control her was her belief in God, which she mediated personally. Yet she survived every set-back she encountered, whether her opponent was the British Empire, Éamon de Valera or John Charles McQuaid. Deeply committed to friends and to principles, what remains most enduring is Kathleen Lynn's practical work towards an equitable Ireland where no citizen's life opportunities would be restricted for reasons of gender, sex, or religious affiliation. James Connolly's words resonate: she was, in many ways, one of 'the most amazing of them all.'

---

[117] Murphy's passport was confiscated: see letter 12 July 1946, FO 171 55532, Public Record Office, London.

[118] Uncatalogued document, Memorial Committee, RCPI.

[119] Noel Browne, *Against the Tide* (Dublin, 1988). James Deeny, *To Cure and To Care: Memoirs of a Chief Medical Officer* (Dublin, 1989).

Hanna Sheehy Skeffington (1877–1946)

Margaret Ward

Irish feminism has had to engage with the reality that gender-based exclusion from the body politic is only one of the many inequalities distorting Irish society. As an aspiration for women's full participation in social and political life, feminism cannot be isolated from the context in which it is developed and put into practice. Hanna Sheehy Skeffington was an Irish feminist, living in a country under colonial domination. She remained acutely conscious of that reality. Her life and career have been considered elsewhere.[1] My focus in this article is in assessing her contribution to the development of a strand in Irish feminism that was radical and challenging in its insistence upon including imperialism within a critique of patriarchy.

Hanna Sheehy Skeffington was a woman whose family history and whose own researches provided her with a profound understanding of the conflicting traditions in Irish political life, and the extent to which women had been marginalised by the various political movements. She realised through first hand testimony that women of her mother's generation had been dismissed as political actors, and this knowledge reinforced her determination to fight for the vote as one marker of citizenship. The suffrage experience was to lead to disillusionment with constitutional nationalism, although never to disillusionment with the possibilities of some form of representative democracy in an independent Ireland. When she applauded the achievements of revolutionary nationalism she maintained her personal yardstick of measuring the degree of commitment to radical principles through assessment of its policies on women's rights. Karen

---

[1] Leah Levenson and Jerry H. Natterstad, *Hanna Sheehy Skeffington: Irish Feminist* (Syracuse, 1986); Maria Luddy, *Hanna Sheehy Skeffington* (Dundalk, 1995); Margaret Ward, *Hanna Sheehy Skeffington, a Life* (Cork, 1997).

Offen, in her influential definition of feminism, has stressed that feminism has no hegemonic model, no single national or sociolinguistic tradition. What is defined as 'the coercive power . . . that upholds male prerogatives' is different in different contexts and may require different strategies to ensure its defeat.[2] Too often we are overshadowed by a dominant Anglo-American discourse surrounding first wave feminism. The Irish variant possesses crucial differences derived from its colonial relationship to Britain. Hanna Sheehy Skeffington's views underwent considerable evolution between the first years of suffrage campaigning to the final intensity of the period between the outbreak of war and the watershed of the Easter Rising in 1916. After that time her political *practice* (although not her convictions) oscillated between promotion of women's issues and support for the republican cause, as she attempted to achieve a harmony of views between what were at times deeply antagonistic interests. The continued evolution of her views was influenced by women's experiences of the hostility of the British state to their demand for citizenship, by the betrayal of women's interests by the Irish Party, and by the opportunities that the republican challenge was to open up for women.

Family influences placed the young woman firmly within a nationalist tradition. Her father, David Sheehy, had been a Fenian for a time in his youth, later becoming a member of parliament for the Irish Party, remaining in that capacity until the virtual extinction of the party by Sinn Féin in the 1918 elections. Her uncle, the Rev. Eugene Sheehy, with whom she had an exceptionally close relationship, remained a Fenian all his life. In 1916 he offered his services as a priest to the insurgents in the GPO, despite age and ill health. What was equally significant about Eugene Sheehy was the fact that during his involvement with the Land League in the 1880s he had shared a platform with Anna Parnell and had urged women to join the Ladies' Land League, despite the recorded ambivalence of most of the male leadership towards the women.[3] Almost thirty years later he revealed continued support for women's political involvement when inviting his niece to stay at his parochial house while she wrote her account of the 'illustrious ladies.'[4] Sheehy Skeffington had a memory of visiting Kilmainham Jail as a small child, witnessing the hampers of food provided by the Ladies' Land League being unpacked. She wrote of women like herself, 'whose father or uncle went to prison in the days of the Land League, whose mother or aunt centred about Fanny Parnell . . . such a girl will have her enthusiasm stirred by family sagas, but how can her enthusiasm be utilised ere it be atrophied or is alienated?' At this stage, in 1909, she called for women to be

---

2   Karen Offen, 'Defining feminism: a comparative historical approach', *Signs: Journal of Women in Culture and Society*, 14, 1 (1988), pp. 119-157.

3   Jane Côté, *Fanny and Anna Parnell: Ireland's Patriot Sisters* (Dublin, 1991).

4   Fr. Eugene Sheehy to Hanna Sheehy Skeffington, 12 July 1904, Sheehy Skeffington Papers, Ms 24, 164, National Library of Ireland, Dublin. [Hereafter SSP].

enfranchised 'even by an alien and grudging parliament' and asked the question: 'Will the Irish Party be bold enough to make this act of faith and help the citizenship of women?'[5]

From the period 1904 until 1912, when she eventually severed all links with constitutional nationalism, she was a member of the Young Ireland Branch (YIB) of the Irish Party. This was a youthful, radical wing, established as a recruiting ground for the parent organisation. In that glittering array of talented individuals were Hanna, her sisters Mary and Kathleen, their future husbands, Tom Kettle and Francis Cruise O'Brien, plus John Culhane, future husband of Margaret, the only sister who was not politically involved. The two Sheehy brothers, Eugene and Richard, were also prominent members. The Sheehy family home was host to the most articulate and intelligent of that generation. However, the YIB was essentially a means of making the party attractive to a new phenomenon in Irish life – university-educated young Catholic *men*. The senior politicians had no interest in women, who were irrelevant because they could not vote or stand for parliament. Were it not for the fact that some of the young men supported the women's struggles for admittance to membership, their application would not have succeeded.[6] However, women were still excluded, even as visitors, from conventions of the United Irish League, the constituency organisation of the Irish Party, and some remained sceptical of the intentions of the parliamentarians.

This was taking place while the development of a movement to improve access to university education for women gathered support. Hanna Sheehy graduated from the Royal University in Dublin in 1899, with a degree in modern languages. In 1902 she received an M.A. with first class honours. That year she was asked to sign a suffrage petition organised by women graduates in Britain and Ireland. She dated her political awareness to this experience, ' Naturally, I signed and became a conscious suffragist from that hour on.'[7] Despite her qualifications, she was unable to secure more than part-time teaching in her old school, the Dominican College in Eccles Street, because religious orders controlled the education system for Catholics and female lay teachers were employed on temporary contracts and low rates of pay. When Hanna Sheehy began to question the rationale for this state of affairs she would find herself becoming estranged from the social and political institutions she held responsible for the maintenance of such inequalities. In 1912, during her first imprisonment, her husband urged her to insist that she had no religion, rather than conform to

---

[5] Hanna Sheehy Skeffington, 'Women and the national movement', typescript copy in SSP, Ms 22,266, published in *Irish Nation*, 6, 13, 20 March 1909.

[6] *Ibid.*

[7] Hanna Sheehy Skeffington, 'Reminiscences of an Irish Suffragette' in Andrée Sheehy Skeffington and Rosemary Owens (ed.), *Votes for Women: Irish Women's Struggle for the Vote* (Dublin, 1975), p. 12.

the official expectation that she was still a member of the Roman Catholic faith, 'let them associate suffragism with atheism if they like – they will be right!'[8] For the rest of her life she described herself as a pagan and rejected all attempts to stage a death-bed reconciliation with Catholicism.

By now she had met her future husband, Francis Skeffington, a committed supporter of woman's suffrage. After their marriage in 1903 they amalgamated their names in symbolic expression of the equality of their union. Skeffington would become editor of the suffrage paper the *Irish Citizen,* and an outspoken campaigner for a number of causes. Husband and wife were active members of the Irish Women's Suffrage and Local Government Association, the only suffrage group in existence in Ireland at that time. After a number of years the Sheehy Skeffingtons became impatient at the slow pace of activities. In Britain the Women's Social and Political Union was bringing attention to women's claims by means of a militant campaign which courted arrest and imprisonment. News of the exploits of the Pankhursts 'stirred a responsive chord in some Irish feminist breasts.' Soon a few would begin to 'start a fire' of their own.[9] In 1908 the Sheehy Skeffingtons helped to found an independent, Irish-defined suffrage organisation, the Irish Women's Franchise League (IWFL). It was the only Irish suffrage group to declare itself militant. Members were prepared to use 'non-constitutional' methods of protest to further their aims and, most crucially, they refused to subordinate women's campaign for the vote to the parliamentary campaign for Irish Home Rule. While constitutional suffragists included supporters of Irish self-determination in their ranks, the IWFL was the only group to define its position on home rule. They wanted 'Home rule for Irish women as well as for Irish men.' Margaret Cousins, co-founder of the League, recognised that the colonial relationship between Britain and Ireland determined the strategy of the Irish militants. They needed to develop a programme of action which would be 'suitable to the different political situation of Ireland as between a subject-country seeking freedom from England, and England, a free country.'[10]

As the women organised deputations to politicians and argued their case, the hostility they encountered led some to re-evaluate their attitudes towards mainstream political life. Irish parliamentarians were as ambiguous as their British counterparts in their attitude towards franchise extension. Irish feminists regarded this as hypocritical, given the party's history of fighting for social justice and national freedom. In 1912, with the third Home Rule bill going through the House of Commons, and women's suffrage bills 'killed' as a result of the Irish Party's opposition, Francis Sheehy Skeffington equated the self-sacrifice of the

---

[8] Frank Sheehy Skeffington to Hanna Sheehy Skeffington, 30 July 1912, courtesy of Andrée Sheehy Skeffington.

[9] *Ibid.*

[10] J.H. and M.E. Cousins, *We Two Together* (Madras, 1950), p. 85.

suffragists with the sacrifices of Irish republican heroes like Robert Emmet and Wolfe Tone, claiming 'There is a stronger and purer Nationalism in Mountjoy Prison at this moment than any Mr Redmond's followers can boast.'[11] For Hanna Sheehy Skeffington, whose father voted consistently against bills for woman suffrage, this was a difficult period, both personally and politically:

> Here were good Irish rebels, many of them broken into national revolt, with all the slogans of Irish revolution and its arsenal of weapons – Boycott, Plan of Campaign, Land for the People, and so forth, the creators of obstruction in Parliament – yet at the whisper of Votes for Women many changed to extreme Tories or time-servers who urged us women to wait till freedom for men was won.[12]

On March 28 1912 the votes of the Irish Party killed off a Conciliation Bill which would have given the vote to women possessing property with a rateable value of more than ten pounds. Their justification was that the woman's bill would have eaten into the time available for discussion on home rule. When, two days later, the Irish Party staged 'Home Rule Day' as a public demonstration of the depth of support for their parliamentary success, the IWFL decided to show the celebratory crowds that they felt women had nothing to celebrate. A Home Rule Ireland would not be one which recognised their rights as citizens. While marching with placards through the streets of Dublin they were attacked by Irish Party stewards. Hanna Sheehy Skeffington said 'Irishwomen were not passive resisters and . . . when she was struck by a steward or official she was inclined to hit back.'[13] Later, a delegation to John Redmond, party leader, elicited what had always been suspected: that he was utterly opposed to a clause in the Home Rule bill giving votes to women. There was now a clear demarcation between suffragists and parliamentarians. It was a divide that touched not only the issue of the franchise but also the whole question of taking the parliamentary road to achieve political ends.

Sheehy Skeffington's immediate response was to resign from the YIB, to urge all women to leave every organisation connected with the party and to threaten that the women of Ireland 'would break the power of the party.'[14] Her relations with her family had already been strained because of her rejection of Catholicism and her refusal to have her son Owen baptised. She now broke publicly from her father and used the pages of the *Irish Citizen* to criticise his refusal to support the suffrage cause. As Barbara Caine indicates so perceptively, in considering new approaches to the writing of biography, 'women's response

[11] *Irish Citizen*, 13 July 1912.
[12] Sheehy Skeffington, 'Reminiscences', p. 13.
[13] *Votes for Women*, 12 April 1912.
[14] *Ibid.*

to personal and familial experiences often helps to explain both the genesis of their feminism and the nature of their particular feminist analysis or commitment.'[15] Sheehy Skeffington's political career had begun with her attempt to have the Irish Parliamentary Party accept women as full members of the Young Ireland branch. By 1913 she had achieved a personal autonomy which enabled her to speak freely on the most difficult of subjects. The House of Commons she described as 'a den of thieves', the members of which had 'overreached themselves in their chicanery towards the women's cause.'[16] Her career from now on was one of increasingly outspoken militancy.

Militancy was a contentious issue within the international suffrage movement. Some constitutionalists argued against the use of force on straightforwardly pacifist grounds, while others believed that 'outrages' like arson turned public opinion away from the women's cause.[17] For Irishwomen, the use of militancy was to assume even more significance when allied to the wider political context of centuries-long resistance to British rule over Ireland. Sheehy Skeffington made a distinction between militancy and militarism which would not be accepted by many within the feminist movement. She always made plain her opposition to militarism (by which she meant the institutionalised response by authority to challenges to its power) but this did not mean that she was opposed to the weak using whatever means at their disposal to achieve their aims. How does this relate to the Irish suffrage campaign? Militancy stopped far short of the taking of life (in actuality, IWFL-organised militancy was small-scale in comparison with the arson campaign of the WSPU), yet acceptance of militant methods in an Irish context had a resonance that was missing from the British experience. Sheehy Skeffington was an 'equal rights' feminist who refused to make a distinction between women's fight for emancipation and the nationalist fight for self-determination. In her eyes, suffrage militancy followed a long tradition in Ireland of oppressed groups fighting their oppressors. On the eve of her first imprisonment, reflecting on the reasons for resorting to window smashing, she recalled the women who had thrown stones upon the Williamites during the Siege of Limerick and those who had defied landlordism in Land League times, 'the stone and the shillelagh need no apologia; they have an honoured place in the armoury of argument.' What was different was that women were resorting to violence on their own behalf, as she noted with irony: 'This element of unwomanly selfishness was repellent to the average man, who only applaud the stone-thrower as long as the missile is flung for

[15] Barbara Caine, 'Feminist biography and feminist history', *Women's History Review*, 3, 2, (1994), pp. 247-61.

[16] *Irish Citizen*, 1 February 1913.

[17] See Louise Ryan (ed.), *Irish Feminism and the Vote, an Anthology of the Irish Citizen Newspaper 1912-1920* (Dublin, 1996).

them and not at them.'[18] It is significant that when they were deciding upon targets she chose Dublin Castle, 'avenging the treasured wrongs of fifty years' and clearly linking together feminist and nationalist causes.

In contrast, Louie Bennett, a member of the non-militant Irish Women's Reform League, argued that 'no real victory has ever been gained by force or coercion.'[19] Bennett held the view that women, when they won the vote, would bring a 'mother element' to government, transforming the ordering of the world. This 'essentialist' feminism counterposed a nurturing, pacifist woman to an aggressive masculine world, creating dualisms very different from the analysis advanced by members of the IWFL. Meg Connery, in the dock for suffrage militancy, explained that 'she had been driven to adopt these methods to draw public attention to the intolerable grievances under which women had to live. She was an outlaw; she was not a person.'[20] Hanna Sheehy Skeffington went further than this in her insistence that those whose status as citizens was not recognised were justified in resorting to violence. Historically, there has been an ambivalence in Irish life towards the use of physical force for political ends. Professor Oldham of Trinity College Dublin, a supporter of the IWFL, at a protest meeting for hunger striking suffragists had told his audience that '[t]he Englishman could never see justice until one took violent action in politics, which was called militancy.'[21] From the nationalist side Thomas MacDonagh, one year before the Easter Rising, declared to a feminist audience that he had 'helped to arm tens of thousands of Irish men for defence because the only justification of war was to end age-long wars such as that in this country. He hoped they would not have war in this country.'[22] This ambivalence, as we shall see, was acknowledged also in the words and actions of Hanna Sheehy Skeffington.

Sheehy Skeffington now became a full-time political activist. Dismissal from her teaching post at Rathmines College of Commerce, a consequence of her jail sentence, intensified feelings of being 'outlawed' from the male-controlled world she challenged. The escalation of WSPU militancy in Britain met with her approval. In early 1913 she declared she wanted no more of the 'resolution-passing, petition-presenting, lobbying and wire-pulling' that the constitutionals insisted on. She wanted 'militant militancy':

Desperate diseases need desperate remedies and if the vote is wrested from

---

[18] Hanna Sheehy Skeffington, 'The women's movement – Ireland', *Irish Review*, July 1912, pp. 225-7.
[19] Ellen Hazelkorn, 'The social and political views of Louie Bennett, 1870-1965', *Saothar*, 13 (1988), pp. 32-44.
[20] Ward, *Hanna Sheehy Skeffington*, p. 105.
[21] *Irish Citizen*, 5 July 1913.
[22] *Irish Citizen*, 22 May 1915.

> Government by methods of terrorism when five and forty years of sweet and
> quiet reason produced only seven talked-out or tricked-out suffrage bills,
> why, who can say it wasn't worth a mutilated letter, a cutwire, a Premier's
> racked nerves?[23]

To those critics who argued that there could be no justification for letter-box
militancy she replied, 'there is none', which was precisely the reason for its
adoption. Reasonable militancy was regarded as 'merely playing at being militant'
and the only sufferers were the women sent to jail in consequence. It was time
for a change in tactics. With heavy sarcasm she quoted the views of a 'recent
able critic' who had protested that this new militancy savoured of 'anarchy and
the final dissolution of society.'[24] Her ready agreement that the militants wanted
more than simple reform of the franchise supports the argument advanced by
Susan Kingsley Kent: 'Their ultimate goal was to bring about a profound
transformation in the sexual culture of Britain, to create a society based upon
reconstruction of masculinity and femininity and of male and female sexuality.'[25]
While possession of the vote would provide the means of overturning the
conventions that confined women in a separate sphere, rendering them unable
to assert themselves in either public or private, the very act of campaigning was
to serve as a catalyst for further radical ideas. The opposition she encountered
deepened Sheehy Skeffington's understanding of the extent to which feminism
had the potential to challenge the deeply entrenched conservatism of Irish society.

She was arrested again in December 1913, despite the fact that the militant
campaign had by then been suspended in Ireland because the Home Rule
situation remained at crisis point. That arrest, on the spurious charge of having
assaulted a policeman while attempting to give leaflets to the Conservative
leader, Bonar Law, and to the Ulster Unionist leader, Sir Edward Carson, revealed
the extent to which the authorities were prepared to connive in order to remove
her from the political scene. They did not want the woman most associated
with the Irish campaign to win female suffrage to be free to express her views
while they courted those Ulster unionists who refused to accept the democratic
right of the majority of the Irish population to self-government. Concessions
would be offered to the Unionist militants while none would be offered to
militant women. The gendered nature of power was clearly discernible. After
hunger-striking for five days she was released, furious over the injustice of her
treatment, and vowing that she would never again go to prison without having
done something to warrant it.[26] It was another defining moment in her political

---

[23] *Irish Citizen*, 4 January 1913.
[24] *Ibid.*
[25] Susan Kingsley Kent, *Sex and Suffrage in Britain 1860-1914* (New Jersey, 1987), p.
212.
[26] *Irish Citizen*, 3 January 1914.

evolution. Through overcoming fears of imprisonment and hunger strike she developed a freedom of the spirit that enhanced her determination to fight against all injustice.

In the summer of 1915 her husband was imprisoned for his anti-war activities, gaining temporary release under the terms of the 'Cat and Mouse Act', which had been introduced in 1913 in response to the public outcry against the forcible feeding of suffrage prisoners. The law enabled the government to release hunger-striking prisoners and to re-imprison them once they had recovered their health. He escaped re-arrest by going to America, and for several months responsibility for the editorship of the *Irish Citizen* was added to Hanna's political commitments. To one close friend she admitted the strain, 'I'm driven to death between *Citizen* and other work but fortunately I'm fairly well just now.'[27] She calculated that during the year the IWFL had held over sixty suffrage meetings, intervened in two by-elections, organised a series of meetings in County Clare, were monitoring court proceedings as part of a widespread campaign to expose the consequences of an all-male legal system and were involved in a range of campaigns on peace and temperance issues.[28] She was not the leading figure in all these initiatives, but she was acknowledged by her colleagues to be irreplaceable. In the annual elections for the League executive she was always returned at the top of the poll. Marguerite Palmer voiced the thoughts of many when she admitted 'I never know an easy moment when your hand is off the ropes.'[29]

The Sheehy Skeffingtons had drawn close to James Connolly, the theoretical brain behind the resurgence of Irish socialism, also an advocate of radical action whenever possible. Connolly had declared that there were no acts of suffrage militancy that he would not support. After his death Hanna would praise him as 'one of those all too rare revolutionaries whose doctrines of freedom apply all round.'[30] When the First World War began Connolly wrote increasingly insurrectionary articles for the *Workers Republic*, calling for an uprising against the British Empire. Francis Sheehy Skeffington disagreed strongly with this attitude and in February 1916 they staged a public debate on the issue. There is no record that Hanna voiced her opinions at the time, but her report on the debate gave a neutral account of its outcome, rather than one which sided with her husband. Privately, she made her views known to some at least of those with whom she worked. Months before the debate, she and Louie Bennett

[27] Hanna Sheehy Skeffington to Meg Connery, n.d., SSP, Ms 22,676.

[28] Hanna Sheehy Skeffington, letter to IWFL members, giving details of 1915 AGM, January 1916. Alice Park Collection, Hoover Institution Archives, Stanford, California. [Hereafter, Alice Park Collection].

[29] Marguerite Palmer to Hanna Sheehy Skeffington, 11 August 1914, SSP, Ms 24,146.

[30] Hanna Sheehy Skeffington, 'Memories of the suffrage campaign in Ireland', *The Vote*, 30 August 1929.

(who took the pacifist side) had corresponded over the issue. Hanna's acceptance of armed resistance to British rule in Ireland, given the appropriate conditions, was unambiguous:

> If I saw a hope of Ireland being freed forever from British rule by a swift uprising, I would consider Irishmen justified resorting to arms in order that we might be free. I should still be radically opposed to war and militarism. This is of course my personal view and in no way represents the League. But I hold no such hopes. I think that freedom for small nations lies in Justice by Arbitration and there is one of my strongest motives in standing for Peace.[31]

Her belief that an uprising against British rule in Ireland could be justified predates the Easter Rising and is therefore unconnected with reaction to her husband's murder at the hands of a British army officer during the Rising. It is often suggested that her later support for the insurgents was a consequence of her justifiable anger at his death. We can see that she believed support for armed struggle to achieve Irish self-determination was consistent with her feminist beliefs. Not many appeared to have taken this position. For example, Meg Connery, in arguing why the task of Irish feminists during the First World War should be suffrage campaigning and not relief work, declared her conviction that 'feminism and militarism are natural-born enemies and cannot flourish on the same soil. As the spirit of militarism (based on brute force) grows and triumphs so must decay the spirit of comradeship, human co-operation, and sympathy for which our women's movement stands.'[32] Her views make an interesting contrast, particularly as her close friendship with Hanna continued throughout their lives. Both women were, as Margaret Cousins described them in 1919, 'non-militarist, non-masculine, ardent nationalists', yet Connery's deeply-felt feminist convictions made it impossible for her to accept the compromises that membership of a non-feminist political organisation would have entailed. When Ireland plunged into full-scale war she continued to plead for an 'independent feminist group to watch women's special interests and keep up a standard for women.'[33] While she campaigned for republican prisoners during the war of independence she worked with members of the woman-only Women's Prisoners' Defence League rather than a mainstream nationalist group. Militancy for Connery was a woman-defined concept which fell far short of the physical

---

[31] Hanna Sheehy Skeffington to Louie Bennett, undated fragment, SSP, Ms 24,134. This contains one of the most significant of all statements ever made by Hanna. It is ironic, because of last-minute revisions to my biography, that those sentences were omitted.

[32] *Irish Citizen,* 19 September 1914, reproduced in Ryan, *Irish Feminism and the Vote,* pp. 97-99.

[33] *Irish Citizen,* March-April 1920.

force methods adopted by the insurrectionists of the Easter Rising. Nevertheless, because of her sympathy for republicanism, she cannot be equated with the 'really pacifist' position of Louie Bennett.[34]

By the outbreak of the First World War the issue of national self-determination had become a crucial element in the feminist campaign to win the right of citizenship. Where would citizenship, if won, be exercised? In the imperial parliament at Westminster, or in a self-governing parliament within Ireland? The priority of ending the war could not be the sole issue for those who also had nationalist aspirations. From this period, in her speeches and by her actions, Hanna Sheehy Skeffington revealed her conviction that citizenship was not only gendered but raced. The Women's Peace Congress at The Hague in 1915 provided an opportunity for the Irish Women's Franchise League to argue the nationalist case on an international stage. In order to accommodate the differing political aspirations of Irish women it was agreed that while there would be a joint committee comprising delegates from the different suffrage organisations, the IWFL would also send its own delegates and would be 'officially represented as an organisation', with the freedom to put forward a separate resolution to Congress.[35] Hanna hailed this as a victory for the nation as well as for women: 'For the first time . . . Irish delegates take their place as representatives of their own country. It is the hour of small nationalities. Long live the small nationalities of the earth! – We have a definite point of view – we see with clearer vision the baleful effect of rule by force, of coercion by the stronger of the weaker – we aim at Peace through Justice and Liberty.'[36] Although it was stated that there was no 'difference in principle' with the joint committee, it was obvious that not all the delegates would have agreed with the following IWFL resolution:

> This International Congress of Women, recognising that Peace, to be permanent, must be founded on Justice and Liberty, and that the government of one nation by another is a frequent cause of war, urges that Subject Nationalities should be offered a path to freedom not involving war or war-like preparations and that to this end international machinery should be provided under the auspices of a world-wide International Council, whereby all subject people shall have the power, by plebiscite of their men and women effectively to declare whether they are contented with their lot or would prefer a change of government.[37]

---

[34] For a sympathetic portrayal of Bennett, see Rosemary Cullen Owens, 'Women and pacifism in Ireland 1915-1932', in Maryann Giananella Valiulis and Mary O'Dowd (eds.), *Women & Irish History* (Dublin, 1997), pp. 220-38.

[35] *Irish Citizen*, 20 March 1915.

[36] *Irish Citizen*, 17 April 1915.

[37] *Irish Citizen*, 24 April 1915.

The hope that Ireland could be included as a small nation in any peace negotiations following the conclusion of war was one harboured by all nationalists. Of the Irish delegates, only Louie Bennett received a permit from the British Home Secretary enabling her to travel to The Hague. However, as the government then closed the North Sea to all shipping until after the end of the Congress, no one was able to sail from Britain. In the wave of protest that ensued, Hanna's denunciation of government action concentrated upon the nationalist rather than feminist implications of the ban, 'Our voice is once more denied in international councils.' She believed the government was 'afraid to let Ireland's voice be heard on the rights of small nationalities.'[38] The Irish women spent a frustrating time besieging the House of Commons as they tried to argue with unsympathetic politicians. Back in Dublin, speaking at a protest meeting, Sheehy Skeffington remained in belligerent mood, 'They would send from that meeting a message to Asquith and McKenna that Ireland was still alive; and apt to kick them now and then. If they had had votes, they would not have been so humiliated.' Once again, the link between nation and gender was clearly articulated.

The Dublin meeting was significant in bringing together a number of advanced nationalists, as well as a wide grouping of feminists, although there was also a degree of tension between the groups. Patrick Pearse, shortly to become commander-in-chief of the Easter Rising, had written a letter of support in which he stated that the 'present incident will do good if it ranges more of the women definitely with the national forces.' From her position as chair of the meeting Meg Connery objected to this 'very masculine inversion.' Loud applause greeted her feminist re-wording, 'The incident ought to have the effect of ranging the national forces on the side of women.' Thomas MacDonagh, director of training of the Irish Volunteers, accepted that criticism. He added that as a Volunteer he hoped he would have a better opportunity than voting to show that by 'people' he meant the women as well as men of Ireland.[39] Louie Bennett and Hanna Sheehy Skeffington once again disagreed over their attitudes to this joint feminist-nationalist protest meeting. Bennett had sat in silence as she heard various speeches being made which equated pacifism with an anti-militarism that was based upon nationalist sympathies. Afterwards, she wrote in anger against those who would justify 'a war for Ireland' as being 'a thoroughly superficial form of pacifism.'[40] In reply Hanna argued that a strategic understanding of political attitudes was essential. If an effective opposition to the war between Britain and Germany was to be organised, then Irish sentiments needed to be stirred up. She explained 'that is why a protest meeting succeeds

---

[38] *Irish Citizen*, 8 May 1915.
[39] *Irish Citizen*, 22 May 1915.
[40] Louie Bennett to Hanna Sheehy Skeffington, 12 May 1915, SSP, Ms 22,675.

where a purely peace meeting would not.' However, she did not leave matters there, but pursued the central core of their difference. While she agreed 'a terrible war for reasons of commercial jealousy admits of no defence', she made a clear distinction between her position and that of what she termed the 'Tolstoyan pacifist.' It is this which is central to her conception of feminism in an Irish context:

> There are pacifists who hold with Tolstoi that resistance to all violence is wrong – I quite see the extreme logic of the position and if you hold to that view of course all war is equally hateful to you. But there are other pacifists (and I am one of them) who hold that while war must be ended if civilisation is to reign supreme, nevertheless there may still be times when armed aggression ought to be met with armed defence.[41]

Her definition of armed aggression included the presence of the British state in occupation in Ireland. An armed uprising, in her eyes, could therefore be defined legitimately as 'armed defence.' It is this which distinguishes her from her husband, who maintained a more rigorous attachment to pacifism, although I would hesitate to call him a pacifist without making some qualification. He supported the Irish Citizen Army obtaining arms for defensive purposes during the bitter lock-out of 1913, for example, but he opposed any suggestion of an armed rising. His wife's attitude was different. During the weekend before Easter she met Connolly, who apparently said 'if you are interested in developments, I would not advise you to go away on holiday just now.' He also said that women had been given equal rights and equal opportunities in the republican proclamation. The confidence that the leadership placed in her can be verified by the fact that they selected Hanna Sheehy Skeffington to act as a member of a civil provisional government which would come into effect if the rising was prolonged.[42]

On the first day of the rising Francis Sheehy Skeffington spent the time attempting to organise a citizen's militia to prevent the wide-scale looting that he feared would discredit the ideals of the insurgents. On the second day the couple walked together into the centre of Dublin. Hanna went to the GPO, headquarters of the insurgents, to offer supplies of food and to give assistance as messenger between the outposts. One of the first people she saw at the GPO was her Uncle Eugene. Connolly then sent her to the College of Surgeons, where Constance Markievicz was a member of the garrison. Markievicz later testified to this role. Mrs Sheehy Skeffington had been at the head of a group of women, whom she described as members of the Irish Women's Franchise League, who had braved the bullet-swept streets to deliver 'all manner of eatables'

---

[41] Hanna Sheehy Skeffington to Louie Bennett, undated fragment, SSP, Ms 24,134.
[42] Ward, *Hanna Sheehy Skeffington*, p. 153.

to the rebels.[43] After meeting her husband, Hanna walked home, worried about the welfare of their son. When Francis set out to follow her a short time later he was arrested by a British army officer and that night, without warning, he and two other journalists were taken out to the yard of Portobello Army Barracks and shot dead. Only after several days of anguished enquiry did his wife discover the dreadful reason for her husband's failure to return home. She had then to endure military reprisal. Her home was raided, her papers confiscated, her son terrified and her maid arrested as the military attempted to concoct evidence to justify the killing of Francis Sheehy Skeffington.

All her suffragist skills were used in petitioning politicians as she threw her energies into a determined effort to discover the truth behind the murder of her husband. Her personal papers contain innumerable messages of support from prominent individuals world-wide. She eventually obtained a meeting with Prime Minister Asquith, turning down his offer of 'adequate and even generous compensation' amounting to ten thousand pounds. It was 'hush money' and she rejected it with contempt. Her husband's death left her as the sole support of their son, but her meagre salary as a part-time teacher had often been the main income in the household and she had recently managed to obtain work as a language teacher. Eventually, through strength of personality, Hanna succeeded in forcing a Commission of Inquiry into the events in Portobello Barracks. The proceedings, presided over by Sir John Simon, were exhaustively covered by the press but the government refused to make public its findings. It was war time and the details of the Simon Commission were too damning, particularly when the British government was attempting to persuade America to enter the war on the allied side. She admitted her shock in having witnessed the 'automatic and tireless efforts on the part of the entire official machinery, both military and political, to prevent the truth being made public' and her anger that no-one in authority was removed from office as a result. Her one consolation was that she had achieved a 'damning exposé of militarism.'[44] She was determined to carry that message abroad at the earliest possible opportunity.

Refused permission to travel, she was forced to smuggle herself and her young son over to America. They arrived there in December 1916. Over the next eighteen months she spoke at a total of over two hundred and fifty meetings in nearly every state in the country, publicising the facts of her husband's murder and mobilising American opinion in support of Ireland's right to be treated as a small nation. Her speech, 'British militarism as I have known it', was reproduced in pamphlet form and reprinted several times, a scorching indictment of the British presence in Ireland. She was the widow of a man whose death was acknowledged to be cold-blooded murder, yet the British government persisted in treating her as an enemy. While in America, British agents kept her under

---

[43] *Irish World*, 3 May 1924.
[44] Hanna Sheehy Skeffington, *British Militarism as I have Known It* (New York, 1917).

surveillance. After America entered the war in 1917 the Department of Justice also took an interest in her activities and the Bureau of Investigation sent agents to infiltrate her meetings. Their reports provide a very clear picture of her personal and political integrity and of her power as an orator: 'The lady, who is highly educated, delivered a very interesting lecture showing why Ireland should be considered at the peace conference at the end of the war. . .'[45] Within a short time she was publicly proclaiming herself a Sinn Féiner and a supporter of the Rising. She applauded the leadership for their support for women's right to citizenship: 'It is the only instance I know of in history where men fighting for freedom voluntarily included women.' Her public lectures made it plain that she regarded herself as an Irish republican:

> I knew the Irish Republican leaders and am proud to have known them and had their friendship. They fought a clean fight against terrible odds – and terrible was the price they had to pay. They were filled with a high idealism . . . It is the dreamers and the visionaries that keep hope alive and feed enthusiasm – not the statesmen and the politicians. . . . The lesson of the Irish Rising and its suppression is that our small nation, Ireland, has a right also to its place in the sun.[46]

Only in the earliest writings of Hanna Sheehy Skeffington can one find any lengthy analysis of her understanding of the relationship between feminism and nationalism. As a suffrage militant she continually linked the goals of the two movements, while criticising nationalists for their failure to support the feminist cause, 'until the women of Ireland are free, the men will not achieve emancipation.'[47] In the post-1916 era, her critique of the gendered nature of nationalism was confined to diatribes against individuals who refused to accept women as 'comrades.'[48] What she retained always was a conviction that women should participate only in organisations that contained equality of citizenship within their objectives and, equally importantly, which included equality between the sexes as a defining principle. This pre-figurative emphasis upon equality while mobilising forces for political struggle explains why Sheehy Skeffington found some groups unacceptable. She would not become a member of Cumann na mBan, the nationalist woman's organisation, because its constitution stipulated its primary role as support to their male counterpart. She would, however, join Sinn Féin, even before its goals were redefined in the

---

[45] Report of meeting in San Antonio, 15 October 1917, United States Department of Justice, file no. 9848 10204, US Archives, Washington D.C.

[46] Hanna Sheehy Skeffington, *British Militarism*, p. 18.

[47] Hanna Sheehy Skeffington, 'Sinn Féin and Irishwomen', *Bean na hÉireann*, November 1909.

[48] See her 1932 critique of Eamon de Valera in Ward, *Hanna Sheehy Skeffington*, p. 304.

1917 Convention, because it appeared to accept women and men on equal terms.

Sheehy Skeffington's success in gaining an interview with President Wilson confirmed her reputation as a leading figure in Irish political circles. Her protracted struggle to return to Ireland in 1918, finally achieved after enduring hunger strike and imprisonment in Holloway Jail, was an indication that the British understood her effectiveness. Once home she found herself inundated with requests from many political organisations, ranging from the Socialist Party of Ireland to Cumann na mBan. She joined Sinn Féin and resumed editorship of the *Irish Citizen*, in uneasy partnership with Louie Bennett. Sinn Féin was now a very different organisation from the small, conservative group founded by Arthur Griffith. Nationalist women campaigned for representation within the Sinn Féin executive by forming a pressure group, the 'League of Women Delegates', which lasted until the escalation of military activity made it impossible to continue. Minutes of their meetings reveal that they looked forward to the return of Mrs Skeffington, hoping that she might agree to organise classes to train women in the art of public speaking.[49] Hanna worked actively to promote women's interests in every capacity in which she operated. If she had not been inside Sinn Féin, adding strength to that feminist pressure being exerted by republican women, an important opportunity to have women's interests advanced would have been lost. At the same time, the pages of the *Citizen* and continued membership of the IWFL afforded her opportunities for outspoken intervention on women's behalf. An editorial declared that women wanted 'equal pay for equal work, equal marriage laws, the abolition of legal disabilities, the right of women to enter the hitherto barred learned professions, women jurors and justices, in short, the complete abolition of various taboos and barriers – social, economic and political – that still impede women's progress and consequently that of the race.'[50] While Louie Bennett would have liked to turn the *Citizen* into a paper for the women's trade union movement, Hanna Sheehy Skeffington was adamant that its independence be retained:

> There is much need in Ireland, as well as in most other countries . . . for a distinctly feminist organ devoted primarily to the advancement of women and holding a watching brief for their interests. It is obvious that such a paper must not belong to any party. . . . We stand for the rights of all Irish women as women, independent of party or sect. But, at the same time, we recognise the right of the majority of the Irish people to mould its own destinies and accordingly like Irish Labour, we stand for self-determination of Ireland.[51]

---

[49] Margaret Ward, 'The League of Women Delegates and Sinn Féin', *History Ireland*, 4, 3, (Autumn 1996), pp. 37-41.
[50] *Irish Citizen*, editorial, October 1919.
[51] *Ibid*.

Dual membership of the IWFL and Sinn Féin enabled her to maintain an autonomous feminist presence, even on occasions when other political considerations threatened to overrule the concerns of women. In 1918, when the IWFL members worked hard to ensure that Constance Markievicz became the first woman to be elected to parliament, there were tensions between feminists and republicans regarding the perceived lack of support being given by Sinn Féin to the Markievicz campaign. In private correspondence Sheehy Skeffington declared to Nancy Wyse Power of Cumann na mBan that the St Patrick's Ward was the 'worst managed constituency in the country', run by a committee so inefficient that the feminists felt compelled to organise their own campaign.[52] From the evidence, it would appear that she too would have liked to have been a candidate in the 1918 elections, the first occasion when women over thirty had the right to vote and to stand for election. It was a notable occasion, particularly for suffragists who had fought hard for this victory. Sinn Féin was willing to nominate her as a candidate, but not, it would appear, for a winnable seat. Sheehy Skeffington rejected such futile gestures as offering women no more than a pretence of equality. When it came to promotion of women's interests it is evident that she refused to be constrained by notions of party discipline. Within Sinn Féin she consistently confronted male unwillingness to accept women colleagues on equal terms, and she also worked to ensure that a heavily male movement became more welcoming to women. For example, in many rural areas, women who attempted to join Sinn Féin were finding themselves directed instead to their local Cumann na mBan branch. Her instructions as organising secretary for Sinn Féin made it plain that women were an important part of the membership: 'An impression exists in some districts that membership of Cumainn is confined to men. This is a mistake and every effort should be made to ensure that women shall not only be on the roll of members, but take an active share in the work of Cumainn and the Sinn Féin movement generally.'[53]

During the War of Independence, when forty two women were elected as councillors in local government elections in 1920, comment in the *Irish Citizen* was sharp. Although Sinn Féin, 'the party of the majority' was commended for its 'good example', the general conclusion was that this was not 'a fair proportion of women.'[54] Sheehy Skeffington herself was elected a member of Dublin Corporation at this time. As Dáil Éireann attempted to supplant the British administrative system, women found themselves appointed as justices in the underground courts established by the Dáil. She was one of those women also. It was a brief opportunity for feminists to try to put into practice some of the

---

[52] Hanna Sheehy Skeffington to Nancy Wyse Power, 1919, SSP, Ms 22,697.
[53] 'Instructions to Sinn Féin cumainn regarding programme of work 1921–22', pamphlet P 2272, National Library of Ireland, Dublin.
[54] *Irish Citizen,* February 1920.

policies they had been urging since the early days of the suffrage campaign, when women called for representation in courts, for welfare reforms and for greater democracy. They were unable to achieve a great deal in the war conditions under which they operated, but Sheehy Skeffington's attitudes towards government clearly favoured a greater radicalism than that being implemented by those in the first Dáil. She believed the British system had 'strangled true democracy', through its cabinet system and elaborate parliamentary procedures, all of which she rejected as 'tosh and piffle.' She preferred the committee structure adopted by 'progressive small nations' in Scandinavian countries, where executive power was not concentrated in the hands of a few ministers.[55] As Arthur Mitchell has noted, she was one of a small vocal group within Sinn Féin in her insistence that there needed to be some assessment of the political direction being adopted by the republican movement.[56]

In September 1920 she editorialised in the *Citizen* her belief 'that we have a mission and a message for Irishwomen as a purely feminist paper and emboldened in that belief we shall carry on.' It was a brave cry, but the reality was that the paper was struggling to maintain its readership in the difficult conditions of the time. It folded soon after this, unable to recover after the Black and Tans had smashed its typeface. The fragmented movement of feminism, still in different ways trying to promote women's issues, lost its last vestige of a coherent identity. Thereafter, it is much more difficult for the historian to trace. However it is still possible to reconstruct the views of Sheehy Skeffington. In July 1923 she was appointed correspondent for the weekly American paper the *Irish World*. She was also an energetic correspondent, with a wide network of friends, to whom she wrote on her opinions of current events. While a truce between the Irish and British was being negotiated in July 1921, she confided her forebodings for the future to Eva Gore-Booth, feminist activist and sister of Constance Markievicz, the Dáil Éireann Minister for Labour:

> . . . there are many who would regard peace short of independence as a defeat – and in spite of my desire for Peace, I am one of these. It's a very difficult matter and one of responsibility either way. Of course, if the country votes Peace on a plebiscite there is nothing to be done but accept for the time being. And a lot depends on how the leaders put it. Democracy to many is only a name and people in masses do as they are told.[57]

On republican and feminist grounds she opposed the Treaty, recognising that those who would vote for acceptance were 'the moderates, and the "safe" people

---

[55] *Irish Citizen*, May 1919.
[56] Arthur Mitchell, *Revolutionary Government in Ireland* (Dublin, 1995), p. 46.
[57] Hanna Sheehy Skeffington to Eva Gore-Booth, 17 July 1921, Eva Gore-Booth Papers, Ms 21,816, National Library of Ireland, Dublin.

with stakes in the country.' None of the women deputies supported the Treaty. Constance Markievicz emphasised that she had fought for a Worker's Republic, not for the interests of capitalism. It was an argument Hanna supported, as she made plain in letters to the press, '. . . the vested interests . . . the propertied classes, the people that boast of "stakes in the country!", are all in favour of the Free State. These will all vote at the election.'[58] Women between the ages of twenty one and thirty still had no vote, so she spearheaded a campaign to have the franchise amended before the Treaty was voted upon, in a final attempt to thwart the forces of conservatism. Dáil deputies were leafleted by an alliance of women from a number of organisations demanding 'Justice for Irish Women.' She wrote to an American suffrage friend, 'the fight for this absorbed all my energies and it seemed like old suffragette times again.'[59] Kate O'Callaghan, a former pupil, was the deputy who introduced the franchise motion into the Dáil. I feel sure that it was Hanna, experienced in drawing up parliamentary legislation, who drafted its provisions on her behalf. No one else had her level of expertise. The majority of deputies had little genuine interest in women's claim to citizenship, so the vote on the motion was in effect another vote for or against the Treaty. However, in accordance with a promise that the suffrage deputation had managed to extract from Arthur Griffith, the franchise was extended subsequently to women over twenty one – but only for elections after the Treaty election. It was the last occasion for many decades when an opportunity for progressive change for women would come before an Irish parliament, but it came too late for many. Hanna summed up the situation with considerable bitterness, 'We may not vote for the Free State or the Republic, but we may vote later when others have voted us into the Free State.'[60] The question of the Treaty, its provisions, and the controversy over who would be entitled to vote on its acceptance revealed, yet again, the extent to which Sheehy Skeffington was uncompromising when she considered that fundamental principles of justice and equality were being undermined by entrenched political interests. An Irish patriarchy, shaped by Roman Catholicism, was victorious. An Irish Free State, in which radicals found themselves increasingly marginalised, was the outcome.

Once the Treaty had been voted upon by a divided people came civil war, with no more opportunities to promote women's needs. A women's peace mission tried to intercede with both groups before hostilities commenced. Sheehy Skeffington negotiated with the republicans. No compromise was forthcoming from either side. Many more women were imprisoned during the civil war than at any other time in the struggle for independence. The pro-Treaty faction,

---

[58] *Freeman's Journal*, 10 May 1922.
[59] Hanna Sheehy Skeffington to Alice Park, 25 February 1922, Alice Park Collection.
[60] *Freeman's Journal*, 10 May 1922.

knowing from first-hand experience what women were capable of, were less chivalrous than the British had been. Under her influence, the programme of immediate work issued to Sinn Féin members again emphasised women's issues: 'special stress should be laid on the imprisonment of women and the treatment of women prisoners.'[61] She travelled to America, appointed by Éamon de Valera as part of the Irish Women's Mission, to explain the anti-Treaty position to Irish-Americans and to fund-raise for the republican cause.

Free State victory was achieved through ruthless suppression of the opposition. Republicans who would not compromise their principles by taking the hated oath of allegiance to the British monarchy found employment in the state sector impossible to obtain. For Sheehy Skeffington, unable to work as a teacher, journalism provided a precarious living. She was an oppositionist in the Free State, aware that the backlash against women's participation in public life, which had begun as soon as the civil war ended, was continuing to have a detrimental impact upon women's hopes for an improvement in their lives. In 1924 women's right to participate in juries was severely curtailed, a foretaste of what was to come. She wrote numerous articles for the British journal *The Vote*, organ of the British feminist group the Women's Freedom League, with which she remained closely linked, informing women in Britain of these changes: 'Women in Ireland still suffer from the effects of the revolution that missed and of the subsequent reaction. What was given at first with gladness has been gradually filched away. Equality has ceased to be accorded to us, save on paper.'[62] Her republican views never affected her friendships or her affection for feminists in England. On the contrary, when in England she often found herself free to stress feminist concerns, without feeling constrained by other political considerations. She was also prominent on the international stage, attending many congresses of the Women's International League for Peace and Freedom, where she stressed her definition of an anti-imperialist feminism. The uncompromising republican views of herself and friends like Rose Jacob and Maud Gonne MacBride created an unbridgeable gulf amongst Irish feminists involved in the League.[63] Internationally, those she felt close to were feminists from India and other countries mobilising against British imperial rule.

For the next decade, the necessity of maintaining a visible republican opposition during the early years of the newly formed state determined her political alliances. The state was anti-republican and anti-woman, and Sheehy Skeffington tried always to emphasise the connection between the two. Her radical republicanism isolated her from many women, while her sister Mary

---

[61] 'Sinn Féin reorganising committee, programme of immediate work for cumainn', n.d. P2260, National Library of Ireland.

[62] Hanna Sheehy Skeffington, 'Irishwomen's place in the sun', *The Vote*, 15 March 1930.

[63] See Cullen Owens, 'Women and pacifism'.

Kettle, a local government councillor, appeared to be more in tune with contemporary attitudes. Margaret Cousins, analysing the situation, believed that the 'great bulk of Catholic women now in the ring of power must be led by Catholic women.'[64] She felt Kettle would be an appropriate person for the task. The feminist groups that still existed attempted to avoid political schism by concentrating exclusively upon feminist concerns. Sheehy Skeffington, a vocal critic of anti-woman legislation, retained membership of groups like the Irish Association of Women Graduates, but there remained a need for a woman's group that would have the potential to draw into its orbit women from all sections of Irish society.

While Hanna's manner of living was outwardly conventional (a widow devoted to her only son, taking in lodgers for much-needed additional income) her continued espousal of radical ideas placed her firmly on the side of those who challenged convention. Belgrave Road where she lived was dubbed 'rebel road', containing as it did so many die-hard republicans. Kathleen Lynn and Madeleine ffrench-Mullen, her neighbours, had both taken part in the Rising. Her sisters (widows also) and their children were an important part of her life, but much of her social and political life was dominated by the same woman friends with whom she had worked over many years. Walking holidays in Ireland in the company of old friends from the IWFL formed a part of her summer holidays once her son had grown up, although Owen, who had his own friendships amongst her set, would sometimes join his mother while travelling independently.

Sinn Féin's policy of abstention from Dáil Éireann became increasingly frustrating for those who wanted to mount a realistic challenge to what was beginning to seem like permanent one-party rule. In 1926, when Fianna Fáil was formed by de Valera, a man whose reactionary views on women she detested, Hanna was a surprising figure in its first executive. Yet other women whose views she respected were there as well, and it might have been that she hoped it would be possible to have some influence within the party. However, it was often an uncomfortable relationship, as her friend Cathal O'Shannon admitted, and one in which she could not have felt happy.[65] The entry of Fianna Fáil to the Dáil before the oath of allegiance to the British monarch was removed provided her with an excuse to tender her resignation. Thereafter she moved closer to the radical republicanism of Peadar O'Donnell and Frank Ryan, helping to edit *An Phoblacht* and providing vigorous propaganda against the Cumann na nGaedheal government.

She had condemned the Treaty from the outset as 'a bad compromise',

---

[64] Ward, *Hanna Sheehy Skeffington*, p. 265.
[65] Cathal O'Shannon, obituary of Hanna Sheehy Skeffington, *Irish Times*, 23 April 1946.

although it was the undemocratic manner in which it was voted into being that had been her initial target. That, and her distrust of the propertied classes, its chief supporters, determined her attitude.[66] Later, as the two separate states on different sides of the border established themselves, people slowly realised the stark reality behind what had been created through the partition of the island. In personal terms, Hanna discovered that the Skeffingtons, her husband's family, living in County Down, were no longer citizens of the same country as she was. Partition had created, as she said to the Women's International League for Peace and Freedom, a 'crazy patchwork frontier', breaking up families in arbitrary fashion.[67] The Unionist government served her with a banning order that forbade her to enter the six county area of Northern Ireland and she found herself unable to visit without fear of arrest. Nevertheless, in 1933, when she was asked to speak on behalf of republican prisoners in northern jails she did so without hesitation, suffering a one month prison sentence in consequence. On her release a motor cavalcade carried her in triumph back to Dublin. She was honoured with civic receptions from Drogheda and Dundalk town councils before arriving at a huge meeting in Dublin's College Green. Leading republicans, family members and friends crowded together onto the platform, where they heard her defiant declaration that 'They had got to break down the border and cut the last link that bound them to the British Empire.'[68]

She supported revolution in Russia and Spain, always open to new ideas but always insistent upon stating her republican-feminist views. After touring Russia in 1929 she applauded their efforts to develop communal ways of living, envying Russian women for their liberation 'from the pots and pans.' She was always outspoken in her dislike of housework, vehement in her rejection of the term 'housewife' and scathing in her criticism of the 'inconveniently-constructed houses' in which male architecture compelled women to live.[69] Every progressive cause found her a willing ally. She was secretary of the Irish Friends of Soviet Russia and chaired the Women's Aid Committee, which organised support for the republican side in the Spanish Civil War. As opposition to the Irish state subsided, radicals like her were left with little option but to wait for more favourable circumstances before the launch of any new campaign. To Eva Gore-Booth's companion, Esther Roper, she admitted that she found no cause for optimism in either Fianna Fáil or Cumann na nGaedheal, 'Here we are rapidly becoming a catholic statelet under Rome's grip – censorship and the like, with a very narrow provincial outlook, plus a self-satisfied smugness. . . I

---

[66] Hanna Sheehy Skeffington to Alice Park, 25 February 1922, Alice Park Collection.
[67] Hanna Sheehy Skeffington, July 1926, speech to Women's International League for Peace and Freedom, Alice Park Collection.
[68] *Irish Press*, 22 February 1933.
[69] Hanna Sheehy Skeffington, 'Random reflections on housewives: their ways and works', *Irish Housewife*, 1, 1 (1946).

have no belief in de Valera. Well meaning, of course, better than Cosgrave, but really essentially conservative and church-bound, anti-feminist, bourgeois and the rest.'[70]

In the meetings of protest against the Conditions of Employment Bill in 1935, she found herself sharing platforms with a variety of women's groups. During that campaign against the exclusion of women from the industrial labour force she called repeatedly for the formation of a woman's party. This call was redoubled during the fight against the 1937 Constitution, with its clauses affirming the primacy of women's domestic role. The Women's Social and Progressive League was the eventual outcome of determined pressure by women to resist the government-led drive to return them to the home. In the spirit of 'first wave' equal rights feminism, Sheehy Skeffington stood for the Dáil in 1943, one of four independent woman candidates. Unlike the others, she did so not simply as a feminist, but as one who declared her support for Connolly's conception of a workers' republic: 'Under the 1916 Proclamation Irishwomen were given equal citizenship, equal rights and equal opportunities but subsequent constitutions had rendered all this meaningless.' Her attitude towards Ireland's right to unfettered nationhood was 'unchanged and unchangeable.' She called for the creation of a community that would care for the welfare of all.[71] Although she received only 917 first preference votes, in public at least she retained her optimism, arguing that their unsuccessful campaign had some positive results. For a while, the streets of Dublin had carried the slogans of 'Equal Pay' and 'A Square Deal for Women.' She hoped that the seeds they had sown would be ready to germinate in the next election.[72] In reality, the aspirations of the succeeding generation of women were more in sympathy with those of Andrée, wife of her son Owen, who co-founded the Irish Housewives Association. In an age where the marriage bar precluded the option of a career, campaigning on consumer issues gave a new generation a means of inserting domestic concerns into the public arena. Although Hanna expressed strong reservations on the wisdom of associating women with housewifery, she was as generous as ever with her public support, urging women to 'educate themselves in citizenship ... become vocal, if need be clamorous ... Go to it, housewives!'[73]

By the time that first issue of *The Irish Housewife* appeared in 1946, Hanna Sheehy Skeffington was dead. Her fatal weakness of the heart was undoubtedly affected by her several hunger-strikes and by the stress of a lifetime of relentless political campaigning. She had participated in what were, for Irish feminists, some of the most important events of the twentieth century. It was she who

---

[70] Hanna Sheehy Skeffington to Esther Roper, n.d., SSP, Ms 24,134.

[71] Maria Luddy, *Hanna Sheehy Skeffington* (Dundalk, 1995), pp. 49-50.

[72] Hanna Sheehy Skeffington, 'Women in politics', *The Bell*, vii, 2, (November 1943), pp. 143-8.

[73] Sheehy Skeffington, 'Random reflections'.

urged the suffrage movement to carry out acts of militancy when all but a few hesitated. When the cataclysmic event of the Easter Rising took place it was Hanna Sheehy Skeffington who immediately grasped its significance as a seminal moment in the long campaign for women's citizenship. Her entire career was focused upon the fight for a society based upon principles of social justice. She had stood for 'complete economic and political freedom for the entire nation both men and women' in an election campaign which exemplified the extent to which her radical spirit remained undiminished by age.[74] She was a feminist who had fought for women's rights for almost half a century. During times of war, insurrection, civil war and fascism, she was always willing to join a new organisation if it appeared that by so doing she could further the causes in which she believed. In Ireland, women have had to contend with the malign effects of fundamentalist religion, authoritarian government and armed resistance and counter-resistance to the constitutional situation. Each element has fed off the other, to the detriment of women. Hanna Sheehy Skeffington did not have all the answers to the difficult questions concerning the relationship between feminism and the movement for national independence, yet she bravely confronted the issue whenever it was necessary to do so. Irish feminists have often argued that the 'national question' has little relevance to the immediate task of improving women's lives. Underlying this has been a fear that it would prove too divisive for a movement based upon assertion of a communality of interests. Slowly, this attitude appears to be changing. Recognition that feminist struggle must interrogate all obstacles to progress and make alliances where it is appropriate to form them is undeniably daunting, but that largeness of vision that defined the feminism of Hanna Sheehy Skeffington remains her most important legacy.[75]

---

[74] Quoted in Ward, *Hanna Sheehy Skeffington*, p. 339.

[75] The Sheehy Skeffington Papers in the National Library of Ireland are an indispensable resource. Without her dedication to preserving the past, the full complexities of those times would be lost for ever. For that foresight as well, Hanna Sheehy Skeffington deserves full recognition.

Margaret Cousins (1878-1954)

Catherine Candy

The story of Margaret Cousins is spectacularly unique in the history of modern Ireland and indeed of the world. A feminist cultural critic in the Irish celtic revival, from 1908 to 1913 Cousins was a leading visionary in the militant suffrage movement. After migrating to India in 1915 as a theosophical devotee she nationalised and internationalised the Indian women's organisations, steering them through the Indian freedom movement of the 1920s and 1930s. A formidable internationalist figure in the interwar global women's movement she also instigated, in 1931, an All Asian women's bloc against what she saw as the misguided interference of western values in Asian feminist movements.

Margaret Elizabeth Gillespie was born in 1878, in Boyle, County Roscommon, into a Church of Ireland family. A manuscript family genealogy compiled in the 1920s suggests that the first Gillespies came to Ireland from Scotland toward the close of the eighteenth century. According to this Hugh Gillespie served in the yeomanry militia in counties 'Wicklow or Wexford' in 1793, while his sister Mary married John Shera, a Methodist farmer in County Leitrim. Successive generations of the Sheras married into the (Church of Ireland) Gillespies. Shortly after joining his sister in Leitrim, Hugh Gillespie married a local woman, Mary Tweedy. Hugh's youngest son, Joseph, inherited what became the mainstay Gillespie farm at Mount Prospect near Boyle. Here Joseph, with his wife Sarah Jenkins, raised five sons and two daughters. Their third son, Joseph, married Margaret Shera in 1875 and three years later Margaret Elizabeth Gillespie, was born.[1] While the family came from land owning stock, Margaret's father was a clerk of the petty sessions in the Boyle courthouse.

Boyle was an important regional business centre, with a population of about

---

[1] Typescript of family genealogy given to author by Ms Darrie Gillespie, Dublin.

three thousand, a maize mill, one of the first post offices in the country, and a newspaper, the *Roscommon Herald*. Middle-class privilege gave Joseph Gillespie's daughters a materially comfortable childhood with two house servants in their twelve-roomed house. An indication of their social world is apparent in the facility with which they travelled the world. The movement of various brothers and sisters to South Africa, Trinidad, and Canada, suggests the Gillespies' sense of global and imperial entitlement which differed strikingly from the more limited options available to most Catholic emigrants. Some of Cousins's siblings stayed in Ireland through marrying into farming and professional families, but none married outside the Protestant church.

Cousins grew up in a genteel atmosphere, acquiring 'a good, sound elementary education' from the Boyle co-educational national school in which such subjects as French and piano were 'taught by two cultured gentlewomen who made an impression for life' on her by their 'cleverness and by their public service.'[2] However, her aspirations to study music in Leipzig were shelved when she won instead a scholarship to the Victoria Boarding School in Derry.

In the joint autobiography, *We Two Together*, published in India in 1950, Margaret Cousins constructed her childhood personality as an embryonic version of qualities which she prized in her adult self-image. She emphasised her independent character, innate sense of autonomy and quick intellect rather than 'conventional feminine' virtues of beauty. 'Everyone decided I had brains and could actually think for myself.' She found early signs of what would later become her lay feminist ministry, such as her preference for biographies of Joan of Arc over dolls. From a young age she recognized the emotional salvation of throwing herself into a challenging cause – 'the more difficult a struggle was the more cheerful I became.'[3]

She gave her Protestant unionist family background short shrift, noting that 'though we were Protestants and Unionists and my Father a Government official,' they never experienced any 'window-breaking' and the like because of her father's 'charm and kindliness.' Her reconstruction of her personal flowering as a nationalist was more effusive. She recalled how as a child her heart 'belonged from the beginning' to 'the fighters for freedom' and how she was awe-struck by the sight of Charles Stewart Parnell.[4]

She mentions no negative influences apart from her resentment at her father's stern control of her mother's finances; '. . . there and then . . . my girlish determination began to try and change the financial status of wives and mothers, who all worked so hard and got no money for themselves.'[5] All the elements

---

[2] James H. Cousins and Margaret E. Cousins, *We Two Together* (Madras, 1950), p. 25.

[3] *Ibid.*, p. 26.

[4] *Ibid.*, p. 24.

[5] *Ibid.*, p. 55.

which would mark the mode and motivation of Cousins's activism are there: crusading zeal for 'freedom' and justice; worship of the staunchness of public and religious servants. Indeed Joan of Arc made a particularly appropriate model for Cousins's later transgressive style of public intervention.

In 1898 Cousins began to study music in the Royal Irish Academy in Dublin. She recalled a 'jolly, widening, cultural period of expansion of mind and experience such as fell to the lot of few girls . . . For the first time I was my own mistress.'[6] Dublin was, she recalled, a magnet for cultural mavericks individually and collectively attempting to redefine Irish identity. One such was a young poet and her future husband. James Cousins was raised in a working-class Belfast Methodist family. Having worked as secretary to the mayor of Belfast and as a part-time teacher of short-hand he migrated to Dublin in 1897 as a largely self-educated young poet with a desire for literary recognition which would last his lifetime. He was already moving in Dublin's literary circles when he met Margaret in July of 1899. They were married in Sandymount, Dublin, in 1903. Margaret tells us how she cried the night he proposed to her. But she had a clear sense of not wanting to become an old maid and wanting a partner to share her life. She knew he was a good man and during their engagement his consistency and affection won her over. The Cousinses conceived their marriage as a co-operative venture in the promotion of a spiritual culture which would unify the world, and presumably also their marriage, in the process.

They earned a reputation in Dublin for their 'high plane of existence', so many were the good causes they championed such as the vegetarian movement, anti-smoking, temperance, pacifism and socialism. By 1906 they had instituted weekly vegetarian social evenings at their home on Sandymount Strand for those interested in the occult – the effort to understand life through a hidden vortex of science, magic and philosophy. Around this time Cousins discovered in herself latent powers of communicating with supernatural forces through automatic writing. Both of the Cousinses were among those in Irish society, like W.B. Yeats, James Joyce and Douglas Hyde, who were drawn to theosophy at the turn of the century.

The Theosophical Society was founded in New York City in 1875 by the Russian Helena Blavatsky. By 1881 the theosophical international headquarters had been established in Madras, India. It had three main objects: 'Universal brotherhood; the study of comparative religion, philosophy and science, and the investigation of unexplained natural laws.' In short theosophy compensated for the materialist, fractured, soulless experience of the modern with a vision of the cosmos as whole, organic, purposive and ordered. Transcending romantically beyond enlightenment deist thinking about the inherent laws of the universe, theosophists reclaimed the occult spiritual powers of 'the ancient wisdom' and

---

[6] *Ibid.*, p. 51.

cited all world religions as expressions of the same wisdom. With the emergence of mass culture, theosophy returned meaning and purpose both to the individual and to the grand history of the universe. Its mix of magic, science and philosophy sought to prove the essential unity of all knowledge both hidden and evident, reconciling the split between the secular scientific universe and the sacred.

While in theory theosophists held that all religions and sciences were part of one organic 'ancient wisdom', in practice they tended to privilege Eastern over Western thought, giving theosophy a particularly orientalist cast. Although theosophists often seized on emergent subversive movements such as feminism and cultural nationalism as the bubbling up of the natural 'Time-Spirit,' their tendency to valorise all that went before as necessary processes of evolution lent a certain conservative, complacent bent to their historical world view, especially in terms of their belief in the essential biological bases of races. Theosophy was, in short, an organic product of empire. Cousins described her encounter with theosophy in terms of an intimate intercourse with a new and enticingly 'virile' universe:

> I entered a new universe and a new universe entered me . . . I got an expansion of consciousness about time, space, ethnology, cosmogony, symbolism, magic and religions that would last me for this life . . . Though I understood so little yet, the bigness, strangeness, newness of the subject matter, the virility of the style, the curiosity it awoke in me, held my interest without flagging.[7]

One reason that Cousins found Theosophy attractive apart from its non-sexist organisational politics was its belief that each soul changed sex as it was reincarnated. This implied that neither sex reigned sovereign over the other and that each individual was an admixture of the masculine and the feminine. She became a proponent of this attempt to renovate a 'traditional' Hindu concept of gender from the bisexual Hindu deity, Ardhanarakishwara, as it appeared to subvert hard and fast boundaries of completely separate sexual spheres. She named this 'new' sexual epistemology the 'femaculine,' explaining that it contained:

> a community of function on the mental side and diversity of function on the physical side and behind both a spiritual unity which coheres all diversity of manifestation . . . a synthesis of the virtues of the masculine and feminine in which the defects of each are balanced if not eliminated.[8]

During the engagement James Cousins had reassured his future wife that 'anything about the coming of children' would be her decision. Soon after

---

[7] *Ibid.*, pp. 103-104.
[8] *Irish Citizen*, 21 May 1912.

their marriage Margaret experienced deep and prolonged trauma on her discovery of sexual intercourse which she found to be degrading and shameful:

> My new knowledge, though I was lovingly safeguarded from it, made me ashamed of humanity and ashamed for it. I found myself looking on men and women as degraded by this demand of nature. Something in me revolted then, and has ever since protested against, certain of the techniques of nature connected with sex. Nor will I and many men and women of like nature, including my husband, be satisfied, be purified and redeemed, life after life, until the evolution of form has substituted some more artistic way of continuance of the race.[9]

Clearly Cousins experienced and saw no value of pleasure in the act of sexual intimacy, casting it in mechanical, Darwinian terms as a 'technique of nature in the evolution of form.' At their wedding banquet she announced her decision to join her husband in his vegetarianism. Both partners seem to imply a certain symbolic reciprocity between their non-sexualized marriage and their non-flesh diet.

Cousins was, around this time, concerned to reconcile her 'femaculine' theory of sex with Christian thinking. A key article that she eventually published in 1915 in the *Theosophist*, the journal of the Theosophical Society, was entitled 'The curse of Eve.'[10] The 'curse' was enforced motherhood and the law of conjugal rights which entitled a husband 'to force his attentions on his wife just as he wishes . . . . The woman suffers shame to her finer feelings, and a gradual hardening of nature through bitterness of spirit' thus degenerating the female form. Cousins calculated that a woman suffers seven hundred times more than a man in her lifetime, hence her view of this 'crucifixion of her sisters' as 'the Curse of Eve.' Continuing the Christian metaphor, she heralded the education and economic independence of women as the 'Angels of Annunication proclaiming the conception of the New Era' which she felt had just begun. Her argument was that the choice of motherhood belonged to the wife – not that motherhood was wrong, but that it was of no virtue in and of itself and should not be compulsory. She was not arguing simply from a liberal individualism: 'The reaction from the present secretly hated sex and maternity slavery may tend to an exaggeration of selfish freedom.' Instead she saw motherhood as a necessary mechanism of evolution which would in the end produce a universal state of androgyny:

> . . . nature has imposed on her [woman] the duty of building forms so that souls will have some necessary means of development. Realising this woman

---

[9] Cousins and Cousins, *We Two Together*, p.108.
[10] Cousins, 'The curse of Eve', *Theosophist* (April, 1915), pp. 21-38.

will become conscious co-creator with the divine will, and evolution will improve at a much increased rate, improvement in the quality of the race being accompanied by its gradual decrease in quantity. . . The new world ideal must be the attainment of the state of the Blessed Virgin. Such perfect purity and chastity can be won by man and woman alike. It was the condition of Adam and Eve in the Garden of Eden, it was the very nature of Jesus Christ – who is considered the first fruits of the perfecting humanity. The Christ was the perfect man-woman.[11]

Such themes of purity and chastity were commonplace feminist strategies against patriarchal sexual culture and were widely articulated in suffragist communities, especially in Britain. Cousins avidly read the British spiritualist feminist writings of Anna Bonus Kingsford and Annie Besant. It was while attending a vegetarian conference in Manchester in 1906, which coincided with a conference of the National Council of Women, that she became aware of the militant wing of the English women's suffrage movement. She followed the militants' campaign in *Votes for Women*, the organ of the Pankhursts' Women's Social and Political Union (WSPU). What attracted Cousins most was what she saw as the soul-stirring spectacle of fusion, movement and solidarity between the women:

> I eagerly followed the doings of the militants with full understanding of their aims, methods and spirit. I felt so much one of them that I longed for some way in which the women of Ireland might be colleagues in such a soul-stirring and needed movement for the freeing of world-womanhood from the shackles, injustices, inequalities and denial of citizen rights and responsibilities under which women suffered.[12]

On her return to Dublin Cousins and six women met at the home of Hanna and Francis Sheehy Skeffington to form the Irish Women's Franchise League (IWFL). In Francis Sheehy Skeffington's view, the meeting was provoked by the County Council bill of 1907 which excluded Irish women but not Scottish or English women from seats on County and Borough Councils, a point Cousins omits in her account of the birth pangs of the IWFL. Francis and Hanna Sheehy Skeffington were well known figures in Dublin intellectual life with whom the Cousinses quickly developed a deep and enduring bond. All were vegetarians, pacifists and broadly speaking, nationalists, although, while they first met at Philosophical Society meetings, the Sheehy Skeffingtons were not as interested in the occult.

The avowed aim of the IWFL was to 'obtain the parliamentary vote on the same terms as men then had it, or as it might be given to them.' It aimed to raise public awareness on the suffrage issue; to obtain pledges from every Irish member

---

[11] *Ibid.*, p. 29.
[12] Cousins and Cousins, *We Two Together*, p. 138.

of parliament to vote for women suffrage bills introduced in the UK parliament; and to include a provision for equal suffrage in any Irish Home Rule bill. This ginger group of IWFL members visited Anna Haslam, leader of the existing Irish Women's Suffrage and Local Government Association (IWSLGA), 'to inform her that we younger women were ready to start a new women's suffrage society on militant lines.'[13] Cousins respected the intent of the by then elderly Haslam, and her husband Thomas, and appreciated the IWSLGA's campaign for women representatives in local government, but found the IWSLGA lacking in the kind of vital energy which had so galvanised her in Manchester.

The IWFL met a need amongst Irish women, judging by its remarkably rapid spread throughout the country by 1910. In less than a year membership totaled 700, although by 1912 official memberships levelled off at 800.[14] While full membership of the IWFL was restricted to women, men could join as associate members. The IWFL became a spearhead to suffragists who favored a more active style of protest, while causing resentment amongst those suffragist groups who disagreed with its tactics and ideology. As the first treasurer and secretary of the IWFL respectively, Cousins and Hanna Sheehy Skeffington became close comrades in the struggle. The day to day business of running the IWFL involved weekly open-air meetings in Dublin's Phoenix Park and around the city, national tours by suffragist speakers who travelled around the country in a side-car speaking from ditches and lorries, and camping out in tents at night. Cousins hugely enjoyed the adventurous theatrical element of creating propaganda, writing letters to the newspapers, and staging pageants of Irish women's history.

Acknowledging the entanglement of the woman question with the national question, the IWFL aimed at a militant suffrage society 'suitable to the different political situation of Ireland, as between a subject-country seeking freedom from England, and England, a free country.' And Cousins adds, later in India, 'besides, we had no desire to work under English women leaders.'[15] The IWFL's perceived position on the national question was consistently a point of contention. Cousins saw the IWFL as a corrective to the sexism of the Irish Parliamentary Party, and furthermore, she was not prepared to wait for a Home Rule government to grant equal suffrage. She charted suffrage as a mere fulfilment of a democratic nationalism:

> The Irish Women's Franchise League . . . is not working to wreck Home Rule, as Nationalists believe, but is upholding the demands of all patriots of the past to the right of the people to govern themselves. If we do not see to it

---

[13] *Ibid.*

[14] Cliona Murphy, *The Women's Suffrage Movement and Irish Society in the Early Twentieth Century* (Philadelphia, 1989), p. 2.

[15] Cousins and Cousins, *We Two Together*, p. 164.

that 'people' included women as well as men, we are only perpetuating the
idea that woman is only property and not a person in her own right. . .[16]

As it became clear that equal suffrage was not a priority for the Irish Parliamentary
Party the IWFL stepped up their campaign of heckling its members. Subsequent
charges of unpatriotism and anti-nationalism forced the IWFL to deny that it
was importing its ideology from the English militants, the 'suffragettes.' Defining
its separate Irish identity was a delicate affair. While the IWFL was partially
inspired by the British example, the IWFL turned militant only in 1912 when
peaceful lobbying tactics were exhausted. Cousins was the chief diplomatic
intermediary between the IWFL and the WSPU as she oversaw the Pankhursts'
speaking tours of Ireland.

Cousins also took possibly the most active part by any Irish feminist in
British protests. With five other Irish women she participated in the 'Parliament
of Women' at Caxton Hall, Westminster in November 1910. The police arrested
over a hundred and injured fifty women. Indignant, the leaders called for a
second deputation for the following day. These few days marked a turning
point in a more radically physical form of militancy for Cousins. She then broke
the windows of cabinet ministers' homes – in Cousins' view 'the property of
tax-payers of whom thousands were women.'[17] She was duly arrested and
sentenced to a month's imprisonment in Holloway Jail. On her release Cousins
poignantly remembered arriving in Dublin on Christmas Eve to be greeted by
a reception committee and torchlight procession which paraded her through
the streets. She was especially moved by the idea of being inducted into what
she saw as the tradition of Irish freedom fighters and capitalized on how suffragists
were appropriating the rituals of the Victorian Irish nationalist to feminist effect.

> It was a stirring and unexpected experience for me to be a figure in such a
> traditional demonstration, the old staging for a new aspect of the age-long
> struggle for freedom, unique in Irish political history in having women at its
> centre.[18]

However when the Liberal Home Rule bill was about to pass in the House of
Commons in 1913, still with no mention of votes for women, Cousins and her
colleagues felt the need of some 'extreme militant action which would assure
world-wide publicity of our protest':

> Three of us volunteered to break the windows of Dublin castle, the official
> seat of English domination. That sound of breaking glass on January 28, 1913
> reverberated round the world and is what we wanted. It told the world that

---

[16] *Votes For Women*, 6 April 1912.
[17] Cousins cited in Cliona Murphy, *The Women's Suffrage Movement*, p. 178.
[18] Cousins and Cousins, *We Two Together*, p. 180.

Irish women protested against an imperfect and undemocratic Home Rule bill.[19]

Although the damage to the windows amounted to a mere five shillings each, the three women, Cousins, Meg Connery and a Mrs. Hoskins were sentenced to a month's imprisonment with hard labour as 'common criminals.' The three demanded to be treated as political prisoners, a classification which Cousins declared 'had been won by men in the Land League and Home Rule clashes with the English Government,' and announced that they would wait a week for the classification to be changed and if not would begin a hunger strike 'as the only form of protest in our power.'[20] They did hunger strike after which they were granted certain ameliorative conditions though the prison insisted that they had not won any legal political status. However, on their release the suffragists triumphantly publicised the bargain with the prison authorities to 'prove' that they had won 'full political privileges.' Characteristically Cousins took advantage of her incarceration to publicise the suffrage cause by writing of her experiences in the *Irish Times*. Her insider's sociology of the jail, written to the press, was an impishly comprehensive institutional report complete with a set of recommendations for the improvement of the running of the jail. In the *Irish Citizen* she underscored how the suffragists were always in control of the situation. Ever the spiritualist she claimed that suffragists were, like Jesus Christ, redeeming humanity by exposing the failure of the 'Emperor's Law':

> We use the tide of the law to serve our own purpose. Thus since we first challenged the law we have exposed its powerlessness to coerce us; we have made its authority a farce; we have injured the prestige of the government which puts in motion old laws to imprison us, instead of new laws to free us. Last month once again, after those Dublin magistrates had given their sentences, we took the helm in our own hands, steered the ship in the exact direction we had on our charts, and started to sentence everyone around us . . . Thus the power of the human will, working on a basis of reason and justice, proved that it could break through a harsh and unjust 'hard labor' precedent, could fix the length of its own imprisonment, could obtain its own release, could face death or torture, could turn that sentence to its own service, through making it a rest for body, mind and soul, could use it for the service of all future reformers, and could make it a source of fresh inspiration and courage in our own work. We know that we are above the law and that in submitting to it according to the terms we ourselves impose on it, we *are* in a far-off way following the example of that supreme crucified one who came not to destroy the law but to fulfill it; that we suffer but to redeem, and that indeed we are co-workers with him for the upliftment of our people.[21]

---

[19] *Ibid.*, p. 189.
[20] *Ibid.*, p. 190.
[21] *Irish Citizen*, 8 March 1913.

The spiritual intensity which underlay Cousins's belief in the moral rectitude of suffragist militance is also apparent from the title *Holy War* which she chose for an IWFL pamphlet in 1913. She saw militance as a necessary phase of evolutionary progress which would balance the masculinity and femininity of womankind.

> Only by militant action (it may be constitutional or non-constitutional) can we succeed in balancing the feminine and masculine virtues in each woman. In doing this, we are winning triumphs for the forces of human evolution.[22]

While Cousins's constant references to the basic androgyny of all human beings might suggest that logically she would also believe in eliminating the Victorian convention of separate sexual spheres, such an attitude is not reflected in her suffragist rhetoric. At least in public she argued that men had for too long controlled the public domain of the feminine such as human welfare, and that suffragists were trying to recover woman's 'natural' and 'sovereign' sphere of influence.

> The common impression was that they wanted to be more like men. What they really wanted was to be more woman-like than they had been. The women's point of view was the welfare of the human life. Men were more interested in the financial side.[23]

On the national question Cousins borrowed the nationalist rhetorical cliché of the lost golden age of Irish sexual equality to shame nationalist constituencies into suffragist support, referring to 'Mother Ireland', and the 'world famous qualities of Irish womanhood' in calculated appeals to nationalist pride. Cousins's idea of woman as the motherly saviour figure of the nation extended to a global vision. She genuinely believed and justified claims for an enlargement of women's power in terms of service to both the nation and the course of human evolution rather than merely in terms of the rights of the individual.

Given their dedication to the suffrage cause it comes as something of a surprise that in May of 1913 both Cousinses emigrated for what they imagined might be five years to Liverpool while the suffrage campaign in Ireland was still very much underway. One reason for their departure was their sudden bankruptcy. In 1907 James Cousins had become became a director of a new co-operative bank which promptly collapsed. He was held partially responsible and declared bankrupt. This was, as James Cousins put it, one of the 'expulsive forces in our lives in 1912 . . . the attracting force came from India.'[24] In 1912 an English vegetarian foods entrepreneur offered James a nine month training

---

[22] *Irish Citizen*, 12 February 1913.
[23] *Leinster Leader*, 18 April 1913.
[24] Cousins and Cousins, *We Two Together*, p. 213.

stint in the town of Garston, near Liverpool, before sending him to open a branch in Bombay. The Cousinses left for Liverpool where they remained for two years. At their formal farewell evening Margaret Cousins presented herself as an occult feminist, as the *Irish Citizen* reported:

> It was not by her seeking that she was going, but as a pawn in the Great Game of Life, she was being moved on to another square by the Eternal Player. She believed that all things were arranged for the ultimate good; . . . and left them as her watchwords: 'Perseverance, Courage, Loyalty, Imprisonment and Love.' . . . Political imprisonment was well understood in Ireland, and imprisonment did more than anything else to forward the cause here. It was not the amount of the damage done it was the fact of high-minded women being in prison that was valuable.[25]

From Liverpool Cousins wrote frequently to Hanna Sheehy Skeffington of how much she missed the vital *élan* of her Irish comrades: 'I am getting plenty to do here in all sorts of directions but I would rather be doing it in Dublin with you.'[26] Instead in Liverpool she turned to religious and philosophical concerns. She founded a new women's church, and created its liturgy. The Church of the New Ideal subverted mainstream churches by having men as associate members only.

When the war broke out in 1914 Cousins reflected on how it was visibly reshaping gender roles. Her reactions followed the popular curve of an initial excitement, arousal, and militant celebration to subsequent disillusionment and horror. As the masculinist chauvinism of the pre-war effort began to wear on her Cousins however became frustrated by the exclusion of women from the army – especially when she felt that women had always faced bloodshed with equally heroic, if less hyped courage in the everyday experience of childbirth – an ignored 'national service.' She felt that women must train for the 'actual field and fighting in the future' as 'a monopoly of the glory and importance of warfare feeds men's vanity.' 'Reading about nothing but men, men, men makes me jealous these days, especially as I know women could do the same work just as well if not better.'[27] By 1914, as the war began, she was looking forward to the disciplining process of mass militarisation: 'We all want licking into shape and peace does not always bring the best out of us as we militants have discovered.'[28] Yet some months later in 1914 when Francis Sheehy Skeffington was arrested in Dublin for his pacifist activism, Cousins' mood had taken a more pacifist turn, even if she still longed for battle. As she wrote to Hanna:

[25] *Irish Citizen*, 24 May 1913.
[26] Cousins to Hanna Sheehy Skeffington, nd, Sheehy Skeffington Papers, Ms 22,665, National Library of Ireland, Dublin. (Hereafter, SSP.)
[27] Cousins to Hanna Sheehy Skeffington, nd c.1914, SSP, Ms 22,670.
[28] *Ibid.*

I really envy you still living so strenuously. I long for life on the great adventure scale again. Only a few days before I got your news I was saying the old longing to be a man had come back to me so that I could fight against conscription and be shot if necessary in support of the Xtian [Christian] and human principle 'Thou shalt not kill.'[29]

Less than a year after the war began Cousins turned more feverishly against the war, scorning 'the frightfulness of militarism' as 'an evil that generates human monsters and mad men' and by 1920, thinking about Christabel Pankhurst, she was particularly appalled by women 'militarists', – 'a woman militarist is appalling, however, unselfish her aims.'[30]

From 1908 to 1913 Cousins had lived for the high drama of the militant campaign and clearly experienced an acute sense of marginalisation and dislocation as the war interrupted suffragist momentum and she found herself excluded even from volunteer service, this time on the basis of her dubiously militant past: 'Winter without the suffrage will be strange.'[31] Clearly the war and the waning of the suffragist drive further heightened Cousins's sense of isolation and dislocation in English culture which left her at something of a loose end during the early war years, frustrating her energy for the cut and thrust of public politics. Both of the Cousinses disliked living in Liverpool for its industrial dullness and its sense of isolation from the cultural avant garde.

In March of 1915 Annie Besant, then international president of the Theosophical Society, accepted James Cousins's offer to work for her new Madras based newspaper *New India*, and duly enclosed two fares and an agreement for three years. The move to India came as a heaven sent opportunity for Cousins to realign herself to the women's cause. Writing to Hanna Sheehy Skeffington in 1914 and 1915 she noted:

I hope I'll find some kind of a career or vocation for myself in India in my own right such as I had in the I.W.F.L and those last years in Ireland. Here I have had plenty to do but it has been of a higgledy-piggledy kind. I prefer straight lines even though they be hard . . .[32] What is going to become of me God only knows! But I am not afraid that I won't find some useful niche before long. I want to help the Indian women, just think only three out of every hundred get any education.[33]

Increasingly horrified by what they perceived as the breakdown of western civilization, the Cousinses transferred their hopes for global regeneration to the

---

[29] Cousins to Hanna Sheehy Skeffington, 8 September 1914, SSP, Ms 22,648.
[30] Cousins to Hanna Sheehy Skeffington, 2 June 1920, SSP, Ms 22,691.
[31] Cousins to Hanna Sheehy Skeffington, 7 September 1914, SSP, Ms 22,667.
[32] Cousins to Hanna Sheehy Skeffington, nd, September 1915?, SSP, Ms 24,102.
[33] Cousins to Hanna Sheehy Skeffington, 8 September 1914, SSP, Ms 24,648.

East. They arrived in theosophical headquarters in November 1915. Margaret went to work in the Theosophical Publishing House while James became the assistant sub-editor on *New India*.

Another figure who landed in India in 1915 was Mohandas K. Gandhi, returning after his years in South Africa and England. The India confronting Gandhi and the Cousinses alike was now straining from its major contribution to the war effort which in turn put great pressure on the ruling structure and resources of the raj. Widespread hardship caused sporadic unrest. Moreover Indian Muslims were increasingly following the anti-British, anti-allied line of their Khalifah, the then Turkish world leader of Islam. Responding to the war time rhetoric of the freedom of small nations, calls for self-government swelled from different sectors of Indian public opinion.

In 1915-1916 two political leaders, Tilak in Bombay and Annie Besant in Madras, formed two Home Rule Leagues to push for self-government with the Indian National Congress, the main constitutionalist nationalist political organisation founded in 1885. Together Tilak and Besant pushed the Congress into a more aggressively nationalist stance. In 1915 however the Cousinses were most closely associated with Besant's rising star in Indian nationalist circles. In England in the 1880s Besant had been a notorious Freethinker, Fabian socialist, strike leader and union organiser, atheist, and feminist activist for birth control before her conversion to Theosophy in the late 1880s. She settled in India in 1895 in order to serve in the Theosophical Society and took over as its international president from 1907 until her death in 1933. Apart from her aspirations for the nationalist leadership Besant was the head of a nation-wide network of colleges and schools whose aim was to revive those aspects of the Sanskritic Vedic culture of ancient India selected by international theosophists and local Brahmans. Besant's radically romantic agenda for the Indian nation was often conservative in its championing of Victorian Brahmanical caste values over democratising lower caste, feminist and regional agendae. This was not lost on a local subaltern movement around Madras who dubbed Besant 'the Irish Brahmani.'[34]

In India Besant made a point of emphasising her Irish ancestry so that importing the Cousinses to work for her in Madras seemed to further authenticate her commitment to anti-imperialism. When Besant became more obstreperously nationalist in 1916 James Cousins chimed in with a ringing celebration of the Irish rising of 1916 in *New India* after which Besant was imprisoned. Promptly hailed as a nationalist heroine she was elected president of the Indian National Congress from 1917 to 1918. In 1917 Besant suddenly presented the Cousinses with their fares home to Dublin. Shocked that their deep-felt vocations to

[34] M.S.S. Pandhian, 'Beyond colonial crumbs: Cambridge school, identity politics and Dravidian movement(s)', Working Paper no. 125, [Adyar, Madras: Madras Institute of Development Studies, 1994].

India could be taken so lightly, they refused to go and both eventually found employment teaching at the Theosophical College and High School in the inland hill town of Madanapalle, well away from Theosophical headquarters in Madras. Their relations with Besant remained delicately respectful, but there was less and less intimate political co-operation, and by the mid 1920s Besant was marginalised in the leadership of the Indian nationalist movement by Gandhi. This seismic shift in the Cousins's political position in a fast changing India meant that being followers of Besant was simply no longer adequate to secure their nationalist credibility, and in rising anti-Brahmanical subaltern circles Besantite credentials could be more of a hindrance than a help.

The move to Madanapalle liberated Cousins from Besant's monitoring eye. While to some extent still tied to Besant and the Theosophical Society, through her involvement in the women's movement she now evolved an independent public identity from grass roots to national levels. Although she had come to India with ideas of extending her cause to that of 'Indian womanhood', she appears to have found little scope while in Madras, perhaps because she was feeling her way into unfamiliar territory, and the 'need' may not have seemed urgent amongst her largely well-heeled, educated, middle class Indian and foreign circles there. At first excited to be away from the metropolitan and European-influenced Madras – ' there will be only one other white person so we will be in the real India',[35] she was soon confiding to Hanna Sheehy Skeffington that she found rural India 'interesting but not wholly satisfying.'[36] Lonely, isolated and bored she began to complain of the lack of 'virility' and 'gumption' in local Indians – 'they are all so cowed out here poor things.'[37] She was also frustrated with her students 'fundamental masculine thought' as she tried to cram feminism into them.[38] In Madras with other British theosophists she had worked to revive the traditional local craft of rattan weaving in rural areas. She began these activities anew in Madanapalle. She also found a particularly rewarding sense of social connection as a sort of alternative mother figure to the girl students in the school, encouraging them especially in sports. Many would stay behind after school illicitly – 'I don't know how many of my students may be pretending that I am their aunt or grandmother they are spending the afternoon with!'[39] In September 1916 she wrote to Sheehy Skeffington:

> Since I last wrote I am thankful to say that I have got into touch with Indian women here. The secretary of the Theosophical Society here, a lawyer, is a fine feminist and an enthusiastic worker. He got about eight women together,

---

[35] Cousins to Hanna Sheehy Skeffington, 21 July 1916, SSP, Ms 27,679.
[36] Cousins to Hanna Sheehy Skeffington, 22 June 1918, SSP, Ms 24,102.
[37] Cousins to Hanna Sheehy Skeffington, 21 July 1916, SSP, Ms 22,279.
[38] Cousins to Hanna Sheehy Skeffington, 21 September 1916, SSP, Ms 22,688.
[39] Cousins to Hanna Sheehy Skeffington, 2 November 1916, SSP, Ms 22,680.

two Sundays ago and I talked to them and made them show me their gold ornaments and sing to me and generally we got on very friendly terms. I am arranging lesson classes twice a week and a general social kind of gathering every Sunday for them with the help of two girl students who are studying for Second Arts and who can speak to them and interpret for me.[40]

At last she was making a connection with Indian women across an enormous divide, caused in part by her inability to communicate in the local Tamil language. Cousins' involvement with Indian women also consoled her with a sense of purpose and connection to the global feminist movement. The very isolation of Madanapalle made it crucial that she make extra efforts to connect locally, nationally and internationally. Throughout her early years in India, she continued to contribute articles and money to the *Irish Citizen* and to the IWFL. In 1918 she wrote to Sheehy Skeffington that the loneliest evening she experienced in India was when she heard of the winning of a partial vote for Irish women, after which she promptly organised a jubilant meeting in Madras.[41]

Having served her apprenticeship to a strain of Irish feminism sensitive to perceived attempts at colonisation by British feminists. Cousins operated in several related modalities as a feminist activist in India. First she was eager to generate a grass roots local feminist consciousness in a range of social reforms issues such as health, maternity, co-operative craft ventures, divorce legislation and birth control. Second she was anxious to connect the different regionally scattered Indian women's organisations into a national organisation, and to connect that in turn to the international women's organisations. Third she was here especially eager to rescue the image of the Indian woman, and indeed of the Asian woman, then circulating in the West from patronising imperial stereotypes. Paradoxically, as she herself stressed the diversity of Indian womanhood, she was also a theosophical believer in the essentially spiritual and healing qualities of an archaic Indian womanhood under cultural retrieval. Much of her time then was spent in communicating with women all over India and the world, through her newspaper columns and her copious level of world wide correspondence. She had herself founded and been long-time editor of the well-circulated multilingual journal of the WIA, *Stri Dharma*, just as she had been centrally involved in the *Irish Citizen*. In addition to writing continuously in provincial, national and international papers, she also published four books at the behest of Indian publishers between 1922 and 1950.[42] On top of this there were her lecture tours and constant travels where she made a point of searching

[40] Cousins to Hanna Sheehy Skeffington, 21 September 1916, SSP, Ms 22,688.
[41] Cousins to Hanna Sheehy Skeffington, 22 June 1918, SSP, Ms 24,102.
[42] *The Awakening of Asian Womanhood* (Madras, 1922); *Oriental and Occidental Music* (Madras, 1935); *Indian Womanhood Today* (Allahabad, 1941); *We Two Together* (Madras, 1950).

out particular like-minded people. Cousins quickly found herself at the centre of an impressive network of international feminist meridians. From there she built an internationalist platform from which Indian woman crucially projected a middle class Indian feminist politics through a range of decolonising global nexes over the next three decades.

A fourth level of operation was her desire to see Indian women represented as full and equal citizens in all levels of government. Her campaigns for women's political representation dovetailed of course with her social reform campaigns but there is evidence of her conscious efforts to moderate a calculated dialectic between them in the national consciousness especially as she herself moved ever more slowly away from her initial passivity on the empire/national question toward a full engagement in the national movement by the early 1930s.

For example, following her initial assessment that India was not ready for a suffrage campaign she switched her focus in 1916 to social reform and joined the local *Abala Abhivardini* – 'the Weaker Sex Improvement Society' in Madanapalle which was soon renamed the Women's Indian Association. Cousins later explained how this title was chosen over the 'Indian Women's Association' to stress how it was a branch of the global transnational women's movement – that it had, as she put it theosophically, 'a larger . . . deeper . . . all inclusive . . . . understanding.'[43] The stated aims of the WIA included both agendas of social and political reform and were loosely couched in a broader agenda of cultural nationalism:

> 1. To present to women their responsibilities as daughters of India; 2. To secure the right of education for every boy and girl 3. To secure the abolition of child marriage and other social evils; 4. To secure for women the vote for municipal and legislative councils on the same terms as it is or may be granted to men 5. To secure adequate representation of women in municipalities, Taluks, local boards, legislative councils and assemblies, 6. To establish equality of rights and opportunities between men and women 7. To help women realise that the future of India lies largely in their hands, as wives and mothers . . . 8. to band women into groups for the purpose of self-development and education, and for the definite service of others.[44]

By 1917-1918 the increasing anxiety of the British administration for stability in India led to a cosmetic gesturing of its desire for a 'gradual development of self-governing institutions' in India. When Cousins in 1917 requested that a deputation of the WIA meet with visiting British officials Edwin Montagu and Lord Chelmsford to discuss educational reform she was informed that they

---

[43] Muthulaksmi Reddi, *Mrs Margaret Cousins and Her Work in India (Compiled By One Who Knows)* (Madras, 1956).

[44] *Stri Dharma*, November 1918, p. 3.

could only accept deputations about electoral reform. Cousins, putting this down to the occult ways of 'the time spirit of the suffrage', promptly asked 'what about votes for women?'

> I can tell anybody who wants to know that to have your finger on a turning point in the history of a vast country is no matter of light refreshments. A month in Holloway jail and another in Tullamore seemed, in retrospect, rest cures compared with the brain-racking job of having to formulate a demand without precedent in the long history of India; a demand far past the understanding of all but the minutest fraction.[45]

Unlike the Irish campaign for the vote, the Indian campaign was more bureaucratic than visceral. The Montagu Chelmsford committee devolved the woman's question along with a host of other electoral reform issues to the provincial legislative assemblies who all voted in the woman's suffrage by 1929. However, if the campaign was a technical success it was also a practical failure as the accompanying property qualification restricted the vote to only about one million women out of a population of three hundred million. From this point on Cousins became deeply frustrated by the machinations of Westminster politicians and British feminists alike in generating 'misrepresentations, ignorance and prejudice' about the capacity of Indian women for citizenship. In national and international newspapers Cousins contrasted the obfuscations of Westminster with the alacrity with which Indian male politicians had championed women's suffrage in order to exert global and especially American leverage on British politicians while ever milking Indian nationalist self-congratulation on 'the woman question.'

After the first suffrage 'victory' in 1919 Cousins realised such cosmetic gestures of good will toward the woman question made precious little difference in most women's lives, so she decided once more to push for educational reform for girls. In 1916 she had been invited to participate as a senator in the first Indian Women's University in Poona, Western India, an institution modelled on Japanese as self-consciously opposed to British lines. Cousins was delighted to meet there a group of 'upstanding, intelligent women,' many of whom would form vital contacts for her subsequent ventures.[46] The most prominent of those subsequent ventures was her foundation in 1927 of the All India Women's Conference, an institution thriving at the turn of the twenty first century. Initially conceived as a singular event to investigate educational reform for girls, it was decided at the first conference to make it a permanent organisation. The AIWC, as a mammoth pan-Indian women's organisation, quickly came to command significant visibility and respect in middle-class India. Cousins's strategy was

---

[45] Cousins and Cousins, *We Two Together*, p. 310.
[46] *Ibid.*, p. 278.

that the AIWC should gather grass roots, élite, government wives and British women together in one comprehensive national umbrella organisation which would function as a quasi parliament of Indian women, while the more nationalist and Madras-based WIA could operate more discretely and executively as a roving political gad fly, possibly pressing the AIWC toward particular stances as circumstances permitted. Whereas the WIA might be dismissed as a theosophical and foreign concern, Cousins was anxious to engage the élite of Indian women within the broad based AIWC, and to affiliate it with all preexisting, grass roots women's organisations to authenticate it as *the* legitimate voice of Indian womanhood nationally and internationally.

This phase of the women's movement in India is inextricably tied to the freedom movement led by Gandhi and others. In the early 1930s as the national question became increasingly urgent the AIWC found its theoretical political neutrality difficult to practice. By the late 1920s Cousins herself was making no secret of her support for Gandhi. She even spent a year in Vellore Women's jail near Madras in 1932 for campaigning publicly in his support. It was partially Cousins's two trips to the U.S. in 1929 and 1931 which pushed her more and more into a pro-nationalist stance. Her shock at the ignorance of the west about contemporary India radicalised her Indian nationalism, where before she had seemed content to follow Annie Besant's slow push for dominion status.

Cousins's shock at western imperialism had two results. First she convened the All Asia Women's Conference at Lahore in 1931, with the aim of 'reAsianising' Asian femininity against what she perceived as the western evisceration of Asian culture. Cousins believed that Indian and Asian womanhood had a crucial part to play in the cultural evolution of the planet by balancing the masculinist capitalism which she saw as choking western culture. The All Asia Women's Conference was not as successful as the AIWC and, despite Cousins's efforts throughout the 1930s was never reconvened. The second result was Cousins's stance in the second round of the suffrage campaign. In 1927, the suffrage question reemerged when the British government, prompted possibly both by the maternalist protectionism of British interwar feminists and their rhetorical competition with the AIWC to represent 'the Indian woman', set up a commission to consider the expansion of the Indian woman's franchise. When no Indian and no woman was invited to work on the commission, the WIA followed the Indian National Congress in boycotting it. To make matters worse, the government then proposed to introduce certain qualifications for Indian women to vote based on wifehood, religion and literacy. Believing it would be seen worldwide as an insult to Indian womanhood if such reservations were attached to the vote, Cousins roused the WIA and the AIWC to mount a protest, hastily dusting off the campaign motto 'free field and no favour' from her IWFL days.

However, some few Indian women, encouraged by the conservative British feminist M.P, Eleanor Rathbone, argued that a piecemeal slow extension of the franchise was the best they could hope for. This wing accused Cousins and her supporters on the executive of the WIA and AIWC of a 'sublime theoretic idealism.'[47] One, Radha Subbaroyan, a wealthy woman from Madras, depicted Cousins as an interfering foreign theosophist who misread the 'real India,' and represented her as the dupe of Congress nationalists. Throughout the early 1930s the AIWC franchise committee followed Cousins's opposition to the reservations issue in a contest between the AIWC, led by Cousins, and the pragmatists led by Rathbone. In the end the government ratified proposals including reservations but these were never implemented because of the instability of the national question. Indian women finally won equal suffrage in 1947 with national independence. Nonetheless the higher ground of liberal 'enlightened' principle which Cousins and the WIA occupied against the procedural pragmatism of the opposition marked a historical 'recovery of nerve' on the part of middle-class Indian feminism. The episode can also be seen as something of a strategic failure on Cousins's part as, despite the WIA's backing of the Congress, the latter effectively withdrew support for the anti-reservations campaign after 1933 and did not support women candidates in elections as Cousins had somewhat naively calculated. Cousins however remained loyal to the Congress, even spending a year in jail in 1932 to 1933 for her part in Gandhi's civil disobedience movement.

Throughout the 1920s and 1930s Cousins managed the election campaigns of several Indian women running for local elections to the provincial legislatures. Declining to run herself, she worked instead to get Indian women elected. Her friend and ally, Muthulakshmi Reddi, an upper class Madrasi woman from a prominent medical family, was famously elected as the first woman to an Indian legislature and subsequently became Deputy President of the Madras Provincial assembly. However Cousins became the first female magistrate in India in 1924.

While Cousins worked on the question of women's access to positions of public power in the media, in correspondence and in national committees, her social reform activism had a more grass roots and visceral character. Like most Indian feminist social reformers she extended the nationalist metaphor of woman's place in the 'home' to cover the newly imagined national public sphere, hoping to reform the master's house with the tools of the kitchen.

The subject of child marriage was raging during Cousins's time in India, particularly in those international circuits which carefully monitored Indian 'progress.' Cousins was privately outspoken to Sheehy Skeffington, believing that child marriage infantilised women and stunted their educational opportunities.[48] In India, while she went to great pains to 'dethrone the present idolatry of the function of motherhood,' she toned down the more abrasive

---

[47] *Madras Mail*, 4 October 1933.
[48] Cousins to Hanna Sheehy Skeffington, 21 September 1916, SSP, Ms 22,688.

language of her 'Curse of Eve' days as she tried to nurse Indian readers towards the idea of marriage grounded on mutual respect and freedom, finding ideal models in the ancient scriptures.[49] She was disappointed with the Child Marriage Act of 1928 which she felt punished offenders after the deed, rather than preventing it. Other successes partially attributable to Cousins are the introduction of compulsory education for both sexes in Madras and a host of social reform organisations which she founded with Indian women for women and children, many of which continue to flourish in the 1990s. Cousins also piloted American birth control activist, Margaret Sanger, through India in the late 1930s, against Gandhi's opposition to artificial birth control. Cousins valued birth control to ease the lot of an overburdened motherhood and to enable the transfer of maternal energy into public service. But her desire for birth control was also problematic in that it was rooted in a strategy to improve the Indian racial stock, particularly by curbing the lower caste birth rate.

By 1937 Cousins was fifty-nine years old and having served a prestigious term as President of the AIWC she was 'retired upstairs,' as the bye-laws demanded. By the early 1940s the political turbulence of Gandhi's massive 'Quit India' movement was making it uncomfortable to have white women fronting an Indian national women's organisation: 'It is an inevitable result of the growth of self-reliance and I honour it.'[50]

In 1941 Cousins suffered the first of several strokes which led to increasing paralysis and loss of speech. For eleven years she was in various states of ill health, nursed by her husband in the hill stations of the Nilgiri mountains and Madras. Characteristically low on funds, the Cousinses were supported by friends, and by an annual bursary from the Indian nation from 1947 onwards in recognition of their work for India. Margaret Cousins died on 11 March 1954 in Adyar, Madras, and her ashes were spread on the Ganges. James Cousins died two years later in Madanapalle.

Margaret Cousins is remembered in India by the generation which succeeded her as a founding 'Mother' of the Indian women's movement. In November 1978 Margaret Cousins's birth centenary was celebrated in Madras by an exhibition of the Cousinses' own art collection and by a new WIA initiative to extend women's education to the city's slum areas. In September of 1994 a plaque to Cousins was unveiled on her birth home in Boyle by then President of Ireland Mary Robinson and Shobha Ranade, then President of the AIWC.

Over Cousins's thirty-nine years in India her relationships with Indian women and men shifted constantly. Initially she eagerly bought in to all of the established imperial orientalist stereotypes of the passivity of 'the Indian woman'

---

[49] Cousins, *Awakening of Asian Womanhood*, p. 48.
[50] Cousins to Alice Paul, 17 March 1942, National Women's Party Papers 1938–1958, Series VII, reel 174, Library of Congress, Washington D.C. (Hereafter, NWPP).

and of the East in general in a way which made herself stand out as ferociously active. For example, anxious to retain her bond with Hanna Sheehy Skeffington in her early years in India she complained in her letters of how Indian women were 'quietist', 'gently submissive,' and irritatingly lacking in 'gumption.'[51] However in India she cannily kept this judgment to herself and instead emphasised the enormous potential agency of Indian feminine tropes in the healing process of the over masculinised West. Paradoxically, although Cousins quickly learnt to debunk western assumptions about the uniformity of 'the Indian woman,' and even while she acknowledged her early naïveté and arrogance on the subject, her consciousness was still ultimately swamped by prevailing ideas of an essentially 'Indian'/'oriental' spiritual quality of the feminine. While she probably used such stock orientalist images to some extent for strategic rhetorical purposes, sometimes, especially during the international fascination in the 1920s and 1930s with the idea of 'Mother India' as the spiritual salve of modern western materialism, it seems that at a deep level she believed in them herself.

At a personal level Cousins tended to bond most closely with much younger protégés whom she mentored as feminist activists, rather than with women of her own age. As she got older she became increasingly disappointed with the relative lack of commitment she saw in the younger cadres. Amongst her peers she had strong relationships with women like Muthulaksmi Reddi and Rajkumari Amrit Kaur but nothing like the solidarity and intensity of the bond she had had with Hanna Sheehy Skeffington. But then apart from the fact that Cousins would always have been regarded to some extent as an outsider (despite the fond and polite protestations of her Indian colleagues to the contrary), she was also forever on the move in India, where national distances were so much greater than in Ireland. Cousins's friendships, made in the first place for the sake of transnational feminist bonding, could never shake off entirely their national edginess. In 1942 she wrote how 'Indian national consciousness is much more touchy about non-Asians like myself taking any initiative or prominent part in Indian progressive movements.'[52] And again her own disappointment is apparent in her closing years as she confided to an American colleague: 'I constantly find that I look at things much more from a world stand point, or from the angle of a world womanhood or of a universal religion or a one God than my Indian or English sisters do.'[53] How did Cousins manage her identity as an Irishwoman in India? Her initial social context in India was organised through local Theosophical connections with other foreigners, Indian Christians and high-caste Hindus, but she made a point of cultivating relationships with many different

---

[51] Cousins to Hanna Sheehy Skeffington, 4 November 1919, SSP, Ms 22,688.
[52] Cousins to Alice Paul, 17 March 1942, NWPP.
[53] *Ibid.*

communities and was especially anxious to make connections in 'native' Indian society. Even amongst the European set she was tickled by how her eclectic profile refused to conform to the simple slot already designed for her in their system of categorisation:

> I was, I gathered, quite an enigma to the various local sections. The Catholics couldn't understand how an Irishwoman could be both a Protestant and a Home Ruler. The Protestants couldn't understand why I was not a missionary. The European club couldn't understand how I could be so jolly and yet be a vegetarian – and a follower of Mrs. Besant![54]

While Cousins was not shy about using the symbolism of her 'natural' Irish sympathy for sundry Indian causes to advance her own agenda in India, it was for example 'as a worthy daughter of Ireland' that she went to jail for Gandhi,[55] yet she was affronted when an Indian nationalist politician claimed her as a fundamental Indian. To Hanna Sheehy Skeffington she wrote in 1919:

> A good Indian tried to grab me publicly in a speech for India, saying he was sure that though on the surface I was Irish, in my heart I was Indian. It would have rejoiced you all to have felt how every atom of me protested against the idea. I had to laugh afterwards at the thought of the strength of my race adherence. Nationalists in every country are selfish, I suppose, but while I remain intensely Irish I have no desire to annex any Indians and claim them as Irish because they happen to sympathise or if need be even serve Ireland. What a queer place the world is and the people in it.[56]

Outside of urban India and those national-international circles where Irishness meant something, Cousins strove to connect with all levels of Indian people in the rural villages, where Irishness generally meant very little. In Madanapalle especially she was more grounded in local grass roots organisations. Personally she and her husband never had any steady substantial income, always living on a shoestring and often depending on the kindness of Indians especially in the later years. She stood out amongst Indian women activists in travelling throughout India in third class rail and is remembered affectionately as having a consistently unkempt appearance, regarded as code-breaking for a white woman in India, which she lightly attributed to having 'been born under a dirty star.'[57]

As she became more involved in women's organisations at the national level she was strategically anxious to engage elite Indian women in the plight of subordinate classes and castes:

---

[54] Cousins and Cousins, *We Two Together*, p. 377.
[55] Cousins, Trial Statement, *Stri Dharma*, January 1933, p. 127.
[56] Cousins to Hanna Sheehy Skeffington, 4 November 1919, SSP, Ms 22,688.
[57] Author's interview with Lakshmi Swaminathan, New Delhi, 18 December 1994.

I was no toady but I recall a touch of pride when at one of these open sessions I counted eight royal ladies on the platform. We were out to liberate what Tagore called 'the poorest, the lowliest and the lost' and I felt that a strong initial pull from above would help the process. [58]

While her theoretical feminist agenda in India tended to solidify the middle class Indian reformist agenda, she was often more attuned to the practical short term difficulties of lower class women than many of her middle and upper class Indian feminist cohorts, as is evident in her defence of women miners' work against the injunctions of international labour organisations to 'protect' women from the abuses in the mines.[59] On the other hand the justification which she used for birth control was that it would improve 'the race' by freeing up lower class women for public service. While rhetorical support for race reform and eugenics was a common feature of 1920s international feminist ideology, it suggests too in Cousin's case that she was somewhat oblivious to the grinding demands imposed on lower caste women to provide a labor force.[60]

Cousins's feminism was often anchored in broader anti-democratic ideological currents. While she was spiritually delighted by her ability to transcend class differences with lower class women, she was particularly anxious that the women's organisations should never be distracted or diffused by a focused class politics. In fact much of her ideology implicitly reinforced the prevailing class structure even if explicitly she advocated class equality. She firmly believed that the resolution of the sex question would eventually in turn resolve all other social inequities.

In India the class, race and national questions interacted in a more immediately volatile way than they did in Ireland. Cousins was a believer in the 'wonderful Aryan race' whose origins she placed in India as the 'Root Stock from which so many races have radiated forth.' Her racial ideology was underpinned by the theosophical universalism which insisted that all was one underneath the superficial differences of culture – a position which made racial diversity seem divinely ordained rather than historically produced. While Cousins's racial romanticism in the Indian context was a replica of her Irish celebration of the Celtic golden age of feminism, the significant difference for

---

[58] Cousins and Cousins, *We Two Together*, p. 459.
[59] Cousins to Hanna Angelo, 15 March 1936, Roll 25, File 12, AIWC papers, Nehru Memorial Museum and Library, New Delhi.
[60] Cousins, 'Margaret Sanger: rebel, scientist, liberator', *Theosophist* (October 1932), pp. 80-84; B. N. Ramusack, 'Embattled Advocates: the debate over birth control in India, 1920-1940" in Cheryl Johnson-Odim and Margaret Strobel (eds.) , *Expanding the Boundaries of Women's History* (Indiana, 1992), pp. 173-202; S. Anandhi, 'Women's question in the Dravidian movement c.1925-1948', *Social Scientist*, 29 (1991), pp. 24-41.

the Indian context was that the ancient Vedic golden age which she held up as the ideal in India was still the basis of contemporary orthodox Hinduism, whereas Celticism provided a relatively safe refuge for both Protestant and Catholic occult narratives of the nation. Cousins's thinking on these lines therefore had a more potentially divisive impact in India than in Ireland. For example, the strategically national, 'All-India' focus of Cousins's feminism was seen in South Indian and Muslim circles as another manifestation of the hegemonic desires of upper caste, north Indian Hindi speakers to define the nation. This national/ subaltern tension was however hardly Cousins's invention. The same tension between the strategic forging of an All-Indian nationalism while simultaneously respecting India's complex multiculturalism also plagued the Indian National Congress, finally resulting in the partition of India and Pakistan in 1947 as well as the assassination of Gandhi in 1949 by the extreme Hindu right. The resurgence of the Hindu right and Hindu-Muslim riots in India of the 1990s are further results of the same dialectic.

What did Cousins achieve in India? She nationalised and internationalised the Indian women's movement. She became a model of the sensitive interlocutor in Indian political affairs. She cast herself in the role of a catalyst who merely supplied critical direction to a latent pool of feminist energy. And indeed there were already several women's reform movements and organisations in India from the mid 1850s. However, they tended to be concentrated regionally and were never as nationally mobilised or internationally visible as the women's movement of the twentieth century.

She helped consolidate the voice of Indian middle class feminism on the international interwar map. Cousins staged productions of 'the Indian woman' on world tours, creating visual spectacles of Asian femininity as she took advantage of the global spotlight on Gandhi. Aware of how American and British feminists could be played off against each other, she used American feminist pressure obliquely as a lever against British conservatism as the 'moral stewardship' of the new world order changed hands. If her scheme occasionally failed as in the reservations controversy of the 1930s when she put all her feminist faith behind Gandhi and the Indian National Congress, thereby diluting the clout of the national women's organisations, it was hardly entirely her fault. What she did do in India and Ireland alike was to redefine the rhetoric, and thus the social meaning, of 'home' and the domestic sphere to stretch across the public sphere.

And what of her achievement in Ireland and for Ireland? How does one evaluate the contribution of an individual to the vagueness of a nation? Especially when she lived so much out of Ireland and yet always through an Irish identity. It might be better to ask what 'Ireland' did for Margaret Cousins. One can easily catalogue her central role in the Irish suffrage movement but what is perhaps more interesting is how her biography sheds light on wider systemic issues of gender, nation, transnationalism and feminist agency. It is beyond doubt that her being Irish, as opposed to British, in India opened some Indian doors for her (while, undoubtedly, closing others) but that was only a beginning, what she did when she got through them was quite often driven by her personality and by her Indian cultural politics. Further, if her identity as an Irish woman enabled her to nationalise and to internationalise Indian feminism and feminists, she was also limited by the grammar of international history that had rules about who could become what. Just as she manipulated international narratives of Indianness to Indian feminist ends, her Irishness worked both for and against her.

Her remarkable adeptness at cultural mediation possibly owed something to the ways in which she was always consciously hinged between a series of unconventional identities, operating always somewhat ambiguously from the fringe. Born to lower middle-class Protestant stock in Roscommon she was not firmly one thing or the other. Growing up on the relatively neutral borders of the midlands and the north west, she centred herself in Dublin's Celtic revival where she mediated between the literary, socialist, feminist and spiritual set. A part-time piano accompanist to James Joyce's first career as a balladeer, she even literally became a medium with the other world of the dead, and the ghostly foundation for Joyce's complex heroine in 'The Dead.' Perhaps it was her compulsion to voice otherness which lent her the enthusiasm to mediate between the Irish and English suffrage movements as much as it would later between Indian and international women's organisations. It was this extraordinarily articulate mediative power and ability to knit several political perspectives and politics into a unified vision which most marked her political performance. Perhaps what drove Cousins more than anything was her unwavering belief in the wholism of everything. Paradoxically it was this addiction to narratives of cosmic coherence which in turn meant that she quite often, but not always, missed the cultural construction of the social categories that she was trying to reorganise. If, with the benefit of hindsight, Cousins's thinking can at times seem to be somewhat theoretically naïve, perhaps it is also a mark of her ingenuity that her thought was only just ahead of her times. While it could be argued that she might have theorised more and romanticised less, she had realised from her early explorations of the cultural *avant garde* how she preferred to keep her feet firmly planted in what she termed the '*terra firma*' of the present, and this she did with resounding impact on real lives.

NOTE ON SOURCES

There is no one single collection of Cousins's papers. However there is a great volume of relevant papers scattered around the world. Alan Denson made some effort to catalog these in his 1967 *James H. Cousins (1873-1956) and Margaret E. Cousins (1878-1954): A Bio-Bibliographical Survey* (Kendal: Westmorland, England, published by the author) which is a useful starting point for research. The published works of Margaret Cousins, *The Awakening of Asian Womanhood* (Madras: Ganesh, 1922), *Indian Womanhood Today* (Allahabad: Kitabistan 1941) and *We Two Together* (Madras: Ganesh, 1950) are enormously rich in both her autobiographical musings on her role in history and for succinct carefully thought out representations of her feminist philosophy. Her more spontaneous published articles range from prolific amounts in the *Irish Citizen* and *Bean na hÉireann; Freeman's Journal; Irish Independent: Irish Times; The Vote; Votes for Women*; the *Irish Statesman*; and from an Indian context *Stri Dharma*, organ of the WIA; Indian provincial newspapers such as the *Hindu; Madras Mail; Indian Social Reformer; Bombay Chronicle; New India; Roshni*, journal of the AIWC; *Amrita Bazar Patrika* and *Times of India*. More revealing of her deeper Theosophical philosophy are her writings in the *Theosophist; Adyar Bulletin; Adyar Library Bulletin* and *Adyar News and Notes*. She wrote a few pamphlets, interestingly entitled, *Women's Place in the Vegetarian Movement* (Theosophical Society, Dublin, 1905) and *Holy War* (Dublin: IWFL 1910?). From India her pamphlets include *What Women have Gained by the Reforms* (Madras 1917) and *Miss Mayo's Cruelty to Mother India* (1928).

Probably the heftiest collection of her letters are strewn through the massive archive of the AIWC, at their headquarters in New Delhi, but also on microfilm at the Nehru Memorial Museum and Library, New Delhi. These papers detail her correspondence with most of the secretaries and executive members of the AIWC from its foundation in 1927 until she bowed out in the early 1940s. The Proceedings and Annual Reports of the AIWC are also invaluable. The records of the WIA are in the Madras WIA headquarters but far less copious. Other important collections of correspondence in the Nehru Museum and library are those of her long time collaborators in India, especially Muthulakshmi Reddi and Hansa Mehta; some of Besant's papers; the Jawaharlal Nehru papers and the papers of the Indian National Congress papers.

The Fawcett library in London houses the most complete run of *Stri Dharma,* the papers of Eleanor Rathbone, and pertinent suffrage collections. The Theosophical library and Archives in Adyar, Madras, has a file relating to Cousins's posthumous profile in the organisation and around Madras, the Indian runs of *New India* and the Theosophical Journals in which she wrote. The Sanger collection at Smith College and Radcliffe Libraries, Massachussets, is useful for her connections with Sanger. The papers of the National Women's Party include her correspondence with Alice Paul and are available on microfilm from the U.S. Library of Congress, Washington, D.C.

For her Dublin years we have in the National Library of Ireland the scant IWFL reports and the rich Sheehy Skeffington collection – especially for Cousins's correspondence from Liverpool and India, and materials in the suffrage exhibition collection. At the National Archives in Dublin the papers of the General Prison's Board are important for her militant period. The India Office Library in London had occasional sidelights on the Cousinses from British politicians and lobbyists. Materials on her Boyle background were at the Public Records Office in Dublin, Parish and County Registers and censuses. The Gillespie family kindly provided the author with a typescript of the family genealogy and gave interviews. Interviews were also conducted in Delhi and Madras with surviving colleagues in Cousins's Indian campaigns such as Lakshmi Swaminathan of the Madras WIA and AIWC; with Sankara Menon, executor of James Cousins's will and director of the Kalakshetra school; with Manda Krishnamurti, niece of Muthulakshmi Reddi, and with past students of the Cousinses in Madanapalle such as Raghunatha T.N Reddy.

We are fortunate in Cousins's case to have her autobiographical recollection of her formative years in *We Two Together*. Quite apart from its inevitable selectivity Cousins also tended to telescope her Irish phase into a prelude to her remarkable Indian and international feminist career. I have kept in mind that she wrote especially the Irish parts of it both from the distance of South India in the 1940s and from her political positioning at that time in Indian and world history. Although she mentions in the autobiography that she compiled it from letters and diaries which she had kept with her from her Irish years, after exhaustive searches such a collection has not been found in Indian archives. I contextualise and measure the reliability of the autobiography against other contemporary sources such as newspapers; collections of correspondence; organisational files of the various bodies with whom she interacted, and other memoirs and government records.

Helena Molony (1883-1967)

Nell Regan

Helena Molony was a leading nationalist, republican, socialist, actress, feminist and trade unionist. Her extensive contribution to Irish society is evident from even a brief account of her career. Landmarks included the editorship of a militant nationalist and feminist paper, combatant in the 1916 rising, leading roles in Abbey Theatre productions, terms as second general secretary of the Irish Women Workers Union and as president of the Irish Trades Union Congress as well as founding member of Saor Éire and the Women's Prisoners' Defence League. Throughout Molony's life she sought to integrate, in the most practical ways possible, the causes of Ireland, women and labour. This is largely a public story since few of her private papers have survived.

Helena Mary Moloney [*sic*][1] was born on 15 January 1883 to Catherine and Michael Moloney of Coles Lane off Henry Street in Dublin. When Molony was two they moved to Rathgar, retaining their grocer's shop on Coles Lane. They moved again soon after but where is unknown. Her mother died while Molony was a child. Her father remarried but died soon after. Her relationship with her stepmother was apparently unhappy and she rarely referred to her family with the exception of her older brother Frank, to whom she was close. Frank emigrated to America when Molony was in her twenties. She probably had a Catholic secondary school education and lived a relatively sheltered lower middle-class life. Later, friends like Maud Gonne, Constance Markievicz, Sydney Czira, Kathleen Lynn and Evelyn O'Brien, became her 'family'. A small bequest from her mother supported her in her twenties. Otherwise she had no family support and earned her living as an actress and a trade union official. Her life

---

[1] Various spellings of the surname are used in different sources. 'Molony' is the one she herself used. Her birth certificate has 'Moloney' but entries in the *Thom's Directory* and her death certificate use 'Molony'.

was financially precarious and unsettled until her late forties. Friends recall a brave, generous and humorous woman given to bouts of depression and heavy drinking as well as illness which dogged her after retirement.

Molony's life of activism began in the summer of 1903 when she was nineteen. At a meeting in the Rotunda she heard Maud Gonne protest at the visit of King Edward VII to Ireland. 'To me she epitomised Ireland, the Ireland of the poets and dreamers – she gathered it all up and made it real for me . . . she made me want to help.'[2] Her brother Frank, whom she later discovered belonged to the Irish Republican Brotherhood (IRB), encouraged her to join Inghinidhe na hÉireann, Gonne's organisation for nationalist women. One day, at the Inghinidhe offices on Brunswick Street (now Pearse Street), she found a note directing members to Gonne's home in Rathgar. She arrived to find the 'Battle of Coulson Lane' underway. Dublin was festooned with Union Jacks for the Royal visit and Gonne had hung out a black petticoat, ostensibly to mourn the death of Pope Leo XIII. Police arriving to remove it were prevented by Inghinidhe members and supporters, including the overawed Molony. After this 'baptism of fire'[3] Molony joined the Inghinidhe and for seven years her life revolved around their activities.

The Inghinidhe were formed in 1900 in response to women's exclusion from existing nationalist organisations. They aimed to re-establish 'the complete independence of Ireland',[4] by fostering national pride through cultural activities, propaganda and force of arms if necessary. Members were mainly drawn from the new generation of young, well-educated, Catholic women. The Inghinidhe were part of the growing movement of cultural nationalism; they ran classes in Irish language, history and culture for children and adults, and organised monthly céilís and theatrical productions. A vigorous anti-establishment campaign was carried out in public houses and on the streets. Leaflets were handed out to prostitutes 'walking' with British soldiers on Sackville Street (now O'Connell Street). Leafleting on Grafton Street, Molony spotted the vice-regal car and pasted a leaflet on the boot. Lady Aberdeen, wife of the Governor General, drove around unaware that she was calling on young Irishmen to stay out of the British Army.

Within months Molony was secretary of the Inghinidhe and largely responsible for running the organisation as Maud Gonne had moved to Paris. For the next two years she dispatched weekly reports and regularly visited Paris to keep Gonne informed of activities. Gonne later described her as 'the most gallant and bravest of my Inghinidhe girls'[5] and they became lifelong friends.

---

[2] R.M.Fox, *Rebel Irishwomen* (Dublin, 1935), p. 120.
[3] *Ibid.*, p. 121.
[4] Margaret Ward, *Unmanagable Revolutionaries, Women and Irish Nationalism* (London, 1983), p. 51.
[5] Seamus Scully, interview with author.

Molony formed another friendship and working relationship when she spotted Constance Markievicz as a potential recruit at a Gaelic League meeting. The countess arrived at an Inghinidhe meeting straight from a Castle function wearing a ballgown. The serious group of young women, dressed in Irish tweeds, received her coolly. Markievicz later said it was 'the first time she had not been kowtowed to' and this had persuaded her to join the Inghinidhe.[6]

Molony's most significant venture in the Inghinidhe was the establishment and editorship of *Bean na hÉireann*. She wanted the monthly journal to be 'a woman's paper advocating militancy, separatism and feminism' which would also counteract the 'reactionary social and dual kingdom ideas' of Arthur Griffith's *United Irishman*.[7] The first edition appeared in November 1908 and, over the next three years, gave the Inghinidhe and Molony an important voice in the nationalist as well as the growing women's and labour movements. It was an eclectic and fascinating mixture. Political articles covered a wide range of national and international issues, there were notes on Inghinidhe activities and other nationalist organisations, gardening, cooking and fashion columns, theatre reviews and short stories and poems by leading writers such as George Russell (AE), James Stephens, Susan Mitchell, Patrick Pearse and Joseph Mary Plunkett. Molony's favourite was Stephens' poem 'The Red Haired Man's Wife', 'perhaps the most complete expression of feminism in poetry . . . nearly all of it applying to the Nation as well.'[8]

> I am separate still,
>   I am I and not you,
> And my mind and my will,
>   As in secret they grew,
> Still are secret, unreached and untouched,
>   And not subject to you.

Bean na hÉireann was the epitome of the Irish-Ireland movement and soon became the primary paper for militant nationalists, male and female, reaching as far afield as England, France and America.

The only body of writing that Molony ever published was her editorials in *Bean na hÉireann*. Her impatience with nationalist contemporaries and her desire for action are palpable. She wrestled with issues of the day, nationalist politics and the emerging women's and labour movements. Nationalism informed her views and she wrote that even the study of Irish, economics and history were all useless 'if there is not behind the great driving force . . . love of Ireland and of everything great and small that belongs to Ireland because it belongs to Ireland.'[9]

---

[6] 'The Green Jacket', 1960, RTE Sound Archive, Dublin.
[7] Fox, *Rebel Irishwomen*, p. 122.
[8] *Ibid.*
[9] *Bean na hÉireann*, July 1909.

The editorials urged Irish women to involve themselves in the cause and encouraged armed resistance to British rule:

> We believe in Ireland there is too much preaching and too little practice. The chief fault we find with men is that they talk very big and do very little and we would like to foster among Irish women a desire to work rather than talk about it in the columns of newspapers.[10]

In the spring of 1909 Molony moved to Belcamp, Raheny, to live with the Markieviczs. She cycled into town to the Inghinidhe offices, Gaelic League meetings and to her brother Frank's house. There she and Frank, with Markievicz and Bulmer Hobson of the IRB, planned the establishment of a national boy scouts movement, the Fianna, which would be the first step towards an Irish army, an Irish nationalist equivalent of the British Baden Powell scouts. In July *Bean na hÉireann* announced that the first branch had been formed. Molony and Markievicz trained and went on camps with the early recruits. Many of these went on to join the Irish Volunteers and fight in the 1916 Rising. Molony, Markievicz and Hobson also tried to establish an agricultural cooperative in Belcamp. This ended in failure and, with rumours of a broken love affair between Molony and Hobson, she moved back to Dublin in early 1910.

In her new year editorial she regretted that, as tensions between Britain and Germany increased, no steps had been taken to organise armed resistance to British rule except for the formation of the Fianna:

> If the German invasion, so much dreaded by England, actually took place have we anything to offer Germany in return for her help? Have we one thousand trained men who could shoot straight or walk thirty miles? If the men really mean what they say let them act. If not let them give up talking of still holding the principles of Tone and Emmet.

She saw little hope of change until 'women come into the National movement . . . and imbue with fresh enthusiasm and vigour the tired warriors who will be glad enough to share some of the fighting at least with their women folk.'[11]

Molony, both a feminist and nationalist, insisted that the feminist cause was part of the nationalist cause, and that '[our] desire to have a voice in directing [the] affairs of Ireland . . . is not based on the *failure of men* to do so properly but is the inherent right of women as loyal citizens and intelligent human souls.'[12] In 1908 the Irish Women's Franchise League (IWFL), a militant suffrage society, was founded in Dublin. Politically non-aligned but nationalist in sympathy, it was soon engaged in debate with the Inghinidhe as to the prior claims of

---

[10] *Ibid.*, January 1909.
[11] *Ibid.*, January 1910.
[12] *Ibid.*, January 1909.

nationalism or feminism. Hanna Sheehy Skeffington argued that discrimination would not end until women achieved the vote. Molony replied that it was 'unworthy and humiliating' to seek the British parliamentary vote and asked 'would the feminist cause be advanced by it?' It was not 'a question of putting nationality before sex or sex before nationality. The two questions do not clash at all although at first sight they appear to . . . the feminist cause in Ireland is best served by ignoring England.' The rights of Irishwomen, she continued, 'must be won in Ireland, not England or any foreign country. Freedom for our nation and the complete removal of all disabilities to our sex will be our battle cry.'[13] Nevertheless, Molony continued to support the suffrage movement both politically and personally. She worked closely with suffrage women on various causes and reported with approval the militant actions taking place in England.

Editorship also brought her into contact with an earlier generation of women activists. Anna Parnell, organiser of the Ladies' Land League, had written her own account of the period, *The Tale of a Great Sham,* and asked Molony to publish it. The Inghinidhe lacked resources to bring out a book, but Molony worked on the manuscript for serialisation in *Bean na hÉireann.*

In 1910 *Bean na hÉireann* introduced 'Labour Notes', co-authored by Molony. It was her introduction to trade unionism and socialism:

> I went to the Trades Hall for my labour notes. ... I knew little of labour ideas. But I was always on the side of the underdog. My attention was turned to Labour matters, when I discovered that one of the best and most intelligent girl members we had was getting 5/- a week as a shirtmaker.[14]

Her knowledge quickly developed and 'Labour Notes' dealt with a wide range of issues. The existing trade union movement was described as 'a living corpse' and the 'Notes' stressed the need for a strong, independent, Irish Labour party and trade union movement. The impact of James Larkin's Irish Transport and General Workers' Union (ITGWU), founded in 1909 to organise unskilled workers, was welcomed. When Larkin was jailed in 1910, readers were urged to join the campaign for his release.

'Labour Notes' paid particular attention to women workers, their conditions and lack of organisation and the ambivalence of prominent male trade unionists to these issues. Molony noted that '[w]hile admitting the needs of the unorganised female worker, the male members of the wage earners look with suspicion on their sisters and are seemingly loath to offer any help.'[15] This was an attitude Molony encountered throughout her career.

Her views on labour and property developed from a variety of sources:

[13] *Ibid.,* April 1909.
[14] Fox, *Rebel Irishwomen,* p. 122.
[15] *Bean na hÉireann,* March 1910.

I had been studying Irish land tenure, and had found out that up to the sixteenth century no chief had an absolute right to the land, and he could not surrender it without the consent of his people. The Irish view of property seemed to be right, and it helped form my Labour views. I also found much support in the Christian moral code of justice and righteousness.[16]

Molony contrasted the nostalgic nationalism of the Celtic Revival with the squalid realities of contemporary Irish life. The *Irish Homestead*, the newspaper of the co-operative movement, suggested that Irish women should wear a national costume for its picturesque value. Molony responded that 'all that about pretty barefooted, red petticoated cailíní is most pernicious nonsense.' The 'cailíní' went bare-foot because they could not afford boots, and red petticoats provided little protection from the wind. Young women would continue to leave rural Ireland while it only offered 'squalid poverty and a certain horror commonly called a 'women's sphere' which includes the dullest work and lowest pay.'[17] She argued that, without an equitable economic base, the *Homestead*'s dream of a 'rural civilisation' could not exist. Molony's thought was developing along these lines when she came into contact with James Connolly. Connolly had a huge impact on her both politically and personally. 'At this period I was fumbling at the idea of a junction between labour and nationality – which Connolly worked out clearly. The connection was always there, though at first we did not perceive it. Labour and the nation were really one.'[18] Connolly argued that English colonisation had destroyed the Gaelic communal system and imposed an alien social as well as political system on the Irish people. Consequently, the 'reconquest of Ireland' must be both social and political.

Connolly was living in America where Molony wrote to him in June 1909, encouraging him to return to Ireland where there was 'a very, very great need for a worker's journal' like the one he was publishing in America, *The Harp*.[19] Connolly was impressed both by Molony's letter and by *Bean na hÉireann*. When he returned to Ireland in 1910, the two became friends and colleagues.

Inghinidhe na hÉireann was winding down as members became involved in other activities, and *Bean na hÉireann* ceased publication in March 1911. Immersion in the Inghindhe and the political life of Dublin developed in Molony a self-confidence and style of politics which stayed with her for life. She always saw direct action, if necessary outside existing organisations, as the best means of effecting change. She continued to use the flamboyant and often melodramatic

---

[16] Fox, *Rebel Irishwomen*, p. 123.
[17] *Bean na hÉireann*, February 1910.
[18] Fox, *Rebel Irishwomen*, p. 122.
[19] William O'Brien Papers, Ms 13,940(ii), National Library of Ireland, Dublin. [hereafter, O'Brien Papers].

methods adopted by the Inghinidhe. Her political thought had developed considerably since 1903 beyond a simple nationalism towards a more complex republican ideal. She believed the causes of labour, women and Ireland to be inseparable and this fundamental analysis informed the rest of her life's work.

By now Molony was well known in activist circles and to the police. It was her actions during the visit of the newly-crowned George V to Ireland that catapulted her onto a wider public stage as she became the first female political prisoner of her generation. Bypassing more sedate methods Molony joined in highly visible forms of protest. At a public meeting in March she and James Connolly called on workers to oppose the adoption of a loyal address. During the visit in July 1911 Molony was arrested for throwing stones at a portrait of the king and queen. The sight of them in the window of a chemist's shop on Grafton street looking 'smug and benign . . . was too much for me.'[20] A charge of high treason was dropped and Molony was sentenced to a month in prison, having refused to pay a 40 shilling fine. Much to her annoyance she was released after fourteen days when an anonymous donor paid her fine. The donor turned out to be Anna Parnell who wanted Molony to continue work on *The Tale of a Great Sham*. The manuscript did not make its way into the pages of *Bean na hÉireann* as it had disappeared, apparently seized during a police raid. It was eventually published in 1987 by Arlen House Press.

After her release, a 'monster demonstration' was organised by the Inghinidhe and the Socialist Party of Ireland. On the platform, Molony referred to George V as 'one of the greatest scoundrels in Europe.' The police rushed to re-arrest her, but in the event the case was dropped – the authorities perhaps gauging correctly its explosive potential. Molony returned to the platform and asserted that the 'Irish National cause is not based on the vices or virtues of an English monarch; it is based on Ireland's inherent right to freedom.'[21] The case attracted widespread attention in Ireland and England. Molony was denounced in an open letter in the English paper *John Bull*, and compared to the suffragettes in England – only on a lower level. Even some of her friends thought her conduct 'reprehensible and rowdy.' In one of few glimpses into Molony's private persona, she recalled feeling 'crushed about this' until a telegram arrived from Maud Gonne in Paris which read: 'Splendid. You have kept up the reputation of Ingheana [*sic*] na h-Éireann'. Twenty years later Molony said, 'I cannot describe how elated I felt when I received this.'[22]

Now twenty eight, Molony began her career as a professional actress. Between 1911 and 1922 she earned her living in theatre with considerable success, alternating theatrical engagements with political and union activities. Theatre

---

[20] 'Green Jacket'.
[21] *Irish Worker*, 5 August 1911.
[22] Fox, *Rebel Irishwomen*, p. 124.

was an integral part of the political movements of the time and her taste for drama and early training had come from the Inghinidhe classes. One of her first engagements was with the Independent Theatre Company run by Count Markievicz. She played Mrs Finnegan, a leading character in George Birmingham's *Elinor's Enterprise*. The *Evening Herald* praised both play and actors, noting that 'best of all was the Mrs Finnegan of Helena Molony.'[23] According to Sydney Czira, Molony's improvised dialogue was so good that Count Markievicz asked her to rewrite the entire script. This largely unacknowledged contribution came in for much praise. One critic wrote that the play's 'dialogue is directly fresh and natural. It is its chief feature and . . . charm.'[24]

In January 1912 Molony was acting with the Abbey's second company where her performances impressed W.B.Yeats. Maud Gonne wrote to Yeats: 'I am so glad you think Helena Molony has the makings of an actress . . . she has the great power of throwing herself completely into different parts . . . She is also, which is quite rare in characters of her type, without jealousy and has a great power of working with others.'[25]

In late 1912 James Connolly offered Molony the position of Belfast organiser in the newly-formed Irish Women Workers Union (IWWU). She declined regretfully on the grounds of incompetence and her commitment to a three-month theatrical tour, while also mentioning 'unsettled personal affairs.'[26] Her brother Frank and his wife had recently emigrated to America and she was now ill. Molony was seriously thinking of joining them. She never did and no further references to her brother or sister-in-law survive. The 1913 lock-out provided her with the 'apprenticeship' she felt she needed, and the next time Connolly offered her a position in the IWWU, she accepted.

The lock-out of members of the ITGWU by the Employers' Federation began in early September 1913 but was preceded by months of tension, strikes and minor lock-outs. Larkin's fiery speeches led to his arrest on 28 August. He was out on bail and had called a public meeting for Sunday 31 August. The meeting was banned but Molony and Markievicz helped persuade him to defy the police. Molony made Larkin up as a clergyman using her stage makeup. In this disguise he passed the police cordons into the Imperial Hotel on O'Connell Street where, from a balcony, he addressed the crowds.[27] The police rearrested Larkin and baton charged the crowd in such a ferocious manner that two people died from their wounds and the day became known as 'Bloody Sunday.' Molony

---

[23] *Evening Herald*, December 1911.

[24] Sydney Gifford Czira, *The Years Flew By* (Dublin, 1974), p. 43.

[25] Anna McBride White and A. Norman Jeffares (eds.), *The Gonne-Yeats Letters 1893-1938, Always Your Friend* (London, 1993), p. 308.

[26] Ms 13,939(ii), O'Brien Papers.

[27] 'Helena Molony, Interview with Proinsias MacAonghusa', August 1963. Private collection.

attended the funeral of one of the dead, James Nolan, and was recorded as one of the 'prominent citizens' who followed his coffin.[28]

Molony was acting with the Abbey's second company during the lock-out. Between performances and rehearsals she worked in the food kitchens in Liberty Hall, the headquarters of the ITGWU, and began to address strike meetings. During the run of *The Mineral Workers* by George Boyce Molony would leave after her first scene to speak on Marlborough Street. Her character did not appear again until the last act so she would return just in time to go on stage. The Abbey management were unhappy with these activities and referred to her disparagingly as 'that girl from Liberty Hall'[29] but she resisted attempts to have her replaced by an understudy. After a long winter strikers drifted back to work. Molony recalled that the 'social battle had been fought with blood and tears . . . Houses were bare of furniture. Hunger was rife. . . .'[30]

The frantic pace of activity told on her health and she went to stay with Maud Gonne in Paris to recuperate from a serious breakdown, the full nature of which is not known. A month after her arrival she, Maud and Iseult Gonne went to the Pyrenees to escape the hot Paris summer. There Molony practised her voice projection 'on the edge of a mountain torrent.' She was anxious to get back to Dublin to work and Maud Gonne wrote constantly to Yeats, stressing that Molony's health was better and asking him to take her back at the Abbey. Seemingly Yeats did not respond and they were still in Arrens when the First World War broke out in August 1914. The three women moved to Argèles 'to help nurse the wounded soldiers of whom the numbers are simply appalling. Every hospital is overcrowded and every public building throughout France is turned into a hospital.' In November Molony was still nursing but 'without enthusiasm'[31] – she wanted to get back to Dublin.

Her guiding principle had always been 'England's difficulty – Ireland's opportunity.' Years earlier, when war between Britain and Germany looked likely, she had decried the lack of an Irish army. In 1914 the situation, from her point of view, was more hopeful. Since the formation of the Ulster Volunteers in January 1913, the Irish Volunteers, the Irish Citizen Army and Cumann na mBan had all been formed. Molony's closest association was with the Citizen Army, set up after the events of Bloody Sunday to defend workers against police intimidation. Connolly had taken over the ITGWU and the army when Larkin left for America in October 1914. He saw war as the opportunity for national and social revolution all over Europe and was transforming the Citizen

---

[28] Jacqueline Van Voris, *Constance de Markievicz: in the cause of Ireland* (Cambridge, Massachusettss, 1967), p.108.

[29] Cathal O'Shannon, 'Recorded Voice of Helena Molony', *Evening Press* 3 February, 1967.

[30] Helena Molony, 'Years of tension', typescript, private collection.

[31] McBride and Jeffares, *Gonne-Yeats*, pp. 348-352.

Army into a viable, if small, force. Molony must have been aware of developments and her determination to get home increased. At the end of the year, the manager of the Abbey wrote to Yeats that he would use Molony as much as possible and by early January 1915 she was back in Dublin.

She moved into a flat on Eccles Street and again appeared regularly in Abbey productions. In February she performed in Lennox Robinson's *The Dreamers*. In April she stepped in to play the 'shrewd, strong minded' Mrs Simpson in *The Bargain* by William Crone, two days before it opened. Reviewers remarked that '[t]he best acting . . . came from a wholly unexpected quarter ... Miss Helena Molony . . . [who] only took up the part a day or so before the production . . . [and] succeeded in extracting every ounce of effect out of the part, getting all the lines home with telling effect and humorous acerbity.'[32] She was soon to be caught up in other events.

In July 1915, Delia Larkin, first general secretary of the IWWU resigned and departed for England. The union and a clothing co-operative were left in the hands of James Connolly. The young union had been devastated by the lock-out and over half of its 1,000 members were unemployed. The co-operative, producing clothing and soft goods, had been set up to provide employment. In August Connolly approached Molony, for the second time, to become involved in the union, this time as general secretary and manager of the co-op. He must have seen her as the obvious candidate with her militant nationalism and socialism as well as her experience as an agitator. Although Molony emphasised Connolly's influence on her and her own lack of experience, there is no doubt that he held her in high esteem.

August 1915 saw the beginning of Molony's high-profile trade union career which spanned over a quarter of a century. Immediately she and Connolly set out to recruit new members. 'I had no experience or idea of any kind of organising and it was really [Connolly] who did the work, coming with me to the various factory gates to try and enlist girls into the union.' She began to revive the clothing co-op at IWWU headquarters on Eden Quay and on 15 November she lectured on 'Women's Wages and Trade Unionism' to the Women's Industrial Conference in the Mansion House, arguing that 'co-operation secured to workers the product of their labour and was thoroughly in harmony with the Irish instinct for communal life.'[33]

Over the next eight, turbulent years, Helena Molony juggled an array of cultural, political, trade union and military activities. During her first year with the IWWU her roles as trade unionist and separatist revolutionary merged as she was at the centre of Citizen Army preparations for the 1916 Rising. After 1917 her different activities began to conflict with each other. By 1923 events

---

[32] *The Stage*, April 1915.
[33] *Irish Citizen*, 20 November 1915.

forced her to choose, firstly between political loyalty to the labour movement and the republic and secondly, between her acting career and the IWWU.

In late 1915 and early 1916, Molony and the women of the co-op (all Citizen Army members) were at the centre of preparations for the rising. Molony, known as 'one of the most militant of the insurrectionist section',[34] was one of four leaders of the women's section of the Citizen Army whom she trained in the use of fire arms and first aid. Most militant nationalist women were in Cumann na mBan, founded in 1914 as a fund raising and medical auxiliary to the Irish Volunteers. It had no part in the decision making process of that body. The Irish Women's Franchise League criticised it for accepting a subordinate position. Although Inghinidhe na hÉireann became a branch of Cumann na mBan, Molony and most of its prominent members did not join and were instead members of the Citizen Army, where Molony stressed that they 'were an integral part of the army and not in any sense a "Ladies Auxiliary."'[35] Cumann na mBan was radicalised by the 1916 rising and its aftermath, but getting their male colleagues to accept them as equals proved difficult.

The nationalist movement was split several ways prior to the Rising. The Irish Volunteers had divided into the National Volunteers and the Irish Volunteers. The former followed John Redmond's call to enlist in the British army, while the Irish Volunteers, under Eoin MacNeill, opposed this but were still undecided about an armed uprising. They were however coming increasingly under the control of the IRB. Finally there was the Citizen Army under Connolly who was trying to force the pace of change. When the ITGWU paper, the *Irish Worker*, was suppressed, Connolly established a new paper, the *Worker's Republic*. This was printed from the back room of the co-op and Molony was its registered proprietor, making her personally liable for any treasonable material published – of which there was no shortage. Connolly's editorials were increasingly critical of the caution of MacNeill and his followers. Molony dubbed them the 'Fan go Fóilles' or the 'wait-a-whiles.' Connolly's calls for a rising and the Citizen Army's increased activity were coming to the attention, not only of the authorities but also of the IRB. Worried that Connolly would pre-empt their own plans they abducted him for three days in January of 1916.

Molony and Connolly were both living with Countess Markievicz in Surrey House, and she recalled his disappearance and return after three days of frantic searching. '"Where have you been?" I gasped, "I have been through hell" he said wearily. "Did they kidnap you?" asked Madame. "Yes" replied Connolly, "but I converted my captors".'[36] Connolly was co-opted onto the IRB Supreme Council and Easter Sunday set as the date for an armed rebellion by the Irish Volunteers and the Citizen Army.

---

[34] O'Shannon, 'Recorded voice'.
[35] Helena Molony, 'Years of tension'.
[36] *Ibid.*

Preparations proceeded apace and central to these was the clothing co-op on Eden Quay. Behind the innocuous manufacture of 'men's shirts and children's pinafores' the co-op women churned out ammunition cartridges and belts, uniforms and flags under Molony's management. The machine gun belts 'gave us women headaches because of the extreme accuracy of the measurements.'[37] In March the authorities, increasingly suspicious of their activites, raided the co-op without a warrant. Molony, Jennie Shanahan and Rosie Hackett were serving behind the counter and the police were prevented from entering the back room by Connolly who appeared with a gun. Constance Markievicz arrived and as the four women were also armed, the police did not pursue the matter. After this Molony and Jennie Shanahan took it in turns to sleep in the co-op and there was a constant armed Citizen Army presence outside Liberty Hall. The co-op, attached to Liberty Hall but with its separate entrance, was an ideal meeting place and private post office for conspirators. Parcels of arms and ammunitions were dropped off and collected and Patrick Pearse, Tom Clarke and Sean MacDiarmada were frequent visitors to meet with Connolly.

Due to conflict among the leadership, and confusion between orders and countermanded orders, the rising took place on Easter Monday instead of Sunday and was much smaller than originally planned. On the night of Easter Sunday, Christopher Brady, the printer from Liberty Hall, finished printing 2,500 copies of the 1916 Proclamation. He brought them tied in two parcels to the co-op and Molony slept that night with the Proclamation under her head.[38] The next morning the Citizen Army mobilised outside Liberty Hall where 'we felt in a very real sense that we were walking with Ireland into the sun.'[39] Molony was posted to City Hall under the command of Seán Connolly, her friend and colleague in the Abbey Theatre. The first casualty of the rising was a policeman shot by Seán Connolly and later that afternoon he himself was killed by sniper fire. Molony whispered a prayer over his body as he was tended to by Dr Kathleen Lynn, now in command. The garrison was hopelessly in need of reinforcement and Molony was dispatched to cross the city to the GPO to ask for help. This could not be spared and the sixteen men and nine women in City Hall were forced to surrender just 24 hours after taking up position and were marched to Ship Street Barracks.

By the end of the week all the insurgents had surrendered and were brought to Kilmainham Jail. Molony heard the daily executions of the seven signatories of the Proclamation and others, men she knew well. One of the last was James Connolly. On 12 May he was executed, strapped to a chair, because of injuries received during the week. The death of the man who had so much influenced

---

[37] *Ibid.*
[38] Christopher Brady, 'Portraits of 1916', 1966. RTE Film Archive.
[39] Van Voris, *de Markievicz*, p.199.

her thought and work, utterly devastated Molony and 'after 1916 the colour went out of life for me.'[40] The anniversary of Connolly's execution would always be a special day for her and she believed that commemoration of his spirit and work could provide impetus for future change. For her, 1916 was the highpoint of the republican struggle – a time of untainted idealism but also of real possibility. Thereafter she would point to the 1916 Proclamation as the basis and inspiration for change in Ireland, encompassing as it did economic redistribution and sexual equality under the banner of Irish nationalism.

From Kilmainham, Molony was brought to England and interned, first in Lewes prison and then in Aylesbury prison with Markievicz and Winifred Carney (Connolly's secretary and friend). She was listed as an 'extremist of some importance.'[41] While Maud Gonne was writing from France to Yeats asking him to procure legal aid for Molony, the only appeals that she and Carney would accept on their behalf were those of the trade union movement. She would soon be disappointed at the manner in which Connolly and Larkin's successors negotiated the turbulent times ahead.

In Aylesbury, Molony kept in contact with the acting world and thought about 'a temptation I have long resisted, in public anyway'[42] – that of writing a play, an ambition she does not appear to have fulfilled. She worried about the IWWU, left without herself and Connolly. In a move that marked the beginning of a productive but fraught working relationship, she asked Louie Bennett to help reorganise the union. Bennett was an active suffragist and, as with others, involvement in relief work during the lock-out developed her already existing interest in the conditions of women workers. Beyond a shared concern for women workers, the two had little in common politically. Bennett, a pacifist, disliked Connolly and believed that the union should not be involved in politics.

Molony was released from Aylesbury two days before Christmas 1916 in a general release of internees. She moved into a bedsit on Leeson Street and renewed her activity on all fronts. Her time in Aylesbury actually renewed her energies, and she confided to Máire Comerford that she had had '. . . so many insults about stabbing [the British] in the back that she came back determined to do it all again!'[43] By February she was appearing in the first Irish production of Anton Chekov's *Uncle Vanya*, was re-elected general secretary of the IWWU and was involved in the growing separatist movement.

In May Molony and a small group of IWWU/Citizen Army women ensured that the first anniversary of the Rising and the executions was remembered by

[40] Fox, *Rebel Irishwomen*, p.131.
[41] Dublin Metropolitan Police Chief Commissioner to Chief Secretary, 8 December 1916, Ms 16,627/18, CSO RP, National Archives, Dublin.
[42] Helena Molony correspondence, August 1916. Earnán de Blaghd Papers, Ms 20,702, National Library of Ireland.
[43] Máire Comerford Interview, Fawcett Library, London.

Dublin's citizens. They pasted copies of the Proclamation all over the city and with the help of a sympathetic steeplejack placed a tricolour on the roof of the ruined GPO. Against the wishes of the ITGWU executive (about whose caution Molony was scathing) she and Rosie Hackett hung a banner from Liberty Hall with the inscription 'James Connolly – Murdered 12 May.' Their emphasis was on raising public conciousness through propaganda, regardless of the dangers involved. The jeers that greeted the 1916 insurgents immediately after the Rising had been replaced by acclaim, even by the time Molony was released. This turnaround was largely a result of the executions and the part played in the subsequent propaganda campaign by the women of the movement, who, as Cathal Brugha acknowledged, 'kept the spirit alive . . . and the flag flying.'[44] Shortly before her death, Molony was asked about the role women played, and retorted 'You might as well ask me what tall red-haired men did or short fair-haired men! We just did what came to our hands from day to day.'[45] She knew that, in reality, the situation was not so straighfoward and constantly defended the right of women to participate fully, whether in politics or the workforce.

In May 1917, a newly reconstituted Sinn Féin party was established as an umbrella organisation for separatist-nationalists and republicans. No women were on the executive so Molony and others, including Jennie Wyse Power and Hanna Sheehy Skeffington, formed a coordinating body of all women delegates to nationalist conferences, Cumann na dTeachtaire. In June the executive was expanded to include returned prisoners but still no women. Cumann na dTeachtaire protested and four women, including Molony, were co-opted. She remained on the executive until the November conference but did not seek re-election.

When the first post-war election was held in December 1918, Sinn Féin were able to run strong candidates in most constituencies. This was the first United Kingdom election in which women (over the age of thirty) were eligible to vote and stand for parliament. Molony canvassed extensively in St Patrick's Ward in Dublin for Markievicz, who became the first woman elected to Westminster. She never took her seat as Sinn Féin abstained and established the first Dáil Éireann. On the day of its first sitting in January 1919, the first shots were fired in the War of Independence which continued until June 1921.

Molony was one of a group of women available for 'special service' to the Citizen Army between 1916 and 1923.[46] However, the Army was torn by splits and never achieved the prominence it had in 1916. Her duties were mainly as a courier for IRA leaders in Dublin where she worked closely with Liam Mellows and Michael Collins. She spent much time on the run, living on and off in

---

[44] Ward, *Unmanageable Revolutionaries*, p. 123.
[45] 'Women of the Rising', 1963, RTE Sound Archive, Dublin.
[46] Document signed P. Ní Dhroinn, Old ICA, 1937, private collection.

Maud Gonne's home on St Stephens Green. Her military activity was carried on alongside union duties and acting engagements. During this period she met Francis Stuart and played a role in the developing relationship between Stuart and Maud Gonne's daughter, Iseult. Stuart recalled Molony with affection. He was struck by an 'ageless' quality about her and her emotional generosity. He was also impressed by her ability to hold her own with Maud Gonne, whose forceful personality often swamped those around her. His lasting impression was that Molony was 'a practical not a theoretical politician.'[47]

Molony could no longer conduct her trade unionism and republicanism simultaneously under the same roof, and her acting and military activity impinged on her duties as general secretary of the IWWU. The union was establishing itself and needed full-time administration. Molony was not primarily an administrator; she viewed the amelioration of horrendous working conditions as a necessity but one which must be connected to more fundamental political and social change. Her commitment to the latter made exclusive concentration on the day-to-day running of the union impossible. Louie Bennett and Helen Chenevix (who had also come to the IWWU *via* suffrage) stepped into this role, and Bennett took over as general secretary. Molony does not appear to have resented her demotion. She was not personally ambitious and being relieved of overall responsibility for the union freed her for other activities and let her concentrate on the most vulnerable sections of women workers.

So, by 1918 Molony had 'retreated' to organise domestic workers,[48] a notoriously difficult task. To attract potential members she rented the Sinn Féin Hall every Sunday and invited prominent speakers such as Hanna Sheehy Skeffington. With Theresa Behan, an official of the laundresses' section of the union, she also spent long days on door-to-door recruitment in the wealthy southside suburbs.

As an IWWU delegate Molony came to prominence in another forum – the Irish Labour Party and Trades Union Congress (ILPTUC). She was one of the most prolific speakers during the twenty years that she attended Congress. She was frustrated by Congress' inaction during the War of Independence. This was particularly evident at her third Congress in 1921 at a time when independent rank and file action was at its height. The upsurge in agrarian and industrial radicalism embarrassed the leadership under Tom Johnson, despite the professed socialist aims of the ILPTUC. Molony accused them of making 'mere pious expressions of opinion.' She and the other IWWU delegates were the only ones to put forward motions calling for practical support for ventures like the seizures by workers of the Knocklong Dairies and the Arigna mines and their (shortlived) attempts to establish soviets, as well as for the rebuilding of the

---

[47] Interview with author.
[48] Mary Jones, *These Obstreperous Lassies: a History of the Irish Women Workers Union* (Dublin, 1988), p. 29.

country. She also defended the existence of a women's union, arguing that segregation was not ideal but necessary while women were 'submerged and inarticulate.'[49]

The signing of the Anglo-Irish Treaty in December 1921 split the country and Molony was a courier for the anti-Treaty side throughout the civil war. She saw the Treaty as a betrayal of the republican ideal and was at the centre of bitter debates in Congress as to whether or not labour should contest the June 1922 election. Molony was elected to the executive in 1921 and was part of the decision-making process over the next crucial year. The executive's recommendation would be critical and, feeling that neither pro nor anti-Treaty Sinn Féin represented Labour's aspirations, they recommended participation, with Molony the only opposing voice. At the Special Congress in February she argued passionately that Labour should again stand aside to let the election be fought on the issue of the Treaty. Her motion was lost by 115 votes to 82. Molony believed that Labour's subsequent entrance into the Free State Dáil was effective support of the Treaty and a betrayal of Connolly's republic. This debate continued into the late 1920s, and it was a measure of Molony's ability to work with others that '. . . she bore no ill will to us in all our differences, nor did we to her.'[50]

Molony's objective was a workers' republic organised around a co–operative commonwealth. While recognising that this was not necessarily the kind of republic envisaged by the IRA and Sinn Féin, she and other left-wing republicans saw them as the only radical alternative to the new Cumann na nGaedheal government. This implied support for Sinn Féin and the IRA politically and militarily, until such time as a full republic was established. For the rest of the 1920s, Molony's republican and trade union activities became increasingly compartmentalised.

Molony had been on the Abbey stage two weeks before the ILPTUC Special Congress, playing the lead in a new play by Lennox Robinson, *The Round Table*. Throughout the War of Independence and civil war, she kept up her acting career, but this caused problems within the IWWU. In late 1921 and into 1922 she was appearing in up to three productions a month and increasingly in leading roles. Molony's comic ability and unusual adaptability was frequently remarked on by critics. On her death her obituary notices commented that had she remained in theatre she would have become 'one of the greats.'[51] Even Molony with her seemingly inexhaustible energy could not combine a successful acting career with a full-time position in the IWWU. It seems that her decision to leave the theatre came under pressure from Louie Bennett and Molony

---

[49] ILPTUC, *Annual Report*, 1922, pp. 118, 192.
[50] O'Shannon, 'Recorded voice'.
[51] *Irish Times*, 30 January 1967.

elected to stay with the IWWU.[52] Her last acting role was also her finest. In November 1922 she took the lead role in the first production of Lennox Robinson's *Crabbed Youth and Old Age*. 'Mrs Swan' was a 'delightfully loquacious and brilliant woman – who keeps attracting the suitors of her dull daughters.'[53] Three years after retirement Molony was still in demand; Sean O'Casey, casting the part of Mrs Gogan in his new play, *The Plough and the Stars*, wrote that he 'would of course like Helena Molony but I suppose this is out of the question.'[54] It is impossible to know what leaving the theatre cost her. Letters written after her retirement show that she retained an active interest in the world of theatre and a fondness for the Abbey.

By 1923 Helena Molony's life was very different. The end of her acting career left her without a creative outlet although this facet of her personality surfaced constantly on public platforms and in her approach to solving problems. The republicans had lost the civil war and she was politically at odds with the direction of the labour movement. She was back in the position of dissident, but this time against an Irish administration. The next few years were unsettled. She moved house several times and seems to have been drinking quite heavily. She was not as busy as in previous decades and was in transition politically.

She was now living with Dr. Kathleen Lynn and Madeleine ffrench-Mullen in Rathmines and earned her living as a full-time official with the IWWU. She caught the No. 25 tram every morning to Eden Quay and often in the evening and weekends on union business or to address meetings of the Women's Prisoners' Defence League and Sinn Féin.

Within the IWWU Louie Bennett was fully established as general secretary and Molony's exact position and duties are hard to identify. What emerges clearly from the executive minutes is Molony's consistent contribution in identifying problems and indicating solutions. Finian Czira recalled that her negotiation skills were renowned as she solved seemingly intractable disputes rapidly.[55] Her commitment was to the most vulnerable sections of women workers; home workers, those affected by increasing mechanisation and the rising numbers of unemployed. There were occasional tensions and differences of opinion between Bennett and herself, for now confined to organisational matters.

Throughout the 1920s increased mechanisation affected the women Molony represented. In July 1924 she reported that, in the printing trade, machinery was displacing workers and employers were imposing wage reductions. Since the union had accepted a reduction the previous year, an increase was sought and strike notice served. Laundry workers faced similar problems. At the 1926

---

[52] Finian Czira, interview with author.
[53] *The Stage*, November 1922.
[54] David Krause (ed.), *The Letters of Sean O' Casey*, vol. 1, (London, 1975), p. 143.
[55] Czira, interview.

IWWU Annual Convention Molony warned that a 'grave crisis' was imminent. Employers were using juvenile workers on new pressing machines, leaving experienced women unemployed. She accused employers of 'dehumanising human life.' In areas where women had exercised skill they were now just 'machine attendants.' Another problem was the 'Magdalen' laundries, established by charitable and penal institutions, which used inmates as unpaid labour. Even the government was contracting work to them and in 'the sacred name of charity, wage earning women were being deprived of their employment.'[56]

In the mid 1920s Molony and the IWWU instigated a campaign to bring public pressure on the government to respond to the growing unemployment crisis. In November 1925 she and Miss O'Connor organised a poster parade outside the Dáil which attracted 'great interest.' The IWWU were deeply critical of their trade union colleagues and resigned from the Dublin Workers Council because of their failure to 'carry out any strong agitation on behalf of the unemployed.'[57] However, their resignation was also a prelude to attempts to reunite the Dublin Workers Council and the Dublin Trades Council. Molony was a member of the Unity Committee drawn from non-aligned unions which successfully achieved this in 1928. She was elected to the executive of the new Dublin Trades Union Council (DTUC) and remained a leading member until 1939.

Molony's other major concern within the IWWU was the organisation of workers. She continually urged a more active approach and was appointed organising secretary in 1929, a position she held until her retirement in 1940. She proposed targeting particular industries in turn to recruit all workers in them – shirt-making and textiles were to be prioritised. She also highlighted a problem particularly affecting the printing trade. Non-union shops outside Dublin were undermining advances made by organised labour inside the capital. A strenuous effort, she believed, should be made to organise outside Dublin and over the next few years she travelled to different towns recruiting for the IWWU. Apart from the usual factory gate recruitment, she proposed public meetings, the use of cinema for propaganda and a weekly manuscript journal.[58]

With like-minded colleagues she was 'concerned with women, not merely as wage earners but primarily as human beings.'[59] The IWWU were particularly concerned with housing initiatives and adult education, and had an active social and civic committee. Molony was an Urban District Councillor in Rathmines and Rathgar and was involved in trying to set up affordable housing schemes.

---

[56] ILPTU, *Annual Report*, 1929, p. 114.
[57] Jones, *Obstreperous Lassies*, pp 68-9.
[58] IWWU Archive, Irish Labour History Society Museum and Archive, Dublin. [Hereafter, ILHS].
[59] Helena Molony, Evidence to the Commission on Vocational Organisation, 19 April 1940, Ms 925, National Library of Ireland.

She was assistant librarian for the IWWU and complained that members were only borrowing fiction; she suggested public lectures and readings and inaugurated a study circle and summer school. She remained, however, aware of the need for more radical and far reaching action, saying that 'individual local activities are not satisfactory . . . the position in Dublin is disgraceful.'[60] She was a trade union representative on the Vocational Education Committee and Technical Education Association in the 1930s.

Outside of the union Molony continued to pursue her republican activities. During the 1920s and 1930s she spoke regularly at the weekly meetings of the Women's Prisoners' Defence League (WPDL). 'The Mothers' had been established during the civil war by Maud Gonne, Charlotte Despard and Molony herself to care for imprisoned republicans and their families and to agitate for the anti-treaty cause. They held meetings on O'Connell St on Sundays after 11 o'clock mass, and usually addressed crowds of between two and four hundred from the back of a horse-drawn platform. The authorities kept a close eye on the meetings but, until 1930, saw them as a nuisance rather than a serious threat. Molony used this platform to attack the new Free State administration.

She was now one of the major figures trying to push the republican movement leftwards. While many of her colleagues, including Markievicz, went with Éamon de Valera into the new political party, Fianna Fáil, Molony urged a socialist analysis:

> The new menace to us small nations is not big armies or big navies but Big Business – except it is controlled in the interest of the nation. We can no longer look out on the world even as we could in 1915. We who have been through a welter of military war have (necessarily) lost sight of certain economic developments. . . .[61]

During the 1930s Molony became a leading figure in the trade union and left-republican movements. She never overtly identified herself as a communist though she was often accused of being one by opponents, especially in the IWWU. In 1929 she visited Russia as part of a Dublin Trades Union Council delegation. They travelled with French and British delegates as guests of the Soviet trade union movement to mark the twelfth anniversary of the revolution. Molony, Robert Tynan and P.T. Daly wrote an enthusiastic but not uncritical report. 'Russia is not a paradise and we do not want to create the impression it is. The delegation submits to the Irish Labour movement that it should support the Russian workers in their struggle for human progress which is essentially the same in all lands. . . . Women are taking their full part in all this work and occupy many responsible positions. Russians do not consider whether it is a

---

[60] ILPTUC, *Annual Report*, 1929, p. 81.
[61] *Irish Freedom*, January 1927.

man or a woman, they are only concerned with getting the best person for the job.'[62] Soon after her return, Molony helped establish a new organisation, The Friends of Soviet Russia, and lectured extensively on the Soviet Union.

This new direction brought her into conflict with colleagues. The trade union movement reflected the hysteria surrounding radical organisations current in the Free State. The report of the Russian delegation ignited a row in the IWWU which quickly centred on Molony's 'public connection with communists.' Molony proposed that the IWWU take one hundred copies of the report on a sale or return basis. The executive refused and Molony, furious, said 'she thought it disgraceful that the IWWU should refuse to take cognisance of the report of their own fellow workers in preference to the reports of the capitalist press.'[63] At the IWWU annual convention in May a motion tabled by Louie Bennett regretting that 'certain principles of religion and liberty . . . aren't upheld by Soviet Russia' was carried by 40 voters to 15. [64] This brought to a head the always fraught and complicated relationship between Bennett and Molony. Bennett suggested that the executive take over the role of organisation, a move successfully resisted by Molony. Two weeks later Bennett told the executive that she intended to resign, citing 'health reasons and . . . friction with staff.'[65] Molony and others persuaded her to stay for another six months and eventually Bennett agreed to remain as general secretary but Molony's non-union activities soon became an issue again.

Molony was one of a small group who appeared regularly in government intelligence reports which examined the links between international communism and Irish organisations. She was named as a committee member of the Friends of Soviet Russia, the WPDL and 'an active sympathiser with the irregular organisation', [66] while a report on the DTUC delegation to Russia described Molony as 'that shrewdest of Socialist propagandists', and noted her association with the IRA.[67] The seeming alliance between the IRA and the left concerned the government most and Molony was to the fore in furthering this. She was on the executive of Saor Éire, founded in September 1931, whose aims included the nationalisation of industry and banking and the abolition of landlordism. Again, Louie Bennett was alarmed and insisted that Molony must resign either as IWWU representative to outside bodies or as executive member of Saor

---

[62] Séamus Cody, John O'Dowd and Peter Rigney, *The Parliament of Labour: 100 Years of the Dublin Council of Trades Unions* (Dublin, 1986), p.160.

[63] Jones, *Obstreperous Lassies*, pp 97-8.

[64] IWWU, *Annual Report*, 1930, pp. 14-15.

[65] IWWU Executive Minutes, September 1930, ILHS.

[66] 'Memorandum on revolutionary organisations', 5 April 1930, Department of Justice, p 24/169, Ernest Blythe Papers, UCD Archive, Dublin.

[67] James Hogan, *Could Ireland Become Communist? The Facts in Full* (Dublin, 1935), p. 111.

Éire. Molony resigned from the executive of Saor Éire but declared she would remain a member.

The strength of these radical groups was greatly exaggerated, both by themselves and the government; they were largely a leadership without a movement. Under a combined church-state offensive Saor Éire disintegrated. On 23 October, twelve different organisations were banned, and most of their members arrested or driven underground. Molony was a member of at least three – the Friends of Soviet Russia, Saor Éire and the WPDL. Only the WPDL openly defied the ban. On the following Sunday crowds assembled on O'Connell Street in anticipation and a lorry drew up with a banner saying 'The People's Rights Association', leaving the police unable to act. To make their identity clear, Molony opened the proceedings by declaring that 'a rose by any other name would smell as sweet!'[68] The Minister for Justice declared that 'we are going to put people like these in prison, and if they persist and if it is necessary we are going to execute them.'[69] However, four months later Fianna Fáil entered government, the ban was suspended and political prisoners released. Immediately Molony, Charlotte Despard, Hanna Sheehy Skeffington with Bob Stewart, Peader O'Donnell and Sean Murray set about reviving the Revolutionary Worker's Groups which led to the founding of the Workers College in Eccles street.

More controversy followed in July 1932 when Molony addressed a WPDL meeting and cautioned against papal intervention in political matters. Her remarks were misquoted in the *Irish Independent* under the banner 'Attack on the Pope.' 'Miss Molony and the Pope' correspondence dominated the letters page for two weeks and revealed the militant Catholic and anti-communist mood in the aftermath of the Eucharistic Congress. The IWWU executive hastily and publicly disassociated itself from her views. She defended her original comments but added that many trade union colleagues were 'in strong disagreement'[70] with her. Molony deplored the fears these controversies aroused. At Congress in 1933 a Scottish delegate declared himself a communist and a trade unionist. Molony's vote of thanks noted that in Ireland they sometimes 'hesitated to nail their flags to the mast. Mr Stevenson's address encouraged them to do so without being afraid of being dubbed with this or that "ism". They could all engage in a common struggle against that common enemy – the capitalist class.'[71] Though she spoke on various anti-fascist platforms, Molony was less involved in the next left-republican movement, the Republican Congress, and directed her energies into the trade union movement.

Here she rose to her greatest prominence during the 1930s. Given

---

[68] Ward, *Unmanageable Revolutionaries*, p. 216.
[69] *Republican File*, 13 February 1931.
[70] *Irish Independent*, July 1932.
[71] ITUC, *Annual Report*, 1933, pp. 131-2.

disagreements over republicanism and socialism as well as women workers, this was a tribute to her effectiveness as a trade unionist and her ability to work with those from whom she differed. It was also a reflection of her personal popularity among her colleagues. Molony was a leading DTUC executive member until 1939. At the time the trades council had many of the functions of the present Irish Congress of Trade Unions. It was the primary arbitration forum for inter-union disputes as well as union-employer disputes. Molony was on various DTUC delegations meeting with national and local government officials on matters ranging from housing to protected industries. She was also their delegate to many outside bodies.

In 1930 the ILPTUC had separated into two distinct organisations, the Labour Party and the Irish Trades Union Congress (ITUC). Molony was the DTUC delegate to ITUC. In 1933 she was elected to its national executive and appointed to the permanent Joint Committee, established to look at matters of joint interest. During Molony's first term they examined the Workman's Compensation Bill and the proposed shops legislation. They proposed extensive amendments and met regularly with the Minister for Industry and Commerce, Seán Lemass, and his officials. Molony was also on the subcommittee that examined the banking, currency and credit system of the Free State and advocated nationalisation. In 1935 she was elected vice-president of Congress and president in 1936. She was only the second woman to be elected president of the ITUC, the first being Louie Bennett in 1932. As president she represented Ireland at the 1937 International Labour Conference in Geneva.

Her personal life remained unsettled. She moved from Dr. Lynn's to Frankfort House, a lodging house run by a family with republican sympathies where Constance Markievicz had also lived. The death of Markievicz in 1927 hit her hard and she continued to disappear periodically on drinking bouts. These may explain her frequent absences from IWWU, DTUC and Congress meetings, absences noted in minutes as 'due to ill health.' A photograph taken at this time shows a haggard-looking woman with hair cropped short, looking older then her years. In 1934 she was allocated a council house in Kimmage, and for the first time had a place of her own where she lived for several years. She continued to go on holidays with the Cziras, as well as visiting the Gonne MacBrides and the Stuarts and could be convivial company. Molony had remained single all these years. There were rumours of love affairs before 1916, but nothing substantial. During the 1930s she began a close and happy relationship with Dr. Evelyn O'Brien, a pyschiatrist in St Brendan's Hospital in Grangegorman. Molony moved into Dr. O'Brien's house on the North Circular Road and lived there until a year before her death when the two women moved to Sutton.

Two major issues faced Molony during her terms on the executive of Congress. The first was the position of women workers. In the 1930s the right of women to employment was facing challenge from both government and male trade unionists. Legislation and attitudes were increasingly restricting women's role in Irish society. In 1930 Molony reflected on

> the sorry travesty [of women's] emancipation. . . . Women, since [Connolly's]
> day have got that once-coveted right to vote, but they still have their inferior
> status, their lower pay for equal work, their exclusion from juries and certain
> branches of the civil service, their slum dwellings, and crowded and unsanitary
> schools for their children, as well as the lowered standard of life for workers
> which in their capacity as homemaker, hits the woman full force.[72]

Molony and others found themselves in a difficult and often contradictory position when defending the right of women to work. 'Work' was usually badly paid and unskilled. Increasingly a part of their argument was that women *would* be better off if it was economically viable for them to concentrate on duties in the home. This did not mean exclusion from civic and political society since the role of homemaker and primary carer of children was a vital contribution. Molony seemed to put increased emphasis on this by 1934 when she wrote that 'Educating for Industry', as demanded by industrialists, left women in a vulnerable position and as 'so much raw material in the manufacturing process.' With the exception of printing and stationery and laundry work, the skilled trades were closed to women. Increased mechanisation would bring ever shorter working days and the 'imperative need for women is to educate them for life and the proper use of leisure, cultural activities. Vocational instruction that will equip her for her special and permanent vocation as homemaker.'[73] Underlying this was the possibility that women might actually be banned from waged labour altogether.

In 1935 Seán Lemass, Minister for Industry and Commerce, published a Conditions of Employment Bill. Section 12 authorised the minister to bar women from industry in cases he saw fit. The IWWU launched a public campaign opposing it. Molony, the only woman and IWWU representative on the Congress executive, fought to persuade her male colleagues to support this opposition. However, male trade unionists tended to see the prohibition of women from industry as the solution to the problem of women's low wages, rather than pressing for equal pay. It had been a problem for the IWWU since their foundation in 1911 and was increasingly voiced in times of high unemployment.

This put the IWWU on the defensive. Molony raised Section 12 again at a meeting of the Joint Committee in Leinster House, convened to determine how the Labour Party would vote on the bill in the Dáil, asserting that it was an

---

[72] Helena Molony, 'James Connolly & women', *Dublin Labour Year Book* (Dublin, 1930), p. 31.

[73] Helena Molony, 'Technical education and women', *Report of the Irish Technical Education Association* (Dublin, 1934), pp. 34-40.

'antiprogressive and antisocial limitation of [women's] rights as citizens to earn their living as such.' William O'Brien supported the section saying that women were pushing men into unemployment. No compromise was reached and at the next executive meeting, in Molony's absence, it was agreed that some form of protection was necessary as 'the incursion of women was a serious social problem.'[74]

In August, at the annual Trade Union Congress, the IWWU tabled a resolution on equal pay and opportunity. The previous year a similar resolution passed unanimously without debate. Now William Norton, leader of the Labour Party, attacked Molony saying that 'the subtle ingenious resolution they were discussing . . . asked Congress to accept certain principles which they could accept in the abstract – if passed, they would be told it implied Congress was committed to opposing Section 12. . .' He challenged Molony as to whether she claimed that women had the right to be carpenters and blacksmiths, and she answered in the affirmative. In the event the result was inconclusive, Congress voting for the IWWU resolution but also for Section 12 – thus making both votes meaningless. Molony was elected vice-president at that same congress and dryly remarked on the chivalry of Irish trade unionists, who would make women 'queens of their hearts and homes . . . but would give them no jobs.'[75]

In September, an IWWU delegation met de Valera. Though 'he listened attentively he could not see that men and women could be equal'.[76] They brought the issue to the League of Nations and the International Labour Organisation in Geneva who blacklisted the Free State. In the Senate Jennie Wyse Power and Kathleen Clarke led an attack against the Bill but Labour deputies swung the vote and it passed. The public campaign continued with protests outside the Fianna Fáil Árd Fheis during which the police intervened. In November, a mass meeting was held and speakers included Molony, Hanna Sheehy Skeffington and Mary Hayden. But by now it was clear that Molony and the IWWU would have to accept defeat on the issue.

Molony turned to older methods of agitation and, with Maud Gonne, Sydney Czira and four other women, established Mná na hÉireann – a successor to the Inghinidhe. Its aims were to 'advance the national cause and to ensure that women will take their place in the political, social and economic life of the country.'[77] They deplored the facts that equal rights and opportunities had been restricted by successive governments since 1922 and based their claims on the basis of women's participation in the national struggle and the 1916 Proclamation. Letters and short articles appeared in the national press but the

---

74 ITUC and LP Joint Committee minutes, 5 June 1935, Irish Congress of Trade Unions Archives, Dublin.
75 ITUC, *Annual Report*, 1935, pp. 146-7.
76 IWWU Executive Minutes, 5 September 1935, ILHS.
77 Mná na hÉireann material, private collection.

organisation never got off the ground. There is no record that Molony was involved in protests against anti-women articles of the 1937 constitution.

The second major issue Molony faced during her term as vice-president and president of Congress, was the serious internal rifts in the trades union movement. The disputes and rivalry between the ITGWU, now led by William O'Brien, and the Workers Union of Ireland under James Larkin had split and weakened the whole movement. In addition conflict between Irish-based unions and those with headquarters in England (the amalgamated unions) resulted in an increasing number of break-away Irish unions and clashes between the ITGWU and the Amalgamated Transport and General Workers Union. Early on Molony argued that 'national self-consciousness was growing and finding expression in the desire of workers to belong to a Trade Union in Ireland rather than across the water.'[78] She supported a solution that proposed the reconstruction of the trade union movement along industrial lines into ten main unions. This would involve the departure of the amalgamated unions and so had a national as well as a purely organisational dimension. Molony was appointed to a Commission of Enquiry set up to examine these issues and try to resolve the disputes. The commission sat for three years but in effect worked on William O'Brien's proposals for ten industry-based unions.

Organisation by industry did not allow for a separate women's union. Molony and the IWWU agreed with the industrial principle but not with merging into the general worker's category. They had no confidence that the interests of women workers would be protected. The annual convention in 1937 passed a resolution opposing 'any suggestion that the IWWU should be merged into the other unions.' Molony was directed not to sign any proposal which included such a merger. In the event she did sign O'Brien's proposal, adding a lengthy reservation stating that organising along sex lines was a 'temporary necessity owing to the fact that women are a separate economic class.'[79]

The commission's conclusions were not unanimous and three memorandums were submitted to the special convention in February 1939. The chaotic meeting that ensued was the last Molony attended. She spoke in favour of O'Brien's proposal, as a member of the commission rather than the IWWU, but it was defeated. In anticipation of this, a council of 'Irish trade unions in affiliation to the ITUC' had been formed just before the meeting and Molony was on the first committee. IWWU policy changed after Molony ceased being an executive member of Congress and in August 1939 IWWU delegates voted against O'Brien's proposal and withdrew from the new council.

Although Molony was only in her early fifties, her health was deteriorating. Bronchitis prevented her from delivering her presidential address to Congress

---

[78] ITUC, *Annual Report*, 1934, pp. 125-6.
[79] ITUC, *Special Proceedings and Report of the Committee on Reorganisation*, 1939, p. 13.

in 1937, and over the next four years she gradually withdrew from active trade unionism. In 1939 she attempted to resign from the DTUC but was persuaded to stay on until the next election. Her last term on the executive of Congress was 1938/39 and she was no longer a delegate after this date.

Molony's departure from the IWWU was controversial and, though the state of her health was central, her non-union activities also contributed. Her IRA involvement at the outbreak of World War II posed problems. In 1940 she was a member of the IRA's Deportees Committee and in 1941 helped draft a social and economic policy for the IRA. Most seriously, Molony took part in hiding the German spy Herman Goertz who arrived in Ireland in May 1940. Goertz initially made contact with Iseult Stuart and, following several abortive attempts to escape, Molony helped him to get to a safe house in Dublin.[80] The IWWU gave her three months leave of absence in September 1940.[81] Angry letters were being exchanged and in April 1941 Bennett reported that police officers had questioned her about Molony's movements. Molony took sick leave again in July 1941 and never returned. In October 1941 the executive accepted her resignation on health grounds and conveyed their regret and best wishes for a speedy recovery.

She did not qualify for a full IWWU pension. The union had recently decided that only officials over the age of sixty-five, who had served for twenty-five years, qualified. Molony was fifty-eight and received a disability allowance of £6 per month. Throughout her retirement Molony was forced into the 'invidious position' of having to request increases to meet rising living costs.[82] Jenny Murray, who joined the union shortly after, recalled that Molony was never mentioned in the IWWU throughout the 1940s and early 1950s.[83] It was not until after the retirement of Louie Bennett, some 15 years later, that she was, in a sense, rehabilitated into the union.

Molony shared the next twenty-six years with Dr Evelyn O'Brien and now had time for other pursuits, including writing, beekeeping and cheesemaking.[84] She kept up contact with a small circle of friends – mostly from Inghinidhe days. She went on holidays with Maud Gonne, Iseult Stuart and the Cziras, and visited the Stuarts in Laragh where the children found her a 'sweet generous funny person' whom they called 'Auntie Chick'.[85]

Throughout the 1950s Molony wrote a series of articles on the events leading up to 1916 and the two people who had such an influence on her life and thought, James Connolly and Maud Gonne. She was particularly critical of the

---

[80] Emo Stephan, *Spies In Ireland* (London, 1963), p. 130.
[81] IWWU Executive Minutes, February 1941, ILHS.
[82] Jones, *Obstreperous Lassies*, p. 204.
[83] Jenny Murray, interview with author.
[84] Czira, interview.
[85] Imogen Stuart, interview with author.

lack of revolutionary spirit in the current labour movement and urged that Connolly's thought and work be their inspiration again. She said little about her career after 1916, saying that she liked 'to avoid lime-light . . . since I have joined the queue waiting for the Styx ferry.'[86] She kept in touch with the arts world in Dublin and in particular the Abbey Theatre. In 1951 she suggested ways of fundraising for a new theatre after the original building was destroyed by fire and floated the idea of a national concert hall.

Increasingly she emphasised the spiritual aspects of struggle for a more just society. In the late 1950s she wrote to Louie Bennett suggesting that veterans of Irish political life, particularly women, take the lead in reinstating spiritual values. For the IWWU their patron St. Brigid could be the symbol of this regeneration. She was invited to the 1960 annual convention and made a life member of the union. Over the next two years at least she continued to urge the idea on the IWWU executive, but with little result.[87]

In 1966 Molony's partner, Dr. Evelyn O'Brien, retired and they moved to Sutton. This year was also the fiftieth anniversary of the 1916 Rising. Molony attended several major functions in her wheelchair and was interviewed extensively for radio, newspapers and books on her role in the 1913 lock-out and the 1916 Rising. Six months later Helena Molony died on 29 January 1967.

Her death was front page news and the list of mourners at her funeral was a who's who of republicans, trade unionists and government, which included President Éamon de Valera and leading representatives of the Minister for Defence and Eastern Command, the ICTU, ITGWU, Labour Party, Abbey Theatre, IRA, Irish Citizen Army and the IWWU. A bugler played the Last Post, while 'a cluster of Helena's nearest friends wept quietly.'[88]

Viewed as a whole, Helena Molony's lifetime achievements are considerable and she contributed much to the political and social life of the country. She consistently refused to accept prevailing orthodoxies whether these concerned the relationship between Ireland and England, the position of women or the class system. Molony, and the small groups of women with whom she worked throughout her life, took up isolated and often unpopular public positions. The very fact of their visibility challenged the orthodoxies of the period and, at the very least, kept alive a vision of an equitable, independent Ireland.

---

[86] Helena Molony correspondence, Cathal O'Shannon collection, ILHS.
[87] Helena Molony correspondence, IWWU archive, ILHS.
[88] *Irish Times*, February 1967.

ACKNOWLEDGMENTS

I am indebted to the few remaining friends and acquaintances of Helena Molony who spoke so warmly about her; Louie O'Brien, Jenny Murray, Imogen Stuart, Anna McBride White, Nora Harkin, Paddy Byrne, John de Courcy Ireland, Niall Murphy, and the late Finian Czira, Francis Stuart and Séamus Scully. Thanks also to Mary Jones, Penny Duggan, Rosemary Cullen Owens, Margaret Ward, Proinsias MacAonghusa and Paidrigín Ní Mhurchú for generous access to primary sources and unpublished research. Special thanks are due to Theresa Moriarty for her generous and insightful help and to Mary Cullen and Maria Luddy for their patience and encouragement.

Rosamond Jacob (1888-1960)

Damian Doyle

All my life I have had a 'complex' against self-constituted authority or assumptions of superior dignity. I hate it in the male sex, in Churches, in humanity as opposed to animals, in aristocracy, in empires, in white people, in everything relating to social ideas of class.

Rosamond Jacob[1]

Rosamond Jacob, known to her friends and family as Rose, was born in Waterford on October 13, 1888, the third child of Henrietta and Louis Jacob. Her sister, Betty, died at age five and Rose and her brother, Tom, born in 1885, were taught by Maria Walpole, a friend of the family, who lived next door to their home on Newton Hill, Waterford. At the age of ten she went to the preparatory class at Newtown School, the Quaker school in Waterford. She was miserable there, being constantly teased by her peers who considered her mollycoddled. After a year she resumed home schooling with a daily governess, and later from 1902 to 1906, learned French and German at the Protestant girls' high school.[2]

Jacob's parents defied the mould of the middle-class Protestant community of Waterford. They were agnostic (though perceived as atheists), anti-British, and socialised little beyond immediate family. Both came from large families. Henrietta Harvey (1849-1919), Rose's mother, was one of five daughters and

---

[1] Rosamond Jacob, unpublished, incomplete autobiography. This and other manuscripts on which I have drawn for Jacob's early life are from the private collection of Rosamond's niece, Mrs. Margaret Shanahan, who kindly allowed me access to the collection. (Hereafter, Shanahan Papers). I am extremely grateful to Margaret for her hospitality, warmth and encouragement on the writing of her aunt's story.

[2] *Ibid.*

three sons of Elizabeth Waring and Thomas Smith Harvey who lived just outside Waterford. Henrietta's father was an orthodox religious Friend. Her mother became an agnostic and her eight children followed. Rose's father, Louis Jacob (1841-1907), was one of twelve in an orthodox Quaker family in Clonmel. He met Henrietta through his sister Huldah, who was married to Henrietta's brother, and they married in 1887. Louis Jacob, and his son Tom after him, worked for Henrietta's brother's and father's house-agency and stock-broking firm in Waterford.

Her father was a major influence in Jacob's life. In her unpublished 'Recollections of Louis Jacob' she writes that he was

> more unique than any other character I have known . . . fundamentally he was like no one else . . . He had two gods, beauty and justice. He was interested in politics because he wished that justice should be done. . . All his life he spent his spare time drawing, modelling, painting in water-colours. . . The pursuit of art was his conception of the most desirable and absorbing activity known to man.[3]

He had two main objections to religion: one was to the Bible, the other was to the lives and deeds of people who professed orthodox Christianity, but did not practice it. He could not respect an orthodox Christianity that supported the British Empire with its greed and cruelty, or a God who ordered the animal creation to be subject to, and in dread of, humans.

Though the parents remained friendly with many of the Quakers in Waterford, their agnosticism led to 'a kind of isolation', while their support for Irish nationalism was 'obnoxious to most Protestants.' At the international level, they sympathised with and supported all oppressed peoples. Her mother worked on the committees of the local Society for the Prevention of Cruelty to Animals, with Jacob later taking her place in this work. Her father never became involved with any clubs or organisations.

In her autobiography, Jacob explains that she 'was reared among middle-aged people with unorthodox minds and artistic and intellectual interests, and [that she] always felt both superior to the children at school and afraid of them.' She was not good at school except for literature and history. She was particularly fond of Irish history and biographies of people like Joan of Arc who fired her imagination. Standish O'Grady's books on Cuchulainn and the Fianna gave her a familiarity with Irish legend and folklore, themes Jacob would return to in her writing near the end of her life. When she was fifteen she began reading books on the United Irishmen, Moore's *Life of Lord Edward Fitzgerald* and Theobald Wolfe Tone's *Autobiography*, and developed an interest which, more than three decades later, would culminate in her history, *The Rise of the United Irishmen*

---

[3] Shanahan Papers.

1791-1794. In literature, her major influences were Charlotte Brontë and George Eliot. In her early years as a suffragist her political influences included Anna Haslam, a Quaker and founder of one of the first Irish suffrage societies in 1876,[4] and the nineteenth-century U.S. feminists, Lucretia Mott and Amelia Bloomer.

Jacob became active in the cultural and political movements in Ireland in the 1890s. She was a member of both the Gaelic League (founded in 1893 by Douglas Hyde) and Inghinidhe na hÉireann[5] (Daughters of Ireland), a nationalist women's organisation founded in 1900. She and her brother Tom were members of the National League, which emerged after Parnell and Davitt disbanded the Land League. In 1906 both were founding members of Waterford's Sinn Féin Club and canvassed for the first Sinn Féin candidate to run for Waterford corporation. In the same year she began learning Irish and spent one month of the next two summers taking Irish at Ring, County Waterford. She was a keen Irish dancer, sought after to teach other students different steps. Though she struggled with the language in the beginning, she was able to speak and write Irish for the rest of her life.

As a member of the Gaelic League Jacob took Irish language classes, was involved in local Gaelic League meetings, and often travelled to Dublin to hear Douglas Hyde and others speak. The League's cultural confines were a limitation in Jacob's view and her wish to see it actively political is evident in her 1908 proposal, 'Should the Gaelic League become Political?' which won the nomination for a debate at one of the League's Waterford meetings. She was also particularly interested in the teaching of Irish history and the use of Irish in the public schools.

In rural areas, often predominantly Catholic, her feminist consciousness and unorthodox religious beliefs contrasted sharply with the ideas of the members of the organisations to which she belonged. It was within the Gaelic League that she 'discovered the docility of Catholics to their clergy and the clergy's determination to control them in all departments of life.' Her frustration emerges in a diary entry where an upcoming céilí is discussed at a meeting:

> A lot of them wanted to have it here in the rooms, so that was settled apparently, and then they got cutting up rough about the foreign dancing. I defended it as well as I could but they were nearly all against me, & I never heard Fr. Ormonde talk so much nonsense in a given time before. He said round dances were strictly barred by the church and that they were immoral, & against the

---

[4] See Mary Cullen, 'Anna Maria Haslam', in Mary Cullen and Maria Luddy (eds.), *Women, Power and Consciousness in Nineteenth-Century Ireland: Eight Biographical Studies* (Dublin, 1995), pp. 161-196.

[5] See Margaret Ward, *Unmanageable Revolutionaries: Women and Irish Nationalism* (London, 1983), pp. 40-87.

6th & 9th commandments, 'or what *you* call the 7th and 10th' (this to me) and to the best of my remembrance cast aspersions on every decent woman that dances them (the men don't matter half so much of course). . . Tom and Mr. O'Neill and I were the only ones that voted for the foreign dances.[6]

She also resented the closing down of W.P. Ryan's weekly, *The Irish Peasant*, in 1910, due to pressure from Cardinal Logue. According to Jacob it had offended him by treating the clergy as ordinary people with whom one could argue and disagree. In losing *The Irish Peasant* Ireland 'lost a splendid organ of civilised national thought and culture' and she noted in her autobiography:

> I became a bitter anti-cleric and freethinker. And my feelings as a woman helped in this; the male monopoly of the priesthood seemed to me an outrage on justice and made me hate the whole institution for its injustice as well as its tyranny, and I never to this day can see why other women do not feel this as I did.

One of Jacob's earliest political activities was in 1911 with Inghinidhe na hÉireann in Waterford. That year the King and Queen of England visited Dublin, and as the Queen's name was Mary, the authorities decided to have all the Marys of Ireland pay tribute through a collection of signatures to be presented to the royal couple. Inghinidhe na hÉireann circulated a repudiation of this to be signed by as many Irish Marys as possible. Going from house to house collecting names was a huge ordeal for Jacob whose shyness made opening the subject afresh to each woman simply agony.

During this time she was also involved with Friends' Relief, a Quaker group in Waterford. The work exposed her to the poverty in rural and urban Waterford and she was elected secretary of the Committee for Social Reform in Waterford City. The committee addressed issues such as gambling in the streets and drinking, which they believed contributed to the poverty of women and children. Members interviewed priests and police in the city, and visited families in the slums to recommend them for relief programs. Her writings show that Rose was sensitive to her class position and critical of the patronising approach of some members of the committee.

Jacob had been visiting Dublin each summer after her father's death in 1907, staying with Josephine and Emily Webb, close friends of her Aunt Hannah. From 1912 to 1919 she travelled to Dublin more regularly, especially for suffrage and Gaelic League meetings and lectures, while remaining in Waterford to care for her semi-invalid mother. She speaks of these visits as highlights in her life, allowing her to make friends with other suffragists and solidifying personal

---

[6] Rosamond Jacob, Diaries, 13 May 1907, Ms 32,582 (14), Jacob Papers, National Library of Ireland, Dublin. (Hereafter, Jacob Diaries).

relationships. The most notable was with Hanna Sheehy Skeffington, whom she first met in 1913 and who became a lifelong friend. Her antagonism towards the church was augmented through her campaigning as a suffragist. After she had read a pamphlet on the position of women by Father Kane she noted, '[h]e gets a bit mixed towards the end . . . but the upshot is that women should have the vote but no more than that, and should be always subordinate to men. It is a deplorable thing to have such a pamphlet circulating with divine authority about the country, but that's what comes of Christianity.'[7]

Jacob became a member of both the Irishwomen's Franchise League (IWFL), founded in 1908 by Hanna Sheehy Skeffington and Margaret Cousins as the first Irish suffrage society prepared to use militant tactics,[8] and of Cumann na mBan, founded in 1914 as a women's auxiliary to the Irish Volunteers,[9] and contributed to the suffrage-first versus nation-first debate among nationalist feminists. In a letter to the suffrage newspaper, the *Irish Citizen*, in 1914 she wrote:

> It has been said, in justification of the *Irish Citizen*'s present policy, that there can be no free nation without free women. This is true in one sense, but the term 'a free nation' may be used in two different senses, either to express a nation of free citizens, or a nation free from foreign control; and a nation must be free in the latter sense before it can be free in the former. Political rights conferred on Irishwomen by a foreign government would be a miserable substitute for the same rights won, even three years later, from our own legislative assembly. The *Irish Citizen* has two theories on this subject, to which it clings with dogged persistence. One is that every nationalist is an obedient follower of Mr. Redmond; and the other is, that so long as women have no votes, they have no duty to their country. The *Irish Citizen*'s idea of public duty is that we nationalists should abandon for an indefinite time, and even oppose, the cause of national liberty for the chance of getting the vote a few years earlier than we might otherwise get it. The woman who does this is a true suffragist, no doubt, but no one can call her a nationalist.
>
> I suppose no self-respecting woman will deny that the members of Cumann na mBan . . . will be much to blame if they do not insist on their organisation being represented on the Volunteers executive, and that all possible pressure should be brought to bear on them to do so. But I do not think any nationalist woman can be blamed for preferring the work of providing rifles for the volunteers to being instructed, by Mrs Pethick-Lawrence or any other Englishwoman, as to the ideals of nationalism for which she should strive.[10]

---

[7] *Ibid.*, 8 July 1913, Ms 32,582 (25).

[8] See Rosemary Cullen Owens, *Smashing Times: A History of the Irish Women's Suffrage Movement 1889-1922* (Dublin, 1984).

[9] Ward, *Unmanageable Revolutionaries*, pp. 88-247.

[10] Rosamond Jacob, 'Letter', *Irish Citizen*, 30 May 1914. Quoted in Margaret Ward, *In Their Own Voice: Women and Irish Nationalism* (Dublin, 1995), pp. 42-3.

While she criticised the *Irish Citizen* for seeing 'every nationalist as an obedient follower of Mr. Redmond', the leader of the Irish Parliamentary Party, she insisted that 'Cumann na mBan . . . will be much to blame if they do not insist on their organisation being represented on the Volunteers executive', arguing that Cumann na mBan needed the same autonomy that Inghinidhe na hÉireann enjoyed and must share decision making at the highest level of the Volunteers.

In 1914 John Redmond insisted on naming twenty-five of his own nominees to the Irish Volunteers' Provisional Committee. Because Redmond had refused to include the women's vote in his Home Rule Bill, the IWFL urged Cumann na mBan 'to declare their absolute opposition to this agreement on the grounds that Redmond . . . forfeited any right to have an organisation of women working on his behalf.' When Cumann na mBan failed to respond, the IWFL deplored 'the silent acquiescence of the executive.'[11] Jacob was opposed to Irish soldiers fighting for England and actively demonstrated against Redmond's campaign in 1914 to recruit Irish Volunteers into the British Army. At a recruiting rally in Wexford Jacob was removed from the platform where she displayed a suffragist poster opposing the war. She was also strongly opposed to World War I, regarding it as an imperialist war, unopposed by the Church, and fought for the benefit of a patriarchal system. In December 1914 she wrote that 'all the Great powers were to blame, Germany not the least, that it is an eloquent testimony to the utter failure of any system of religion or morals to civilise the human race, and a melancholy example of masculine government.'[12]

Many of the issues Jacob was involved with surfaced in her first novel, *Callaghan*, written in 1915 and dealing with the period 1912-14. Its central focus is the relationship between Frances Morrin, a Protestant suffragist and Aloysius Callaghan, a Catholic landlord and nationalist who joins the Irish Volunteers and opposes Redmond's strategy of supporting Britain in the war. Callaghan assumes that Frances will give up her work after their marriage, but is forced to grapple with the concept that 'a woman might have public duties which seemed to her so [*sic*] important as a man's.'[13] The novel also deals with several of the other conflicts within Irish life at the time: the suffragists' campaign for the vote; the involvement of the Irish Volunteers in the world war and the resistance to British recruitment in Ireland; and public reaction to Protestants marrying Catholics. The novel ends in an atmosphere of destruction, despair and chaos, reflecting the turbulence in the lives of those living through the period, particularly those who chose to be political. *Callaghan* did not find a publisher until late 1920. Both its contemporary political content and Jacob's location in Waterford may have contributed to the delay.

---

[11] Ward, *Unmanageable Revolutionaries*, p. 100.

[12] Jacob Diaries, 31 Dec 1914, Ms 32,582 (27).

[13] Rosamond Jacob, *Callaghan* (published under the pseudonym F. Winthrop) (Dublin, 1920), p. 174.

In 1917 she was chosen to represent Waterford as a delegate at the Sinn Féin Convention[14] where she won a commitment to women's suffrage.[15] She had asked Arthur Griffith on what franchise would the future Constituent Assembly be elected, and 'Griffith answered plainly that whatever the franchise was, it would include them, which is the straightest statement he has ever made on the point.'[16] Before the convention Jacob and other women members had discussed the need that the Convention 'should declare unmistakably for a republic, and the danger of Griffith's non-republicanism and autocratic spirit: and the extreme trouble they had in forcing six women onto the executive against the will of Griffith and Milroy etc.'[17] For Jacob and others a 'republic' meant one based on the French and American democratic models rather than Griffith's aim of home rule under a monarchist constitution. During the convention Countess Plunkett, wife of Count George Plunkett, the first Sinn Féin candidate elected in 1917, and mother of the executed 1916 rebel, Joseph Plunkett, hosted a reception at her home for the women delegates which aimed

> to link up all the women in Sinn Féin clubs and encourage them to be active and educate themselves and take part in all political life of their districts – and to link up other women's organisations too and encourage all to do Feminist work together.[18]

During the 1918 elections Jacob canvassed for de Valera in the Waterford area, but was particularly interested in Sinn Féin women candidates as she wrote to Hanna Sheehy Skeffington:

> I hope I'll see your name in the list of candidates . . . I hope the Dublin women at least are stirring themselves to get women candidates selected – women in most other parts of the country are too scattered to do much. . . It seems to me the important thing for Irish suffragists to be doing at present. I hope they won't try to run women as independent candidates. . . That would be hopeless everywhere, I should think, and would give the impression that they didn't care about the national issue.[19]

---

[14] The annual meeting of the Sinn Féin Party. This convention was held after the release of the 1916 prisoners and saw de Valera's election to the presidency of Sinn Féin.

[15] Ward, *Unmanageable Revolutionaries*, p. 126.

[16] Jacob Diaries, 25 October 1917, Ms 32,582 (32).

[17] *Ibid.*, 1 October 1917, Ms 32,582 (32).

[18] *Ibid.*, 26 October 1917, Ms 32,582 (32).

[19] Sheehy Skeffington Papers, Ms 24,108, National Library of Ireland, Dublin. Quoted in Ward, *In Their Own Voice*, p. 81.

However, by the following year Jacob and Sheehy Skeffington were concerned at 'the lack of feminism among Sinn Féin women in the provinces.' [20] And by the time the first Irish Dáil met in 1919 Jacob had 'lost a great deal of interest in it on account of there being no women in it, and couldn't respect it very much either, for the same reason.'[21] From this point on, Jacob's political energies increasingly turned to issues that were ignored by the nationalist momentum sweeping the country. The following lengthy, but telling, quote gives her analysis of the historical and psychological impact of colonialism and of the love colonised nations can develop for authority and censorship:

> All nations are subject to this desire to enforce the will of the majority without regard to individual rights, and those who are not troubled with foreign interference have less excuse than we for yielding to it. But the less liberty we allow each other now, the more will habits of persecution and mental and moral slavery flourish among us after foreign incubus is removed. . .
>
> In a nation situated like Ireland, which can only avoid national extinction by maintaining a perpetual state of defensive resistance against the efforts to absorb her of the stronger state who claims authority over her, one of the dangers most difficult to guard against is the lowering of the value set upon individual liberty. . .
>
> The network of British prohibitions and permissions which surrounds us seems to breed in us not a dislike to the whole troublesome insulting tyrannous spirit of the thing, but a desire to set up a similar system of prohibitions and permissions of our own. We must have our own permits, our own censors. In spite of – or perhaps because of – our perpetual fight for national freedom, the principle of authority has ten times more weight with us than the principle of liberty. We love authority. We don't feel comfortable except when we are told by our own native authorities what we may do and what we may not, what cinema pictures we may see, what Sunday papers we may read, what dances we may dance, what men we may speak to. It is one of the evils of foreign domination that by the state of war which it occasions, it strengthens the natural learning towards authority and mass action, and weakens its victim's sense of the importance of individual liberty. We find that nothing can be done without union, we must act together; and to ensure this a certain compulsion – of 'pressure' – seems necessary. Evil breeds evil, necessitates evil.[22]

In 1920, one year after her mother's death, Jacob moved to Dublin. For the first year she lodged with Hanna Sheehy Skeffington in Rathmines, strengthening

---

[20] Jacob Diaries, 30 August 1918, Ms 32,582 (34).

[21] *Ibid.*, 21 January 1919, Ms 32,582 (35).

[22] Excerpt from an article 'Individual liberty' by Jacob written in 1920 for *An Gabail Timpal*, hand-written on piece of paper inserted in diary, Jacob Diaries, Ms 32, 582 (37).

their relationship, and growing extremely fond of Hanna's eleven-year-old son, Owen. She had been strongly influenced by both Frank and Hanna Sheehy Skeffington's work with the *Irish Citizen*, to which she herself regularly contributed. In addition to friendship Hanna provided an intellectual engagement which Jacob valued. Both were committed feminists, republican-nationalists, activists and writers who regularly consulted each other on current issues, often reading drafts of each other's writing or letters to the press.

Once in Dublin, she began to actively seek a publisher for *Callaghan* and by March she got her first refusal from Maunsell's, remarking in her diary, 'I wish they would give some idea of why they refused it.' By September of 1920 Martin Lester had accepted the novel though they insisted that Jacob remove 'most of the suffrage lecture.'[23]

Jacob's move to Dublin also led to her increased activity in the Irishwomen's International League (IIL), founded in 1916 as the Irish branch of the Women's International League for Peace and Freedom (WILPF).[24] She had become involved in the League when living in Waterford. In 1920 she was made secretary, a position she held for much of the following decade. In the summer of 1921 Lucy Kingston and Jacob were the Irish delegates to the WILPF conference in Vienna. While they were in Vienna, the truce in the War of Independence came into force on 11 July and was followed by negotiations between the British government and Sinn Féin.

Jacob, like many republicans, opposed the Treaty that was signed in December and accepted by a Dáil majority in January 1922. She regarded dominion status and the oath of allegiance to the crown required of Dáil deputies as a betrayal of the republic ratified by Dáil Éireann in 1919, and wrote in her autobiography: 'I had felt how wrong it was to have no women among the delegates, and felt then that, had there been even one woman, that treaty would never have been signed.' However, her friends and colleagues were thoroughly divided on the issue. Many members of IIL, including Lucy Kingston, supported the Treaty. So did her brother Tom and, from then on, they differed a good deal on political issues.

The civil war followed. On the morning of 28 June 1922, after hearing 'ferocious firing all the latter part of the night, close by apparently', Rose found on buying a newspaper 'that the Free State Army was attacking the Four Courts.' She went down to the quays 'to look, and stood a while with a crowd at the corner of Parliament St. listening to the big guns and watching the dome of the

---

[23] Jacob Diaries, 23 September 1920, Ms 32,582 (37).
[24] The International Committee of Women for Permanent Peace was founded in 1915 and in 1919 renamed the Women's International League for Peace and Freedom (WILPF). See Rosemary Cullen Owens, 'Women and pacifism in Ireland 1915-1932' in Maryann Valiulis and Mary O'Dowd (eds.), *Women and Irish History* (Dublin, 1997), pp. 220-38.

Four Courts in a senseless sort of way . . . I went most of the afternoon wandering around High St, Bridge St etc. from a diseased spirit of curiosity.'[25] Within two days she had made inquiries about the Red Cross and 'found a Trade Union place called Tara Hall, full of girls making bandages. They showed me how and I worked there til dinnertime.'[26]

Jacob was part of the women's delegation organised by Maud Gonne, which attempted to negotiate peace between the Republicans and the Free State at the outbreak of hostilities. The women met on 1 July 1922 at the Mansion House, three days after the bombing of the Four Courts:

> Then the more or less Free State women; Mrs Despard, M. McBride, Agnes O'Farrelly, Edith Webb, and L. Bennett as a neutral went to interview the government and came back reporting as follows – they spoke of the suffering of the people and the need for peace and got the usual sort of answers from Griffith, Collins and Cosgrave. Cosgrave seemed anxious for the Dáil to meet and said it could be summoned for Tuesday, but Griffith nudged him to make him shut up. Miss Bennett and M. McB asked if they would let the Republicans evacuate without giving up their arms – Griffith said no, they must give up their arms. Mme Mc Bride said that they certainly would not do, and that it would be better to let them go with their arms than to shell the city. They were firm on this (though Collins said he didn't know why the republicans didn't go home with their arms now, as there seemed nothing to stop them) and Griffith said the lives of all the ministers were in the greatest danger. . .
>
> It didn't seem much use sending a deputation to the republicans, but Miss Bennett said it would be very unfair not to – should at least show them there were some republican women who wanted peace , and not put all the burden of guilt on the government – so Mrs. Sheehy-Skeffington, Mrs. Connery, Mrs Johnson, Miss Bennett and I went.[27]

In late December of the following year, Jacob would find herself imprisoned by the new Free State government. Hanna Sheehy Skeffington departed on a republican lecture tour, and asked Jacob to stay at her house and take care of Owen. Hanna had given her leave to shelter any IRA members who asked and Jacob lent a room to some republican typists. Just after Christmas the house was raided by Free State detectives who discovered republican publications. Jacob was arrested and brought to Mountjoy prison, where she shared a cell with Dorothy Macardle, the republican writer and friend of de Valera. In prison Jacob's main fears were of being kept there indefinitely and of being expected to go on hunger strike if some serious grievance turned up. After a month of

---

[25] Jacob Diaries, 28 June 1922, Ms 32,582 (41).
[26] *Ibid.*, 30 June 1922, Ms 32,582 (41).
[27] Jacob Diaries, 1 July 1922, Ms 32, 582 (41).

incarceration, a petition signed by over forty relatives and friends obtained her release.

Jacob's arrest was undoubtedly an embarrassment to WILPF, which felt compromised to have its honorary secretary imprisoned because of her alleged association with the republican army.[28] Nevertheless, Jacob and other republican women continued to campaign for better conditions for the republican prisoners in jails and internment camps throughout the Civil War (1922-23) and until their release in 1924. In the late spring of 1923 Dorothy Macardle and the other republican women were released. Jacob and Macardle became close friends, sharing a flat in Rathmines in the later years of the decade.

The same issues that consumed Jacob's political activism continually surfaced in her fiction. *The Troubled House* was written in the early 1920s but not published until 1938. Set in 1920 during the War of Independence the novel explores a number of themes through the eyes of the narrator, Margaret Cullen. One is the sacrifice of a woman's identity to that of the men in her family:

> What a queer thing it was that my life should be spent thus, almost entirely in love and care and fear and thought and anxiety over three men and a boy. Was I nothing but a being relative to them without real existence of my own? Each one of them led his own life, had his centre in his own soul, as a human creature should, but I had no purpose or driving force in myself: nothing that was independent of them.[29]

This theme is juxtaposed to the less constrained lives and strongly suggested lesbian relationship of two artists, Josephine and Nix, whose lives intersect those of the Cullens. Debates about the merits of pacifism versus physical force pervade the book. Conflict develops around the solicitor father's 'worldly prudence', the IRA activism of one son, Liam, the pacifism of the eldest son, Theo, and the hero-worship of Liam by the fourteen-year old Roddy who runs messages for the IRA, all observed through the eyes of their mother, who acts as mediator and negotiator.

The plot centres around the Croke Park killings by the British forces on 21 November 1921, a reprisal for the previous night's killing of eleven undercover British agents. By choosing to harbour Liam (on the run after assassinating a British undercover officer) Nix and Josephine have their studio raided and their art destroyed. Theo is involved in an IRA ambush when Liam is ill, and the Cullen home is raided by the Black and Tans who beat Theo in front of his mother and Roddy. At the end of the novel Liam accidentally kills his father in an ambush on the British army. This act of patricide suggests the removal of the old establishment – the colonial servants, represented by the father and his

---

[28] See, Cullen Owens, 'Women and pacifism in Ireland'.
[29] Rosamond Jacob, *The Troubled House* (Dublin, 1938), p. 45.

established law practice – to make way for the emergence of a new nation. Throughout the book troops patrol constantly; people live in fear, and life is disrupted by curfews and raids. Without either glorifying or condemning war, Jacob calls into question its very nature, the killing of other human beings. On another scale, she examines the emotional and psychological impact of war on the individual, the family and society. It seems likely that the realistic portrayal of the period and its volatile material delayed publication of *The Troubled House* until 1938 after the success of her history, *The Rise of the United Irishmen*.

As the Free State became more conservative and insular in its policies during the 1920s, Jacob and others began looking to Europe and beyond. In 1926, as honorary secretary of WILPF, Jacob was among the organisers of its International Congress held in Dublin. As one of the few republicans within WILPF, and conscious of the politicisation of the congress, she attempted to use her influence to see what benefit the republicans could gain from it. She even met de Valera to discuss the possibilities, but did not feel the meeting achieved much.[30]

At the congress's Minority commission, Jacob presented the Irish Minority Report and expanded on the oath of allegiance to the crown of England taken by Irish Dáil deputies under the 1922 Treaty. Hanna Sheehy Skeffington 'made an excellent *resumé* of British Imperialism in Ireland, past and present' to the Imperialism commission though Jacob noted that 'many of our own committee would have highly disapproved.'[31] Many of the Irish members of WILPF disagreed with Jacob's and Sheehy Skeffington's view that Ireland's dominion status and the oath of allegiance made the Treaty unacceptable.[32] In a later diary entry for the same congress Jacob notes, '[I]mportant resolutions and such all this morning, interesting to see how it was the republicans only in the Irish delegation who voted for anything advanced, such as a resolution against special legislation for the "protection" of women in industry [and] resolutions against colonisation etc.'[33]

In April of 1926 Jacob resigned from the Sinn Féin party, just weeks after the Ard Fheis at which de Valera resigned. She later joined Fianna Fáil, the new party which de Valera established to enter the Dáil and overturn the Treaty by constitutional means. In May of 1927 she was appointed official secretary of the Gaelic League. She resigned the WILPF secretaryship, finding both positions too much work. However, she continued to spend much of her energy in WILPF and, in 1929, she and Hanna Sheehy Skeffington represented Ireland at the WILPF congress in Prague. These conferences allowed Jacob to meet and interact with women of different nationalities and ethnicities. She was particularly concerned with the conditions of women workers in industrialised nations and

---

[30] Jacob Diaries, 28 January 1926, Ms 32,582 (51).
[31] *Ibid.*, 10 July 1926, Ms 32,582 (53).
[32] See Cullen Owens, 'Women and pacifism in Ireland'.
[33] Jacob Diaries, 15 July 1926, Ms 32,582 (53).

the autonomy of small industrial nations in the face of rising imperialism across the globe. At the same time she continued to work for women's rights in the new Free State. In this context an ongoing issue for Jacob throughout the 1920s was the government efforts to remove women from jury service,[34] especially in cases of sex offences. By 1928 she writes that the '[w]hole jury panel for Dublin called – not one woman on it.'[35] She was a member of the Irish Women Citizens' and Local Government Association (IWCLGA),[36] one of the main feminist pressure groups keeping a close eye on legislation affecting women as citizens in the Free State. Strategies included writing 'to the Press, [lobbying] of the Oireachtas and circulating leaflets.'[37] But by 1936 the situation was no better. When a joint committee of women's organisations sought an audience with de Valera to discuss women police and women in the new constitution, Jacob recorded with irony 'how [de Valera] could receive no deputation – but he could receive the German footballers all right.'[38]

During the years 1928-36 Jacob's diary entries often mention depression. While reasons for the depression are not offered, it is not difficult to imagine her feeling marginalised as she saw the nation to which she had given over twenty years of campaigning for women's rights and independence moving towards a cultural ideology imbued with Catholicism in which women were expected to confine themselves to the home. On a personal level she was experiencing growing tension between herself and her immediate family and friends at home in Waterford, reflected in the following argument during a Christmas visit:

> Went back to the Limes and began talking of [Aunt] Maya – Tom started on how men can't stand her, and when I said it was partly their own fault, he rounded on me and told me I was like her and it was getting impossible to talk to me because of my anti-men obsession. . . When I protested that everyone didn't see me like that, and that people in Dublin could get on with me all right and liked me. . . Tom I think said yes but what sort of people were they? It didn't occur to them that any of the wrongness might be on their side. . . [They] think I am wasting and fretting away my life among these intolerable Dublin people.[39]

---

[34] See Maryann Valiulis, 'Defining their role in the new state: Irishwomen's protest against the Juries Act of 1927', in *Canadian Journal of Irish Studies*, viii, 1, (July 1992), pp. 43-60.

[35] Jacob Diaries, 6 October 1928, Ms 32,582 (60).

[36] For more on this period (1922-1937) and the IWCLGA see Mary Clancy, 'Aspects of women's contribution to the Oireachtas debate in the Free State, 1922-1937', in Maria Luddy and Cliona Murphy (eds.), *Women Surviving: Studies in Irish Women's History in the 19th & 20th Centuries* (Dublin, 1990), pp. 206-232.

[37] *Ibid.*, p. 207.

[38] Jacob Diaries, 29 October 1936, Ms 32,582 (80).

[39] *Ibid.*, 5 January 1927, Ms 32,582 (55).

However, despite these differences she remained extremely close to Tom and his wife, Dorothea, and continued to visit them in Waterford throughout her life.

Resistance to women's progress in society is the theme of Jacob's unpublished third novel, 'Third Person Singular'.[40] Written in the late 1920s and set between 1918-1920, it tackles the conventions surrounding marriage, adultery, love and friendship and a parochial versus cosmopolitan view on life and relationships. The protagonist, Violet, is married to Mr. Ambrose, who is domineering, arrogant, conceited and has little respect for his wife. When the unmarried Hugh MacNevin confesses his love for her, she reciprocates. Neither see what they are doing as immoral; rather, they argue it would be immoral if they were not true to themselves and allowed the pressure of family, friends and societal norms to override their decision to be together. Instead of the self-sacrificing Victorian style heroine who tells him she loves him but has to remain with the husband out of duty, Jacob's protagonist stays true to her instincts.

The 'third person singular' is Constance Moore, who also loves Hugh MacNevin. Constance is unorthodox in every sense of the word and not unlike Jacob. She is agnostic, seen as unfeminine, confrontational, speaks her mind, does not care for fashion and does not date men. She has been secretly in love with Hugh for six years. Instead of the two women competing for the man, Constance provides sanctuary to Violet at her cottage by the coast in Co. Waterford. The two women become close, and the refuge provides the space, conversation and support to return some individuality and identity to Violet.

Both *The Troubled House* and 'Third Person Singular' are women-centred and their protagonists speak their minds on topics such as sexuality, religion and ethics. In a very real sense these novels are a direct response to the emerging state. Under the restrictive conditions that followed the first Censorship of Publications Act in 1926, such a text as 'Third Person Singular' posed a direct affront to the 'revised' directive and morals of the Free State, which perhaps explains why the novel was never published. Three decades later, after Jacob's success with the historical fiction *The Rebel's Wife*, she revised 'Third Person Singular', yet failed again to find a publisher. Jacob's fears about the mindless following of authority, voiced in her earlier essay on 'Individual Liberty', appeared prophetic.

For Jacob and others the censorship act was a major step in the Free State's departure from the aspirations in the struggle for independence. During the divorce debates in 1928 she again noted her fear that the 'state is to be mentally governed by authority: any attack, for instance, on the institute of marriage, will be banned.'[41] Both Lucy Kingston and Jacob felt that the Eucharistic

---

[40] Rosamond Jacob, 'Third Person Singular' (unpublished manuscript). Jacob Papers, Ms 33,113.

[41] Jacob Diaries, 6 October 1928, Ms 32,582 (60).

Congress of 1932 marked the take-over of Catholic and conservative thinking in the Free State.[42] If 'Third Person Singular' can be regarded as Jacob's personal statement, she also let those in power know how she felt. In a letter to Frank Gallagher, who became the first editor of the *Irish Press* in 1931, regarding the proposed Censorship Bill of 1930, she explained: '[J]ust because I think the censorship bill so ridiculous, I would refrain from saying a word about it outside Ireland, because it's so humiliating that the world should learn that that is the sort of thing the Irish do when they get the power.'[43] And in a later letter she expanded:

> What I object to was simply the clear implication in the article that all the books censored were written for the sake of indecency. That is what seems to me so essentially unfair; that is the attitude that puts censorship people so in the wrong, and gives the impression that they are ignorant of what they are writing of.[44]

In 1929 Jacob formed a Protection Committee to 'investigate the arrest and continual re-arrest of certain republicans, but also for those republicans who were losing their jobs to employers and to send deputations to these employers.'[45] This was at the request of her friend Frank Ryan, whom she had met in 1926 in a Gaelic League Irish class taught by him. An I.R.A. member since he was sixteen, he had been in prison camps in 1923. When Rose met him he was a student at University College, Dublin, and one of the leaders of its republican element.

Jacob's politics also brought her into contact with activists around the world. In 1930, at the request of A.E. Russell,[46] Jacob was invited to become a member of the Dublin Committee of the One Hundred of the Threefold Movement – Union of East and West League of Neighbours Fellowship of Faith, which worked 'for the realization of peace and brotherhood – through understanding and neighbourliness – between people of ALL Nationalities, Races, Cultures, Classes, Conditions and Creeds.'[47] In 1930 after attending a lecture by Mr. Chakravarty of India on non-violence, she travelled to England with Lucy Kingston as WILPF representatives to interview Chakravarty and learn more about Gandhi's use of non-violence for political purposes. In 1932 Jacob was elected to the committee of the Indian-Irish Independence League. During

---

[42] *Ibid.*

[43] Frank Gallagher Papers, Ms 18,353, National Library of Ireland, Dublin.

[44] *Ibid.*

[45] Jacob Papers, Ms 33, 230.

[46] A. E. (George) Russell was a central figure of the Irish Literary Revival, which included Douglas Hyde, W.B. Yeats and J.M. Synge, among others.

[47] Jacob Diaries, 6 August 1930, Ms 32,582 (65).

this period she was involved with the International Disarmament Declaration
Committee. The committee collected 6,000 signatures for total disarmament of
all the military powers in the world, which was sent to a disarmament conference
under the auspices of the League of Nations in 1932. They received support
from Quaker meeting houses, and also by canvassing cinema queues, where on
one occasion Jacob and Lucy Kingston 'toiled away for one and a half hours,
and did well, getting ninety names on their disarmament petition.'[48] At Jacob's
request the Committee also wrote a letter 'protesting against military show at
the Eucharistic Congress.'[49]

In 1931, as an Irish delegate for the Friends of the Soviet Union (FOSU),
Jacob travelled to the USSR at the invitation of the Central Trade Union
Council of the Soviet Union. Her interest dated back to her participation in a
famine relief fund for the USSR in Dublin in the early 1920s, and she was a
longtime supporter of socialism and admirer of James Connolly. Of the original
delegation of seven, only two succeeded in getting passports, the majority being
refused 'on the grounds (given by the Minister of Justice) that they were not
suitable people to be allowed visit the USSR.'[50] She travelled as a writer and
journalist, accompanied by Meg Connery travelling as a working housewife.
Meg Connery had been a member of the IWFL and WILPF, and also, with
Louie Bennett, a key organizer of the Irish Women Workers Union. They
sailed from London to Leningrad with the English FOSU delegates. The main
issues Jacob wished to investigate were, 'the progress of women in the USSR,
the every day home life of the workers and peasants, and the means by which
religious tyranny has been overthrown.'[51] In a meeting with Soviet officials she
inquired about the number of women in high positions, and was informed of
women chairing 'The Union of Medical Health and Sanitary Works, the Textile
Union and Commissar of Finance in the Russian Republic.'[52] As religious
persecution was the chief issue in anti-Soviet propaganda in Ireland, she visited
four churches within a mile of their hotel 'with services proceeding' and 'in the
cathedral of the Redeemer, prelates in magnificent vestments were officiating
before a considerable congregation.' She knew it was not possible in one month

---

[48] Daisy Lawrence Swanton, *Emerging from the Shadow: the Lives of Sarah Anne Lawrenson and Lucy Olive Kingston, Based on Personal Diaries, 1883-1969* (Dublin, 1994), p. 122.

[49] Jacob Diaries, 24 March 1932, Ms 32,582 (69).

[50] *Ibid.*, 21 May 1931, Ms 32,582 (66). The diary entries and notes on her trip extending over a three-week period record observations contradicting traditional assumptions of the Soviet Union.

[51] Draft report of the Irish Friends of the Soviet Union (FOSU) delegation to the Soviet Union, May 21, 1931, Jacob Manuscripts, Ms 33,229. [Hereafter, Draft Report].

[52] Jacob Diaries, 23 May 1931, Ms 32,582 (66).

to see much of so vast a country or know first hand of conditions beyond what appeared on the surface. She thought the system of the Red Army 'extraordinarily wise and unmilitaristic; especially the attention paid to keeping the Red Army men in the closest touch with the life of the community, and the provision made for the exemption from military services of men with genuine religious convictions against war.'[53] The most spectacular event of the visit was the demonstrations at Revolutionary Square on 1 May. From a hotel balcony she 'watched for three hours, four processions at once converging on Red Square – no end of banners and slogans and caricatures of Popes and wreckers, capitalists and politicians, and the people walking so casually and so full of spontaneous enthusiasm – it was the most stunning evidence of popular feeling imaginable.'[54] When Jacob eventually joined in and walked through Red Square she noted there was 'not one woman in the government group on the Lenin tomb.' She believed 'that the new order [had] gone far to abolish poverty, that it [had] whole hearted support of the people, and that they [were] showing a degree of sanity in the work in building up a new civilisation which no other people [had] yet approached.'[55] In her end-of-year notes she recorded that she had given four lectures on Russia after her return, one with Connery at the Mansion House.

In 1935 Jacob and Hanna Sheehy Skeffington attempted unsuccessfully to form an anti-capital punishment group in Dublin. The Civil War had seen many executions of republicans by the Free State, leading to bitter divisions within the country. Jacob's thoughts on the subject of state-sanctioned killing are expressed in her essay, 'The right to kill', written as a reflection on seeing *Vigil* by A.R. Fanning at the Abbey Theatre, in which three prisoners of war, technically 'rebels', are captured by the government army. In the play a law has been passed 'that all prisoners taken in arms are to be shot.' To Jacob this law 'takes such murders entirely out of the realm of crime or violence, making them acts of loyal obedience to the state.' She argues that soldiers 'obeying orders from above', relinquishing them of personal responsibility is not morally justifiable.

> People may have to subordinate their judgement to that of the state, but must they subordinate their conscience? It is not quite the same thing. They may obey laws which they think are ill-contrived for securing their objects, but that is rather different from committing, in obedience to orders, acts which are in themselves obvious crimes. Murder, for instance. When authority commands the violation of all human and kindly feeling, authority ought to be left to do the job itself. Let legislators and judges who believe in capital

---

[53] Draft Report.
[54] Jacob Diaries, 1 May 1931, Ms 32,582 (66).
[55] Draft Report.

punishment be the hangmen, let military governments murder their rebel prisoners with their own hands, let ministers who decide on wars be deprived of all special protection, or better still, put in the most dangerous place that can be found.[56]

After the referendum which passed the 1937 Constitution, Jacob joined the Women's Social and Political League (soon to be renamed as the Women's Social and Progressive League), which aimed 'to monitor legislation affecting women.'[57] Her response also included letters, articles and stories which she wrote during the 1930s. She was a regular contributor to newspapers throughout the decade, most frequently to the *Irish Press*, which published five of her stories in 1935. Among their themes were Irish history, Irish folklore and free speech. However, her most articulate and extensive response to the erosion of democratic rights was a book that would reflect the international scope and secular intentions of those who began the struggle for independence. From the late 1920s to the mid 1930s she put much of her energy into the research and writing of *The Rise of the United Irishmen 1791-1794*, parts of it appearing weekly in the Republican newspaper, *An Phoblacht*. Published in 1937, the book's main focus is from 1791, the founding year of the United Irishmen, to 1794, when they were outlawed by the British government.

The Rise of the United Irishmen is Jacob's most important work of non-fiction. Her research on the period took almost a decade to complete, a decade that coincided with the glaring reversal of democratic and progressive thinking in the Free State. From the divorce debate in 1928, to the rewriting of the Irish Constitution in 1936-7, Jacob was compiling and rewriting for a contemporary audience an interpretation of a pivotal period in Irish history 'where people devoted their lives to Independence, freedom of religion, and the right of all men [sic] to vote.' Her focus on the past was an attempt to illuminate the misdeeds of the present.

The book offered an explanation of the United Irish movement, its impact on the period and its relationship with the various organisations in the country, including the Catholic Committee, the Volunteers and the Defenders. The comprehensive introduction provides a brief summary of events from the plantations of the seventeenth century up to 1791. She saw the plantations and the penal laws as creating a split country where 'two civilisations, two languages, two nations, two ways of life, dwelt, conflicting together, in a country, one conquering and possessing, the other enslaved; and the broad line of demarcation between them was religion.'[58]

---

[56] Rosamond Jacob, 'The right to kill', in *Ireland Today*, April 1937.

[57] Hilda Tweedy, *A Link In The Chain: The Story of Irish Housewives Association 1942-1992* (Dublin, 1992), p. 19.

[58] Rosamond Jacob, *The Rise of the United Irishmen 1791-1794* (London, 1937), p. 13.

The 1791 Declaration of the United Irishmen called for 'a cordial union among all the people of Ireland', and a radical reform of the representation of the people in parliament to include Irishmen of every religious persuasion. Jacob viewed the declaration as a turning point in Irish history, writing that 'before 1791 there were in the country only the British colonists and the enslaved Irish; after [1791] parties took a new division – those who stood for privilege and foreign government, and those who stood for an Irish nation, democratic and self-governed.' While this quotation did not make it into the body of the published text, Jacob's colonial analysis permeates throughout. From a democratic viewpoint, she found one fault with the United Irishmen's declaration: that it 'takes it for granted, in perfect good faith, that there is but one sex in humanity, and that male. The idea that women were human beings, with human rights, had not occurred to anyone, except Mary Wollstonecraft and Thomas Paine.' A chief tenet of the United Irishmen was international brotherhood, and one chapter specifically deals with the friendly relationship between the United Irishmen and the societies springing up in both Scotland and England as a result of the French Revolution.

Following the success of *The United Irishmen* Jacob finally found a publisher for *The Troubled House*, though Jacob herself funded the printing costs. Having waited seventeen years to be published again she enjoyed the renewed interest in her work, and in 1938 she was invited to give a radio broadcast on 'Dublin in 1798.' In December she gave a lecture on 'The Women of 1798.' In 1939 she was a participant in a broadcast on 'Nationality', and during the same year presented a talk on 'Androcentric Culture.'

The 1940s were a difficult period in Jacob's life. In financial terms the cost of living had risen due to the war.[59] She also lost several close friends. The first was Frank Ryan, with whom she had worked during the late 1920s. Ryan had fought in the International Brigade for the republicans in the Spanish Civil War, 1936-39. He was taken prisoner but, because he was a general in the brigade, Franco refused to release him after the war. In 1940 Jacob headed a campaign to free him. Though operating through the highest diplomatic channels, which included L.H. Kenny, the Irish Ambassador to Spain, the request went unheeded. By the following year Jacob lost contact with Ryan, and in 1945 she received the news of his death.

She moved in with Helen McGinley, a friend since the 1920s, to care for and nurse her, as her physical and mental health deteriorated for several years

---

[59] When Jacob lived in Waterford she did not need a job, as there was income set aside for her while she cared for her mother. After her move to Dublin in 1920, it is not clear whether this income covered her increased expenses. By the 1930s she supplemented it by journalism, history and fiction. Never able to afford her own apartment, she shared with different women during her forty years in Dublin and lived modestly.

before her death in 1949. During these years Jacob also lost her close friends, Hanna Sheehy Skeffington and Lucy Kingston's husband Swik. She found consolation in the fact that her only niece, Margaret, and nephew, Chris, had moved from Waterford to Dublin, affording her the opportunity of getting to know them better. She continued to write and to be politically active. By 1942 she had completed 'The Naked Truth', a play which sketched the life of Wolfe Tone, which was never published. For much of the decade she was honorary secretary of the Women's Social and Progressive League. By 1945 the end of the war signified for Jacob the end of 'a constant nightmare of thinking what is going on abroad, and makes a slight brightening of material prospects', though she noted that the '[A]llies are as repulsive as victors always are, and the Russians do themselves no credit.'[60]

In 1949, she moved to Charleville Road, Rathmines, to share the top floor of the house with Lucy Kingston. Here she spent the last eleven years of her life. The arrangement worked well for both women who had been friends and political colleagues for almost thirty years. Lucy was then chair and Rose honorary secretary of the Women's Social and Progressive League. In her early sixties at the time, Jacob lived an active physical as well as intellectual and political life. Her bicycle continued to act as her main form of transport in the city, and she regularly hiked in the Dublin and Wicklow mountains.

During the 1940s she published a number of articles in the newspapers, though much of her energy went into producing three texts: 'The Naked Truth', *The Raven's Glen* and 'Matilda Tone: A Memoir'. All went unpublished. The last was the most ambitious. Her interest in Martha Witherington, known as Matilda Tone, the wife of Wolfe Tone, developed during her research for the *Rise of the United Irishmen* when she noted:

> All we know of Matilda Tone is contained in her husband's autobiography, in two of her letters and an account she wrote of her life in France with her children between Tone's death in 1798 and her marriage to Henry Wilson in 1816. But from the materials, tantalisingly incomplete as they are, we know her, and we see her as a human being surpassed in quality by scarcely any character in our history, although in that history, technically speaking, she has no place.[61]

Martha Witherington, at the age of sixteen, eloped with Theobald Wolfe Tone. Their relationship was based on mutual respect, trust and understanding. They discussed everything, shared the same political opinions and his achievements owed much to her support. Matilda tolerated what Marianne Elliot characterises

---

[60] Jacob Diaries, 31 December 1945, Ms 32,582 (116).
[61] Jacob Papers, Ms 33,107-33 (246).

as the eccentricity and impulsiveness of Tone.[62] She took responsibility for raising and educating their children. After Tone's death, the twenty-nine year old Matilda was left destitute in France with three children to support. With the help of Thomas Addis Emmet she secured a widow's pension from the French Army. Having lost two of her children through fever, Matilda won a guarantee for her son William's French naturalisation by personally presenting a letter of appeal to Napoleon. This secured William a place in the Imperial Cavalry School at St. Germain. For eighteen years in France she was sustained by her love for her son and the support of Thomas Wilson, a Scot she had met on her voyage to France from America, and whom she married after nineteen years of friendship. When William moved to the United States, the couple followed, first to New York and then to Washington, D.C. There Matilda lived until her death in 1849, aged seventy-nine.

Jacob had finished 'A Memoir' by 1950, but, failing to find a publisher, she rewrote the text as historical fiction, which in 1957 was published as *The Rebel's Wife*. The following year, to Jacob's delight, it was awarded 'Book of the Year' by the Women Writers' Club. She was honoured at their 25th Anniversary Banquet, where Owen Sheehy Skeffington's speech on Jacob was, for her, 'the best thing in the year.'[63] It is curious to see how the literary critics viewed the work. The review in the *Irish Times* offers an example:

> At the present time, when from one reason or another the rising generation in Ireland seems to be forgetting the deeds and sacrifices of the brave men who rose in dark and evil days, it is a relief to find the story retold with such sympathetic understanding and historical accuracy.[64]

The reviewer elides the centrality of the female protagonist and misses the point. While the story is indeed 'retold with sympathetic understanding and historical accuracy', Jacob's focus is not on 'the brave men,' but on the strength, bravery and endurance of Matilda Tone.

During the 1950s Jacob continued to be politically active, working closely with Lucy Kingston in WILPF, and both women attended its 1956 conference in Birmingham in England. In the same decade the remaining members of the IWCLGA, including Jacob and Kingston, merged with The Irish Housewives Association (IHA). Founded in 1942, the original aim of the IHA was 'to unite housewives, so that they may realise, and gain recognition for, their right to play an active part in all spheres of planning for the community.'[65] Its first focus

---

[62] Marianne Elliot, *Wolfe Tone: Prophet of Irish Independence* (New Haven and London, 1989).
[63] Jacob Diaries, 31 December 1958, Ms 32,582 (164).
[64] *Irish Times*, 15 February 1958.
[65] Tweedy, *A Link in the Chain*, p. 112.

was on consumer rights, but it soon adopted a feminist agenda committed to 'a real equality of liberties, status and opportunities for all persons.'[66] In 1961, one year after Jacob's death, Lucy Kingston's comments about a meeting of the IHA offer some insights into the role Jacob had played in the organisation:

> Very retrogressive atmosphere on many questions, including school meals, nursery centres etc. I never miss Rose so greatly as on these occasions, she never let anything in the nature of a backwash towards anti-feminism pass without protest. Wish there were more 'protestants' in this sense.[67]

In the last couple of years of her life, Jacob was a member of the Campaign for Nuclear Disarmament (CND). She believed that nuclear testing was harmful, especially to unborn children and was concerned with the dissemination of truth, as opposed to what she perceived as a conspiracy to keep the population ignorant about 'large areas of nuclear physics now kept secret', and their use in creating 'large scale weapons ... which destroy people indiscriminately', rather than 'for useful work.'[68] However, the CND's efforts to educate the Irish public became entangled with other politics. At a Civil Liberties Council meeting in 1958, when someone suggested a public meeting against nuclear weapons, 'Dorothy Macardle object[ed] to anything definitely against them and talking of "the enemy" meaning Russia. It was decided better to have a public meeting on Freedom in the Theatre.' Jacob commented with some irony, that '[n]uclear weapons are not exactly connected to civil liberty here.'[69] Until the end of her life she was also a member of the Anti-Vivisection Society, a continuation of her earlier work with the Society for Prevention to Cruelty to Animals, and both, no doubt, directly connected to her lifelong commitment to vegetarianism. In 1959 Jacob lost her brother Tom, after a long illness. Kingston noted that 'something is gone out of Rose's life – quite irreplaceable.'[70] What was gone was the special friendship they had shared throughout their lives. Their early years of isolation from other children, their parents' unorthodox beliefs, and their physical proximity until Rose moved to Dublin all contributed to their closeness.

In 1960 *The Raven's Glen,* written in 1945 but repeatedly rejected by publishers, finally appeared in print. After the success of *The Rebel's Wife* Jacob had revised both 'Third Person Singular' and *The Raven's Glen. The Raven's Glen* moves outside the confines of Christian Ireland and reinvents a tradition of matriarchal lineage since erased from Irish history. Its intended audience

---

[66] *Ibid.,* p. 18.
[67] Swanton, *Emerging from the Shadow,* p. 157.
[68] Shanahan Papers.
[69] Jacob Diaries, 7 February 1958, Ms 32,582 (161).
[70] Swanton, *Emerging from the Shadow,* p. 154.

appears to be adolescents and it centres on the adventures of a group of teenage cousins on holiday in the Glen of Imaal in County Wicklow. They encounter a Miss Kelly, whose real name is Mor a' Chaillighe, a direct matrilineal descendant of the Cailleach, original keeper of the Raven's Glen, who dates back to a pre-Christian era in Irish history. Mor lives alone at the top of the glen, and is considered a witch by the locals.

The children meet Mor, when one of the boys cuts his leg, and she treats it with herbs from her garden. When the children accidentally stumble upon a hidden tomb at the end of the 'hag's road', the 'oldest path in the glen', Mor reveals her true identity. She explains that the tomb is 'the grave of the woman that was the first keeper of the glen, more centuries ago than anyone knows … The Cailleach they call her.'[71] Characteristically, Jacob does not ignore the role of the Catholic Church in the destruction of the old culture and religion as Mor explains that the little church across the river was built on the site of a clochán belonging to the Cailleach which was pulled down to build the church. Mor's greatest fear, that when she dies 'there'll never be another [cailleach]' is relieved when her niece, Moreen Kelly, becomes her apprentice and the tradition of the Cailleach is secured.

On 24 September, 1960, Jacob and Lucy Kingston spent four hours at the Ideal Homes Exhibition 'trying to interest people in *The Irish Housewife* magazine, and encourage them to join the association.'[72] From there Jacob was making her way to Harold's Cross Hospice where she regularly visited some elderly people, reading and talking with them. As she was crossing a street she was knocked down by a motorist. She was brought to the Meath Hospital unconscious, suffering from head injuries and broken legs. She never recovered consciousness and subsequently contracted pneumonia. She died in hospital on October 11, 1960, politically active to the end. Of her funeral Lucy Kingston would later reflect: 'very large number, a 'representative' funeral, but so many things to represent!'[73] These words aptly captured the breadth of activities that encompassed Rose Jacob's world.

Jacob's work and life have been neglected by Irish literary critics and historians perhaps because both were so uncompromising with regard to the issues of Irish independence, religious freedom and women's rights. Both her writing and political work challenged the ruling ethos in the country. Her agnostic and republican beliefs differed in almost every respect from those of most of her class and contemporaries. Jacob's work was too volatile, too critical, for the sensibilities of an emerging patriarchal state. The resistance to her kind of political convictions are mirrored in the reluctance to publish her work. Today, all her previously published work remains out of print.

---

71 Rosamond Jacob, *The Raven's Glen* (Dublin, 1960), p. 145.
72 Swanton, *Emerging from the Shadow*, p. 156.
73 *Ibid.*, p. 156.

The threads that weave through all Rosamond Jacob's years of political activity are her feminist consciousness and her unwavering insistence on educating both men and women on their rights and responsibilities as citizens. Representing a continuum of political action spanning half a century, her work was accomplished within a nation which was first a colonial state, later the Irish Free State, and then the Republic of Ireland. Over the years Jacob's writing reflected her acute awareness of patriarchal control of institutions of power, and the intersection of this power with gender, sexuality, class, ethnicity and nationality. She was a visionary and a global feminist, who spent her life forming coalitions by crossing class, gender, ethnic and national boundaries. Her politics, principles, ethics and humanitarianism are relevant to many current issues, including women's reproductive rights in the Republic, the peace process in Northern Ireland, the Republic of Ireland's relationship to global capitalism, animal rights, and the continued threat to public health and the environment from nuclear weapons and industrial pollution. Four decades after her death perhaps we are ready for a new appreciation of Jacob's life and writings.

Published Books:
Callaghan (published under pseudonym F. Winthrop), (Dublin: Martin Lester Ltd., 1920).
The Rise Of The United Irishmen 1791-1794 (London: George G. Harrap & Co. Ltd., 1937).
The Troubled House (Dublin: Browne and Nolan Ltd., 1938).
The Rebel's Wife (Tralee: The Kerryman Ltd., 1957).
The Raven's Glen (Dublin: Allen Figgis & Co. Ltd., 1960).

Unpublished Books:
Third Person Singular
Matilda Tone: A Memoir

Short Stories:
'Two days long ago' (published under the pseudonym F. Winthrop), *Green and Gold.* 2, 6, (March/May 1922), pp. 1-6.
'Trailing clouds of glory', *Green and Gold,* 2, 9, (December 1922), pp. 309-316.

Essay:
'The right to kill.' Letter of the Month in *Ireland Today,* (April 1937), pp. 58-60.

Index